GREAT AMERICAN
TRACTORS

BIG GREEN
John Deere GP Tractors

Text by Robert N. Pripps
Photos by Andrew Morland

MBI Publishing Company

First published in 1998 by MBI Publishing Company,
729 Prospect Avenue, PO Box 1, Osceola, WI 54020-0001 USA

MBI Publishing Company books are also available at discounts in bulk
quantity for industrial or sales-promotional use. For details write to Special
Sales Manager at Motorbooks International Wholesalers & Distributors,
729 Prospect Avenue, Osceola, WI 54020-0001 USA.

Library of Congress Cataloging-in-Publication Data Available
ISBN 0-7603-0651-6

On the front cover: A 1952 International Farmall Super M.

On the back cover: Top: A 1946 Ford-Ferguson Model 2N;
Bottom: A 1929 John Deere GP.

Photo on page 128: For the serious antique tractor collector, the serial
number is the important thing. This allows, first of all, recognition of a rare,
or unique, version of an otherwise common machine. Secondly, it allows the
collector to determine the unit's original configuration so that accurate
restoration can be made. Shown here is Bruce Keller's John Deere BWH,
Serial Number 57718. A check of the manufacturers records indicates that it
was built in 1938, and was one of only fifty made.

Photo on page 131: Lady, a registered Guernsey, appears to be
appreciating the classic lines of the Farmall Super H. Lady is one of several
Guernseys on the Langy farm near Lena, Illinois.

Photo on page 257: A British-built Fordson, owned by Keith Dorey of
Wareham, Dorset, England.

Printed in China

Contents

BIG GREEN

FARMALL TRACTORS

FORD TRACTORS

Acknowledgments

My thanks and appreciation go to the following people who helped immeasurably in making this pictorial history possible:

First of all, to Andrew Morland; without his excellent photographs this book would be hard to sell!

Next, to helpful equipment companies:

Meridian Implement, my Rockford, Illinois, John Deere Dealer.

Polacek Implement, Phillips, Wisconsin, who did the work on my John Deere B.

And to Deere & Company; especially Dr. Leslie Stegh and Ms. Vicki Eller in the Deere Archives and Records Services Department.

Thanks to the following tractor collectors who generously gave of their time and energies to provide information and photo opportunities for this book. Despite their best efforts, some of their tractors did not get photographed because of weather and scheduling difficulties. In other cases, due to circumstances beyond their control, pictures taken do not appear in this book; for these omissions, we heartily apologize. For those that do appear, the pictures speak for themselves as to the loving dedication of the owners to their hobby. Andrew Morland and myself, as well as the staff and management of Motorbooks International Publishing, extend our thanks to the following collectors:

Lyle Pals, Egan, Illinois;
Rich Ramminger, Morrisonville, Wisconsin;
Walter and Bruce Kellor, Forest Junction, Wisconsin;
Orv Rothgaard, Owatonna, Minnesota;
Jim Quinn, East Peoria, Illinois
Bruce Johnson, Maple Park, Illinois;
Clarence (Bunky) Meese, Freeport, Illinois; and
Jim Kenney, Streater, Illinois.

Finally, thanks to Michael Dregni, Editor in Chief, and the staff at Motorbooks International. Their talent and professionalism never cease to amaze me!

Introduction

The words "John Deere," like the word "Tahiti", conjures a mental image complete with sounds, smells, and feelings. Especially to the older agriculturist, the included "sound bite" is one with the distinctive music of a laboring two-cylinder tractor engine. It is our intention to add to the visual image through the pictures in this book.

Photographer Andrew Morland and I traveled the states of Wisconsin, Minnesota, and Illinois to photograph the beautifully-restored historic tractors appearing in the following pages. In the text, I have attempted to infuse the tempo of the times into the history of the John Deere company and it's General Purpose tractors. These were times, as they say, to try men's souls. They were also times of great realization of the efforts of gifted men, both in the industry and on the farm.

This book includes only John Deere General Purpose tractors simply to limit its scope and so to concentrate on the general, or all-purpose, concept in tractors born in the late Twenties. The definition is stretched to include the Utility concept of the Forties.

This is my second book on John Deere tractors (the first was *John Deere Two-cylinder Tractor Buyer's Guide*, also published by Motorbooks). I hope it will not be my last. My associations with Deere & Company, its tractors, and the John Deere tractor collectors have only served to heighten my already high regard for the great Green and Yellow machines.

Robert N. Pripps

Foreword

Ralph C Hughes retired from Deere & Company in 1992, after thirty-eight years with the firm. When he retired, he was Director of Advertising. Ralph started with Deere in 1954 as a writer for their *Furrow* magazine. He co-authored the book *How Johnny Popper Replaced the Horse* with Donald S. Huber, in 1988, and authored the book, *The Toy and the Real McCoy,* in 1990. Ralph grew up on a family farm in Indiana and is a graduate of the Purdue University School of Agriculture.

In 1963, Deere & Company passed International Harvester (and all other U.S. and Canadian manufacturers) in total sales of farm and light industrial equipment. Since then Deere has never relinquished its position of "Leader in the Industry." The significance of this achievement can only be fully appreciated by knowing how far behind International Harvester Deere was at one time. Many factors contributed to this important advancement, but significant among them were the development of the John Deere General Purpose tractors, starting in 1928; and the introduction of the "New Generation of Power" John Deere tractors in 1960. The author of this book details the genealogy of these tractors and the events that helped shape their design, special features, and specifications. He also chronologizes the history of John Deere, the man; John Deere, the company; and several competing companies and their tractor lines.

Tractor design during the Twentieth Century has indeed been a never-ending "leap-frog" process with one company's tractor gaining temporary advantage over its competitor with superior features; just to have another manufacturer design a tractor with superior features, more power, or greater productivity. Fortunately, the end result has worked to the advantage of the North American farmer with a steady improvement in tractor capability and reliability. This competitive process continues today, but with fewer companies vying for tractor sales in a continually shrinking worldwide market. This process, of course, extends to other farm equipment as well: combines, planters, haytools, etc.; and even to dealership organizations and the caliber of services provided by them to the farmer customer.

In this book, the author has compiled many facts and figures, specifications and interesting details from a variety of sources. The net result is a handy reference that the farm tractor aficionado or agricultural historian will find exceedingly useful for years to come.

Ralph C. Hughes
former Director of Advertising
Deere & Company

Chapter 1

Origins of Deere & Company

"Who made that plow," asked the farmer?
"I did, such as it is," replied John Deere, "woodwork and all."

John Deere The Blacksmith

Who was John Deere, and what gave him such a prominent place in history? What was so special about him that his name should still grace the finest agricultural implements after 156 years?

John Deere was a legend in his own time. The company he founded in 1837 is also a legend. Deere & Company is one of America's oldest companies in continuous business. It has survived political, economic, and business crises from well before the Civil War with a series of gifted leaders, outstanding technical talent, and by attention to quality. Today, Deere & Company is the only U.S. farm machinery giant still operating under the same name.

John Deere was born February 7, 1804, in Rutland, Vermont, and grew up in Middlebury, a few miles away. His father, William Ryland Deere, was a tailor who had come

Charles Deere was born in 1837 in Vermont after his father had left for Illinois. He was over a year old before he and his mother joined John Deere in Grand Detour. Charles started with the firm at age 16 and took over day-to-day management at age 21. Charles's management style fostered independent branch houses that wielded much influence with the company and its products. *Deere Archives*

from England, and his mother, Sarah Yates Deere, was the daughter of a Revolutionary War British soldier who had stayed on after the fighting. When John was eight years old, his father made a trip to England. While waiting for his ship to depart, William Deere wrote a poignant letter to his son John, perhaps out of a sense of foreboding. The letter has been preserved.

"Take good care of your mother," he wrote. It was the last word of him the family ever received. Although the ship and his trunk

Right, the founder of the company, John Deere. After the Civil War, John Deere's role in managing the company was minimal, son Charles having taken over in 1857. While John Deere retained the title of president, Charles saw to day-to-day operation. John spent his time tinkering in the shop, farming, and being mayor of Moline. *Deere Archives*

The Gilpin Sulky plow, circa 1875. The picture shows an aging John Deere and his dog observing the testing on a site overlooking the plow factory. The Gilpin plow was the invention of Deere shop manager Gilpin Moore. Moore was also a stockholder in the company. *Deere Archives*

Above, a drawing of the original John Deere plow based on records and surviving similar plows. The plow share was made from a piece of broken steel saw blade. Deere fashioned the handles and beam himself from pieces of hardwood. The smooth, shiny steel share did not adhere to the sticky gumbo soil like the cast iron shares did. *Deere Archives*

reached England, William did not. Speculation is that he was washed overboard during the voyage.

Sarah Deere continued the tailor business to support the family, but young John was soon earning money himself. His mother insisted that he attend Middlebury College, which he did for a time. But young John was bent toward the practical, rather than the theoretical, so he apprenticed himself to Captain Benjamin Lawrence, a blacksmith. Workmanship was Captain Lawrence's creed, and it soon became John's, as well. The apprenticeship was completed in 1825, and afterward, Deere was employed as a blacksmith, either for others, or in shops of his own.

In his own shops, in Leicester Four Corners and in Hancock, Deere began specializing in tool manufacture. His shovels, hoes, and pitchforks were known for their quality. Deere not only made tools

to order, but made them to stock for later sale, thus gaining insight into the factory business.

In 1827, Deere married Demarius Lamb from Granville, Vermont. However, this was not a prosperous period—the shop in Leicester Four Corners failed, leaving the thirty-two year-old blacksmith with no alternative but to leave Vermont to avoid his debts. In 1836, with four children and a fifth on the way, John left Demarius and the children temporarily in Vermont and went to Illinois. He traveled by canal boat and stage coach to Grand Detour, a village about 100 miles west of Chicago (where the Rock River makes a sweeping horseshoe turn). There he found a need for his services by another Vermonter, Leonard Andrus, who operated a saw mill in Grand Detour.

Difficult Times in the 1830s

Two major factors in the first decades of the Nineteenth Century directly affected John Deere. The first was a migration of Easterners west. This migration was caused, largely by the second factor: bad economic times.

The economy of the Eastern States had matured somewhat during the first fifty years of the Union. General agriculture had been the mainstay, especially in the northern regions. Second generations farmed the lands, but the third generation was growing up. Due to the geometric progressional increase in family size, there were too many sons to inherit too little land.

As people pulled up stakes and moved west, first to Ohio and then to Indiana, the economy of the East was drained. Times were worsening, especially in Vermont, where John Deere lived. Because of the shortage of hired labor, many land owners switched to a less labor intensive discipline: raising sheep. But raising sheep dramatically cut the need for blacksmiths' services, which was primarily tool fabrication.

In his blacksmith venture in Four Corners, John Deere had taken in a silent partner, Jay Wright. In addition to the difficult economic times in Vermont, Deere was struck with his own misfortune. A series of fires burned out two of his shops. Although he received additional capital each time from Wright to rebuild, he was forced to take employment at another shop in order to support his family. When he could no longer pay Wright anything against what he owed, Wright, concerned for his investment, had papers served on Deere. Deere was now threatened with imprisonment and attachment of all his property.

At about the same time, Deere's employer, Amos Bosworth, closed

William Butterworth, Charles Deere's son-in-law, succeeded Charles Deere as head of Deere & Company. Butterworth joined the company in 1892 after he married Katherine Deere. Butterworth stayed with the firm for the rest of his life. From 1928 on, however, he occupied the ceremonial post of Deere Board Chairman once he accepted the presidency of the U.S. Chamber of Commerce. Butterworth's concern for the intense competition of International Harvester guided much of his term as head of Deere. He was reluctant to enter the tractor-making fray, and withheld encouragement from Deere's early endeavors, but ultimately acquiescing to the purchase of the Waterloo Boy Line. *Deere Archives*

his shop and emigrated with his entire family to Grand Detour, Illinois. Bosworth's daughter was married to Leonard Andrus, owner of the Grand Detour sawmill. With complete economic disaster imminent, John Deere had no choice but to follow.

Opening the Prairies

Southern Illinois was well populated in the 1700s, but the immense prairies of the north were ignored. The sticky gumbo soil of the prairie spawned such a thick bed of grass and roots that everything else was

choked out. Breaking this land with the tools of the day was virtually impossible. Unbeknownst to all, the black rock-free humus soil beneath the tangle of sod extended as far down as seven feet in some areas of the northern Illinois prairie. This soil, and the climate, would prove ideal for the growing of corn.

By the late 1830s, about the time of John Deere's arrival in Grand Detour, the benefits of prairie soil were being recognized. The rich, black humus soil was analyzed to be rich in natural nutrients from centuries of decaying prairie grass. This thick mat of grass, often shoulder-high, was a formidable obstacle, however. The new phrase "prairie-breaking" described the overwhelming task of tilling this earth. Indeed, sod-breaking was not new, with "breaking plows" having been brought from Europe with the New World settlers. But this was more than sod breaking. As Wayne Broehl states in his book *John Deere's Company*, "The term 'prairie breaking' captures the essence of the arduous, physically demanding fight with nature that was demanded of early settlers."

Sod breaking was just the first step in prairie breaking. It was the initial attack in the effort to wrest the land from nature and turn it into farm land. Many methods were tried, from starting prairie fires to plowing under the sod with huge breaker plows pulled by as many as eight yoke of oxen. After the thatch was finally overcome, periodic re-plowing was required to break up the clods of sod and to keep the prairie grass from starting again.

In today's no-till, or low-till environment, we sometimes forget the importance of the plow, and plowing, to the farmer of even just a few years ago. Before the age of chemicals, two of the main jobs of the farmer were plowing and cultivating. As the use of herbicides is frowned upon more and more for their deleterious ancillary effects, plowing and cultivating (and their impact on the configuration of the tractor) will be making a come-back.

The purpose of plowing was to pulverize the soil and to cover field trash. The tilled soil had to have good contact with the subsoil to facilitate the rise of moisture. Air spaces, bunches of trash, and sod clods were undesirable, as they impeded root growth and broke the contact with the subsoil. The plow also accomplished the job of covering and mixing in manure fertilizer.

Crude iron plows appeared in the Near East about 1000 B.C., but it wasn't until the eighteenth century A.D. that the cast-iron plow was known in the western world. Charles Newbold obtained the first American patent for a cast-iron plow in 1797. With typical resistance to anything new, however, the American farmer feared the iron plow would poison the soil and promote the growth of weeds. Yet, the superiority of iron over wood was quickly recognized, and by 1819 a cast-iron plow maker named Jethro Woods was turning out 4,000 per year.

Ordinary cast-iron is by nature rough and full of surface imperfections known as blow-holes. It does not take a polish and is prone to rusting, which further pits the surface. The ordinary cast-iron plow worked well enough in the light, sandy soils of the eastern states, but as one went west, the soil got heavier. Brown silt loam was found on the plains of Indiana and a sticky black gumbo in Illinois and further west. The North included a full complement of gravel and rocks (winter potatoes). Cast-iron plow makers added, as standard equipment to their plows, a leather pouch containing a wooden paddle,

Charles D. Wiman's portrait. Charles Deere Wiman, grandson of Charles Deere, assumed the presidency of Deere & Company in 1928. He continued in that capacity until 1955; almost the end of the two-cylinder era. Wiman's bold management during the depths of the depression of the 1930s led to the development of the General Purpose Models A and B tractors. *Deere Archives*

not unlike a modern-day windshield ice scraper. In many cases, the plowman could only travel a few yards before it was necessary to roll the plow on its side and scrape the "mud" from the moldboard.

Before 1864, when Bessemer steel was first made commercially in the United States, steel cost about twenty-five cents per pound. Thus, while it was available throughout the Nineteenth Century, because of its high price it was only used where its superior strength, or other properties, were essential.

Steel is an alloy of iron and small, but definite quantities of carbon and other materials. It is stronger than iron and can be formed in ways that iron cannot. The surface of steel is smooth and it takes a high polish.

The Grand Detour Business

When Deere arrived in Grand Detour he was thirty-two years old. He had brought with him the necessary tools of his trade, and immediately put them to use. He was able to get a job at the Andrus sawmill to repair a broken pitman.

Soon Deere had his blacksmith shop built and had a good business going. He also built a small house and sent for his family. Demarius arrived carrying their new son, Charles, born after John had departed. Charles would grow up to play an important part in the John Deere Company. What was the key to his success in Illinois when he had failed at the same thing in Vermont? The improved economic situation and the "gumbo suprema:" the sticky humus sod of the Great Plains.

Shortly after Deere had set up his shop, he spotted a shiny broken saw blade laying on the floor at the Andrus mill. With a flash of intuition, he connected the shining surface to the problem of plow scouring in the gumbo soil. Deere asked Andrus for the broken blade, which he then took to his shop and fashioned into a steel plow share. The plow was tried on a neighbor's farm, and did indeed scour!

Deere's business now turned more toward the steel plow trade, and he did less ordinary blacksmithing. His first plows were not the huge breaking plows, but rather the small plows that the farmers used every spring and fall on land that had already been broken. As time went on, Deere developed new plow shapes and used combinations of cast iron, wrought iron, and steel in his plows. Eventually, obtaining materials at a reasonable cost became a problem. To help offset the rising financial problems, Deere took in partners, including Leonard Andrus. By now, general blacksmithing had been left behind.

Portrait of William Hewitt, who took over as president of Deere & Company in 1955. Hewitt was the son-in-law of Charles Deere Wiman, and the last of the Deere family members to head the company. Hewitt's attributes for the position were more than just hereditary; he was well educated, experienced, and had a contagious good humor that endeared him to those around him. It was Hewitt who presided over the successful transition to "The New Generation" tractors; tractors with engines that had more than two cylinders. *Deere Archives*

In 1847, Deere began complaining to his partners that Grand Detour was not the best place to continue the plow business. By then, production was up to 1,000 plows a year. Although situated on the Rock River, Grand Detour was not afforded steamboat service except in periods of very high water. Thus, coal for the forges had to be brought in by wagon from LaSalle, some 40 miles away. Steel and other metals came up the Mississippi from St. Louis, but had to be hauled overland to Grand Detour. Later that year, Deere announced his intentions to move the business to Moline, Illinois, on the Mississippi River. His partners, unwilling to give up their Grand Detour homes, balked, and so the partnership was dissolved.

John Deere Finds A Home

In 1848, Deere moved his plow business to Moline, where he could get steel directly from St. Louis. Here again, different partnership arrangements were undertaken, with various degrees of success.

In 1853, John Deere's oldest surviving son, Charles (then sixteen) joined the firm, to remain with it for fifty-four years, until his death in 1907. Charles, who later followed his father as chief executive officer, had an inestimable influence on the success of the firm. He was a "hands-on" kind of manager, often going into the fields to personally test the product.

After coming into the firm, Charles Deere had his first company experience in the accounting department. His father, meanwhile, was becoming involved in what would one day be the tractor business. The year was 1858. A man by the name of Joseph W. Fawkes, a Pennsylvanian, had built a steam traction engine that was gaining some recognition. By combining it with a gang plow made by The John Deere Plow Works, the Fawkes Steam Plow won the gold medal at the Chicago Fair in 1859. Surprisingly, the plow was of the "mounted" variety, as sulky, or wheeled plows, had not yet been invented. The senior Deere was becoming enamored with the traction engine beyond a doubt, as company records indicate Deere had hired some steam experts to begin work on one in his shop. Whatever became of the effort seems, however, to have escaped the recording historians.

The Last Half of the Nineteenth Century

By 1853, the firm was known as "John Deere," and annually produced about 4,000 plows plus various other implements. In just three more years, plow production jumped to almost 15,000, and the firm employed about 70 workers. John Deere was referred to as the "Napoleon Plow Maker" among the 400 plow companies in the country. As the firm headed into the spring selling season of 1857, everything seemed rosy. No one foresaw the coming economic disaster later called the "Panic of 1857."

The Panic of 1857 was triggered by the failure of the New York branch of the Ohio Life Insurance and Trust Company. This, in turn, precipitated a run on banks and a general downturn of the nation's economy. Prices, especially of farm produce, fell sharply. Many farmers decided not to sell their crops, even though they owed money for their equipment. Instead, they would subsist on what they could grow. The ripple-effect was felt all the way back to John Deere. The firm owed a large sum to its steel supplier, which it was unable to pay.

To stave off bankruptcy, for both the company and John Deere personally, reorganization was undertaken. New partners with cash were taken in. John Deere's assets were separated. Ownership of the company was now in the hands of four partners, of which 21 year-old Charles Deere was principal. The Company was renamed "John Deere & Company."

Through the years of the Civil War, and the decades following, the company prospered under Charles Deere's leadership. John Deere, himself, was never very far from his beloved plow shop. With others running things he was free to tinker. He obtained several important patents for the firm during those years. In 1868, the partnership was changed to a corporation, with John Deere as titular president and Charles as vice president. The official name of the firm was now "Deere & Company." The product line consisted of walking and riding plows, both single and gang; riding and walking cultivators; harrows; drills and planters; wagons and buggies (and around 1890, bicycles). Probably the most important product of this time period was the Gilpin Sulky plow, invented by Deere's shop manager (also a stock holder). It was patented in 1875 and although not the first riding plow, it was probably the best. It was a big seller and led the way for subsequent plow developments.

The End of the Era

After the end of the Civil War, and the firm's incorporation, John Deere's role was minimal. Nevertheless, he remained active, tinkering in the shop, farming acreage of his own, banking, and he even served a term as mayor of Moline.

In 1866, Demarius Lamb Deere, John Deere's wife and the mother of his nine children, died at the age of sixty. Later that year, John returned to the Lamb homestead in Vermont to commiserate with the family.

While there, he became reacquainted with Demarius' maiden sister, Lucenia. When John Deere returned to Moline, he brought Lucenia with him as his new wife.

On May 17, 1886, John Deere died at the age of eighty-two. His funeral in Moline was attended by 3,000 people. A floral plow graced the coffin with the words "John Deere" on the beam. John Deere was not much of an inventor, certainly not a financial genius, nor was he a diplomatic leader. He did however, have the charisma known to many self-made people. He was a man of great personal bearing and dignity. He personified the company's integrity and dedication to quality. He also instilled these qualities in his son Charles.

Charles reared no sons to follow in his footsteps, but his two daughters, Anna and Katherine, married well and each union would have great influence on Deere & Company. Anna married William D. Wiman in 1890 and Katherine married William Butterworth in 1892. Butterworth began at the company right away, eventually succeeding Charles Deere after his death in 1907. Anna and William Wiman had a son whom they named Charles Deere Wiman. Charles Deere Wiman succeeded William Butterworth at the controls in 1928 where he continued almost to the end of the "Two-cylinder Era." Following Wiman at the helm of Deere & Company was the last Deere family president, William Hewitt, Charles Deere Wiman's son-in-law.

Chapter 2

Easing into the Tractor Business

The Turn of the Century

"The period from about 1898 to the World War I era has generally been regarded as one of exceptional stability and relative well-being for the American farmer," says noted economist Harold F. Williamson. This twenty-year period also witnessed the most profound societal changes in history. The period is referred to by some historians as the "Fecund Years," because they were so intellectually productive and inventive, and to such a marked degree. There are still a few hardy souls who remember those days first hand, but most, like myself, first heard about them from parents and grandparents. Farm equipment manufacturers employed agents called "Travelers" to demonstrate and sell the various pieces of equipment. One can only imagine the difficulty in getting buyer and seller together on a major item of equipment, such as a thresher or binder, in those days.

Left, the difference in the drive configuration of the Model R Waterloo Boy is clearly shown here. Compared to the Model N, the drive gear is much smaller in diameter.

In the 1890s, during the height of the bicycle craze, Deere marketed a line of bicycles, the trade-mark for which is shown here. *Deere Archives*

The Travelers and the Machinery Wars

In his book, *The Century of the Reaper*, C.H. McCormick, Jr. recounts a tale told to him by a McCormick agent about an incredible scrap over the sale of a binder.

"A dealer telegraphed me saying the Champion outfit was trying to break up a sale he had made of an eight-foot binder. They had pulled their machine onto the farm and challenged the farmer to a competition.

"When I got there, the farmer was having trouble with our machine, and the Champion boys were giving him plenty of poison about it and me. I got the machine fixed so that it worked satisfactorily.

"Meanwhile, Champion had notified every farmer around to come see them beat the McCormick binder in a contest set for the next day, thus hoping to get them to cancel any orders for McCormick machines.

"I got up at three o'clock in the morning and drove out to the farm and woke the farmer up. He put on his pants and came out to the barn where I gave him such a sales talk that he was absolutely convinced the Mc-

Cormick was the best machine.

"A big crowd of machine men had come to the hotel that night. The Deering men said they would join the contest and show us both up. The next morning there were at least a hundred and fifty farmers there. The Deering outfit was the first to start. They had a new machine, all decorated with flags, and four big gray horses. But when the first bundle of tangled barley came through it choked and they were done.

"The farmer, driving our binder, was having no trouble, but I caught a Champion man trying to put a handful of straw in our elevator chains to foul them. I grabbed him by the neck and he fell down in the stubble. Then the whole Champion crew started after me, but somebody got between us. They started to abuse the farmer, a big powerful man, and he struck the Champion dealer. The farmer's old father stopped the fight, but the whole competition broke up into a row. Finally, Champion left in disgrace without having driven us from the field."

The Travelers, often operating out of regional branch houses, would load a box wagon with as much of a manufacturers small equipment as it would hold. The wagon and a team of horses would be loaded into a box car for the rail journey to his territory. He'd then unload the wagon and horses and make his way to the neighboring farms. The Traveler would actually sell his stock, plows, harrows, cultivators and the like, off his wagon until it was all gone. Then he'd load up for the rail journey and return home.

Larger items, such as a thresher, or a traction engine, were usually demonstrated at county fairs. The binders, or harvesters, as they were called then, represented a special challenge to the implement companies.

Local dealers would canvass their territory seeking farmers with both the need and means to buy a harvester. When several prospects were lined up, the dealer would arrange for the branch house, or factory, to send out a machine, and the necessary horses and men to put on a demonstration. Agents from competing outfits would often get wind of these demonstrations, and bring in their own equipment.

At about this time, a "bicycle craze" swept the country, even prompting John Deere to get involved in their sales. The proliferation of bicycles, and the new freedom of mobility they provided, gave impetus to improving the roads. These were then available to the emerging gas buggies.

The Otto-cycle (4-cycle) engine began to supplant the steam engine in providing non-animal farm power. A large crop of 1-cylinder stationary "gas engines" came up in the last decade of the Nineteenth Century. In 1902, Hart and Parr made the first production "tractor"

A replica of the 1892 Froelich tractor stands in the Display Building at the Deere & Company Headquarters. John Froelich started the company which later produced the Waterloo Boy tractor. In 1918, Deere & Company entered the tractor business by acquiring the company. *Author Collection*

A Big Four tractor pulling five John Deere harvesters; circa 1912. The Big Four was big! It sported drive wheels 8 feet in diameter! A four-cylinder vertical engine of 30 horsepower provided the motivation for the 10 ton monster. In 1912, the Big Four appeared in some branch house catalogs giving the impression that it was a Deere product, although it was not. *Deere Archives*

The Melvin tractor. Pressure from the branch houses and competition with International Harvester prompted the board of Deere & Company to commission C.H. Melvin to build an experimental tractor in 1912. It was a three-wheeled affair with three plow bottoms mounted underneath. The single (steering) wheel was behind for plowing, but went first for hauling. Two seats were provided for the operator, for either direction of travel. It was patterned after the 1911 Hackney; a 40 horsepower four-cylinder machine, which included a power lift for the plows. Lack of traction and unreliability caused Deere to abandon the tests and the concept. *Deere Archives*

Left, the all-wheel drive Dain tractor; the first production tractor to bear the John Deere name. In 1914, board member Joseph Dain Sr. was given the task of coming up with a viable $700 tractor. The result of his efforts was the 3-wheel, all-wheel drive machine shown. The remarkable 3,800 pound tractor had a maximum drawbar pull of over 3,000 pounds. It began life with a four-cylinder Waukesha engine, but this was later replaced with a more powerful McVickers engine. Testing, and reluctance by the board, especially President Butterworth, delayed production until 1917. By then Dain had died; with him died much of the push for the tractor. Also, by that time, it was determined that the price would have to be around $1,200, and the $850 Waterloo Boy tractor line was available for acquisition. Over 50 Dain-John Deeres were completed and delivered to customers, however. *Deere Archives*

and became fathers of a great industry. The automobile pioneers, Duryea, Benz, Olds, and Daimler, were joined by the upstart Henry Ford. By 1900, there were 8,000 auto buggies on American streets. But there were still 8,000,000 horses in the United States. In 1891, the Canadian implement giants Massey and Harris merged. In 1902, in the U.S., McCormick and Deering joined, and together with others formed International Harvester.

Origins of the John Deere Tractor

From approximately 1850 to 1950 the farm machinery business saw almost constant dramatic

Above, the Velie 12-24 tractor, built and marketed by a Deere & Company board member during the time Deere was struggling to come up with a tractor of their own. Apparently Velie did not exert much pressure to have his machine taken over by Deere, but instead, used it to pull and sell Deere plows. *Deere Archives*

change. Each new invention spawned the next. Thus, reapers begat threshing machines, and when the threshing machine required more power than could be conveniently provided by horses, farm steam engines were developed. The portable steam engine soon became the traction engine, followed by internal combustion traction engines.

A Waterloo Boy Model R owned by Tony Ridgeway of West Unity, Ohio. The tractor is shown at the John Deere homestead in Grand Detour, Illinois, during the Two-cylinder Days exposition in 1991. Ridgeway also owns a Model N.

Agricultural historian, R.B. Gray, credits Obed Hussey with the invention of the steam engine plow in 1855. Hussey, from Baltimore, Maryland, is remembered as the inventor who first patented a reaper, much to the chagrin of Cyrus Hall McCormick. Hussey's reaper was, however, more successful than his steam plow.

Three years later, a Mr. J.W. Fawkes, of Christiana, Pennsylvania, introduced a more successful steam plowing outfit at the Illinois State Fair. It was based on a vertical-boiler steam engine of 30 horsepower. It used a roller-type driving wheel 6 feet in diameter by 6 feet in length. It pulled a mounted six-bottom makeshift plow with "power-lift." Observing that the plow was the rig's weak-point, John Deere made contact with Fawkes and over the summer of 1859 developed an eight-bottom steel plow for it. In the Fall of 1859, the outfit was entered in the U.S. Agricultural Contest in Chicago, where it won the Gold Medal. Despite this victory, the great ungainly Fawkes engine did not prove serviceable and none were sold to the public. Nevertheless, Deere & Company had its first taste of the tractor business.

The Waterloo Boy

By the early 1900s, giants of the industry were International Harvester, J.I. Case, and Massey-Harris, then known as the "Long-line" companies. Deere, with its five lines, was not yet in their league. By 1906, International Harvester was making a gasoline traction engine.

23

The Waterloo Boy Model N was introduced in 1917 and produced until 1924. It is interesting to note that in 1920, the Model N was the first tractor to be tested by the University of Nebraka. *Author Collection*

The final version of the Waterloo Boy tractor, the Model N can be distinguished from its predecessors by the size of the large drive gears attached to the rear wheels: on the N it is nearly as large as the wheels; on earlier versions, it was much smaller. The reason for the change was that the N employed a two-speed transmission while earlier models had only one speed. Thus more reduction was taken in the final drive on the N version.

The Model N Waterloo Boy, the second version produced by Deere, had a two-cylinder, kerosene-burning engine that operated at 750rpm. The N can be distinguished from the earlier Model R by the larger diameter drive gear inside the rear wheel. The Model N had two forward speeds, while the R had only one. *Author Collection*

The pictorial logo of the Waterloo Boy tractor. The Waterloo Gasoline Engine Company was taken over by Deere & Company in 1918. Their primary product, prior to the success of the R version of the 1915 tractor, was a line of farm stationary engines. The Waterloo Boy tractor was started on gasoline, but normally operated on kerosene.

The Model N Waterloo Boy was produced into 1924, overlapping the first two-cylinder production tractor to bear the John Deere name: the Model D. When the serial numbering system was started for the Model D, production of the Waterloo Boy was expected to die out. But instead, demand continued right along with the successful D until the Waterloo Boy serial numbers caught up with the first of those taken out for the D. Therefore, Deere officials took a block of ninety-two numbers out of the D sequence. The resultant numbering system is thus not easy to follow. Further complicating things, Waterloo Boy farm engines also shared the numbering system, and Waterloo Boy Model R tractors were produced simultaneously with Model Ns for a while, all on the same numbering system.

Case had been a pioneer in the steam engine business from 1892. Canadian Massey-Harris delayed entry into the tractor business until 1916. By 1918, Henry Ford was mass producing more Fordsons per year than the output of all the other tractor-makers combined. One might think, given its position in the industry, that Deere would have been reluctant to step in, but that was not the case.

Deere had been very successful in providing plows for neophyte tractor companies. One of the best was made by The Gas Traction Company of Minnesota; a 19,000 pound monster known as the Big Four. In 1912, the Big Four appeared in the catalogs of the John Deere Plow Company with the implication that it was actually a Deere product. In fact, in a color spread, the predominant color was a green very close to that used on subsequent John Deere tractors.

The arrangement with The Gas Traction Company did not last long, but it did give them a taste of what having their own tractor would be like. In 1912, the Deere board commissioned internal trac-

tor experiments. The resultant machine, known as the Melvin tractor, was disappointing in field trials, however, and was dropped in 1914.

The Velie 12-24 was marketed by Deere for a time. It was developed by a Deere board member, but he more or less did it on his own. The Velie tractor used primarily by the branch houses to demonstrate Deere plows.

Up to 1914, large tractors (with weights as high as fifteen tons) were the industry norm. Many farmers simply had no way to use such a monster. The directors of Deere next commissioned a fellow board member, Joseph Dain, to develop a small tractor, one that would sell for around $700. By early 1915, Dain had a prototype ready for the board to see. It was a three-wheel, all-wheel drive machine with a four-cylinder Waukesha engine. By the end of the year, six prototypes were in the field, proving themselves to be quite successful. After a year of testing, and with a more powerful McVicker engine, it was decided to build one hundred for the market.

Unfortunately, Dain died in 1917, and with him, much of the "push" for the tractor. While the tractor was considered a great success, and indeed it was much ahead of its time, it turned out to be too expensive. The target price of $700 had become $1700. With the Fordson now on the market at, or below the first figure, the Dain machine was no longer viable. And especially since the Waterloo Gasoline Engine Company's 25 horsepower tractor, the two-cylinder Waterloo Boy, was selling for just $850. Also, the company was available for purchase.

The Waterloo Boy was a direct descendent of the world's first truly successful internal combustion traction engine developed by John Froelich in 1892. Froelich mounted a single-cylinder Van Duzen engine on a Robinson steam engine running gear and devised his own drive arrangement for the wheels. With this tractor, Froelich completed a fifty-day threshing run, both pulling and powering the thresher, and threshing some 72,000 bushels of small grain.

Later that year, Froelich joined with others to form the Waterloo Gasoline Traction Engine Company which would become the John Deere Tractor Company twenty-six years later. Four tractors of the Froelich design were built and two were sold to customers. Neither proved satisfactory and both were returned. To generate cash flow, the company developed stationary engines, which they sold successfully. Therefore, when the company reorganized in 1895, the word "Traction" was dropped from the company's name. With the name change, Mr. Froelich also left the company. By 1906, six engine models were in production, which carried the trade name "Waterloo Boy." Despite the name change, tractor experiments continued. In 1911, a man by the name of Parkhurst, from Moline, joined the Waterloo Gasoline Engine Company, bringing with him three tractors of his own design, each with two-cylinder engines.

From 1911 to 1914, many variations on the theme were tried. Model designations and serial num-

The Waterloo Boy Model N was built between 1917 and 1924. The 465cid two-cylinder engine produced 25 belt horsepower at 750rpm. Some Model Ns, such as this 1920 version, had chain steering, while others had "automobile" steering. There were also several different fuel tank and radiator configurations employed. Its engine had a 6.5 inch bore and a 7 inch stroke in its final form. Earlier versions used a 5.5 inch and a 6 inch bore although the stroke was always 7 inches. The horizontal two-cylinder engine was preceded by a horizontally-opposed version and by two-cycle versions.

bers from this period are rather confusing, as test articles were often rebuilt and redesignated.

Finally, in early 1914, the design of the Waterloo Boy Model R tractor was frozen; it was to be a four-wheel, rear wheel drive, with one forward speed and one reverse. The engine was a two-cylinder, four-cycle, overhead valve type, with a bore and stroke of 5.5inx7in giving it a displacement of 333ci. Operating speed was 750rpm, which produced 25hp at the belt (the drawbar rating was 12).

The Model R was sold in thirteen styles, A through M, until 1918, the year Deere & Company purchased the firm. Style M, which became Model N, was introduced in 1917 and produced until 1924, when it was replaced by the first mass production two-cylinder tractor bearing the John Deere name: the venerable Model D. (The four-cylinder Dain also bore the John Deere name, but there were only about 50 made.)

The Waterloo Boy experimental tractor which became the prototype of the John Deere Model D. By the time this picture was taken, 1919, Deere engineers had converted the final drive from gear to roller chain, no doubt capitalizing on experience with the Dain tractor. The subsequent Models D and GP also used chain final drives. *Deere Archives*

The Waterloo Gasoline Traction Engine Company

In 1892, John Froelich and his associates formed the Waterloo Gasoline Traction Engine Company. As founded, the company did not last long, nor were many tractors built (a total of four). Also, Mr. Froelich did not continue with the firm after it was reorganized as the Waterloo Gasoline Engine Co.

Nevertheless, the original company made a bold venture into the traction engine business. Their venture was based on a machine invented by John Froelich earlier in 1892. Froelich was driven by problems associated with farm steam power, and saw the gasoline power plant as the solution. As stated in an early sales brochure for the tractor, necessity was the mother of invention "It was dire necessity, resulting from an unfortunate investment in the apple business on the part of our old friends Adam and Eve, that led to the invention of clothing..."

Advantages claimed for the new machine were:
1. No possibility of explosion
2. No danger of fire
3. No tank man and team necessary
4. No high-priced engineer required
5. No early firing to get up steam
6. No leaky flues
7. No broken bridges on account of weight
8. No running into obstacles as the operator is in front
9. No runaway teams on account of steam blowing off
10. No long belt to contend with

Chapter 3

Making Tractor In The Twenties

Competing with Steam

"If it hadn't been for the free publicity given by our friends, the enemy, I really don't know if we should have pulled through." These are the words of Charles Hart, of The Hart-Parr Company, when he saw the laughing scorn of the steam engine salesmen turned back on them as the gas tractor gained ground. Their derision was apparently along the line of the Shakespearean quotation, "Methinks you protest too much."

This Model C, like the subsequent Model GP, used an unusual post-type seat support. The C was an "experimental" forerunner of the GP. The designation was changed primarily to better counter the new McCormick-Deering Farmall and Oliver Hart-Parr general purpose tractors that were ravishing the marketplace in the late twenties. The second reason for the change was, due to the quality of the telephone system of the time. It was difficult to distinguish "Model C" from "Model D" over the phone.

By 1910, there was approximately 28 million total farm horsepower, animal and mechanical, in the United States. Of this, about 15 percent was provided by steam and 8 percent by internal combustion. Steam power was a maturing technology, finding routine use in ships and on railroads. With few exceptions, the internal combustion (gas) engines used for farm power was of the 4-cycle type, with automatic intake valves and hit-miss governors and low voltage, battery-powered ignition. The first "Gas" tractors were basically steam engine chassis with a gas engine mounted. There were 600 of them operating in 1910. The next twenty years would see almost a million more in use.

There was, in 1910, no conventional configuration for gas tractors, other than that most of them tended to look like steam traction engines. Almost all of both types, steam and gas, were large, with drive wheels of 8 to 10 feet in diam-

eter. Weights approached 50,000 pounds in many cases. By the middle of the century's second decade, many gas tractors were using multi-speed transmissions.

Rumely, Hart-Parr, and International Harvester were the big gas tractor producers during these years. Hart-Parr sent three and Rumely sent two trainloads of their gas tractors to the emerging wheat lands of Western Canada in 1912.

The John Deere Light Draft Binder was built around 1920. It was one of the first designs to come out of the East Moline "Harvester" plant. *Deere Archives*

Henry Ford, and his son Edsel, stand before an early Fordson tractor. With the Fordson, Henry had intended to do for the farmer what he had done for the motorist with the Model T car. That is, build a lightweight, inexpensive model that all could afford. What the Fordson lacked in traction, it made up for with a low price; as low as $395 in 1921. This set off a tractor price war that eliminated all of the weaker competitors. *Author Collection*

The John Deere Model D was produced from 1923 to 1953 without much in the way of changes. A third transmission speed was added in 1935, and sheet metal styling in 1939. Belt horsepower rose from 30 in 1923 to 42 in 1953 through minor engine improvements. More than 160,000 Model Ds were built. Other than the ill-fated four-cylinder Dain-John Deere, the Model D was the first tractor to bear the John Deere name. *Author Collection*

Rumley was also a steam engine maker, as were Case and Minneapolis. At the turn of the century, the steamer was so reliable and steady in its power, compared to the gas tractor, that many farmers held the gas tractor in derision. Especially in the Canadian prairies, the big steamers were winning converts to power farming. Records such as 160 acres plowed in 24 hours (with a 40 horsepower Reeves) were made. At the 1909 Manitoba Fair, a 25 horsepower Garr-Scott steam traction engine recorded a plowing rate of an acre in 7 minutes 58 seconds.

Although at first glance this looks like a John Deere GP, it is actually a Model C, the forerunner of the GP. This example, Serial Number 200109, is owned by the Kellers, of Forest Junction, Wisconsin. The Kellers, father, son, and grandson (Walter, Bruce and Jason) own over 160 collectible tractors.

Nevertheless, with more and more of the better gas tractors coming into the field, the tide began to turn. In 1908, the Winnipeg Industrial Exhibition began sponsoring comparative tractor trials. Now the public could witness and compare the performance of the various brands of steam and gas tractors. The obvious convenience and versatility of the gas tractor became apparent. Yet, as late as 1920, there were still 15 brands of steam tractors available, and in that year they produced 1766 machines.

Deere management watched the unfolding tractor events with detachment. They were in the plow business, and were selling plows of all sizes and types to go with the new tractors, both steam and gas.

In 1900, Deere's competition was The Oliver Chilled Plow Company in the U.S., and Cockshutt in Canada. After the 1902 formation of International Harvester, Deere management became concerned. Their concern was not about product competition, but about IH winning the hearts and minds of the independent dealers. If this happened it would either force Deere out of business, or force them under Harvester's control. William Butterworth was probably more concerned by the later prospect. Not only was he Deere's President, but he was also a trustee of the Charles Deere estate. As such, he was responsible for the fortunes of the family members, as well as for the reputation and memory of John Deere, himself.

Butterworth led the Deere board of directors toward a policy of aggressive defense. To prevent being swallowed up by IH, they would have to become too large a bite. Yet, the tractor part of the business still presented a quandary. The management of Deere struggled with the question of whether to enter the

tractor market, or to continue to tailor their implements to the tractors of others. To enter would alienate some of their best customers; not to enter would leave Harvester with a big advantage.

Competing with International Harvester

Following the Harvester merger in 1902, Deere & Company at first took a hands-off, self-effacing stance, emphasizing to dealers and farmers that the two companies' product lines didn't compete. International Harvester made harvesters and mowers and the like; Deere made plows and cultivators. Many independent dealers sold both lines of implements. In fact many of Deere's branch houses had been handling non-competing lines of wagons and hay-making tools, planters and spreaders.

By 1906, however, IH took a more aggressive competitive posture by encouraging exclusivity of their product lines at the dealers. Harvester also began to market farm wagons, gas engines, and manure spreaders by buying the companies that made them, sometimes surreptitiously. To defend itself from further monopolization of the market place by International Harvester, Deere made its first acquisition of another company; the Fort Smith Wagon Company. This acquisition was made just before the death of Charles Deere in 1907. Later that year, the John Deere Plow Co., Ltd., was formed in Canada.

The Canadian John Deere company was formed after an aborted attempt by Deere to buy the venerable Canadian house of Frost and Wood of Brockville, Ontario, (which later became Cockshutt). When International Harvester got wind of the Deere interest in Frost and Wood, a harvester (binder) maker, it became suspicious of Deere's intentions. Direct meetings between IH president C.H. McCormick III and the new Deere president William Butterworth did not allay Harvester's fears, especially when Deere pirated away one of their top harvester designers.

Finally, January 6, 1910, the Deere directors issued a decision on reorganizing the company into a more consolidated entity. The same written decision included the statement that Deere & Company would enter the harvester business.

In 1911, Deere entered upon an aggressive policy of acquisition. Companies were added which made shellers, elevators, spreaders, and hay-making equipment. Some of these companies were moved to the Moline area. Finally, in 1912, ground was broken in East Moline for a new "harvester" plant. Now the cat was out of the bag. Deere had taken on International Harvester head on. It was almost a foregone conclusion that tractors would be next, as IH was by then the number one tractor maker in the world.

It's hard to believe, now that the words "John Deere" are almost synonymous with "farm tractor," that it was such a struggle for the company to get into the tractor business. But, following Deere's purchase of the Waterloo Boy in 1918, the company found the "Boy" to be an immediate success, and it continued to be successful during the years of World War I. Over 4,000 Waterloo Boys were exported to England to aid in overcoming food shortages. English tractors used the brand name "Overtime" rather than Waterloo Boy.

Prosperity continued for a time after the November 11, 1918, Armistice. Deere sold more than 5,000 Waterloo Boys in 1920. But Henry Ford had begun producing

Fordsons in earnest in 1918. His 1920 production was 67,000!

The Fordson Phenomenon

What was a Fordson? Anyone over fifty years old who lived in farming country, knows! For those who don't, the Fordson was a new concept in farm tractors pioneered by the Model T car king. It was a 2,700 pound tractor of 20 belt horsepower and 10 on the drawbar. It was in almost all respects a very worthy tractor, especially for the price; about half that of the 25 belt/ 12 drawbar horsepower, 6,200 pound, Waterloo Boy. There were two detriments to its worthiness. First, its traction suffered because of its low weight in relation to its power. This weight versus traction problem became dangerous when the wheels could not slip for some reason; then the tractor rotated backwards around the stationary axle. This rearing action was often so rapid that the operator was pinned under the tractor.

The Fordson's second problem was in its ignition system. It used a

A John Deere GP tractor with a check-row corn planter. The spool of wire, mounted to the left side of the tractor, is pulled out as the tractor proceeds across the field; evenly-spaced knots in the wire trip the planter. Check-row planting allowed cultivating both ways. *Author Collection*

flywheel magneto and voltage step-up coils similar to the Model T. When it worked, it started well. When it was "off," the farmer with only a Sunday School vocabulary was at a severe disadvantage!

Why the name, Fordson? The Ford Motor Company, at this time, was a stockholder company. Henry Ford was chafing under the board of director's control. He had made enough money by then to start a separate company to build tractors, but did not yet have enough to buy out the stockholders of the car company; that would have to wait several more years. Meanwhile, a group of Minneapolis-based entrepreneurs, which included a man whose last name happened to be Ford, had launched a tractor named "Ford." This was an obvious attempt to try

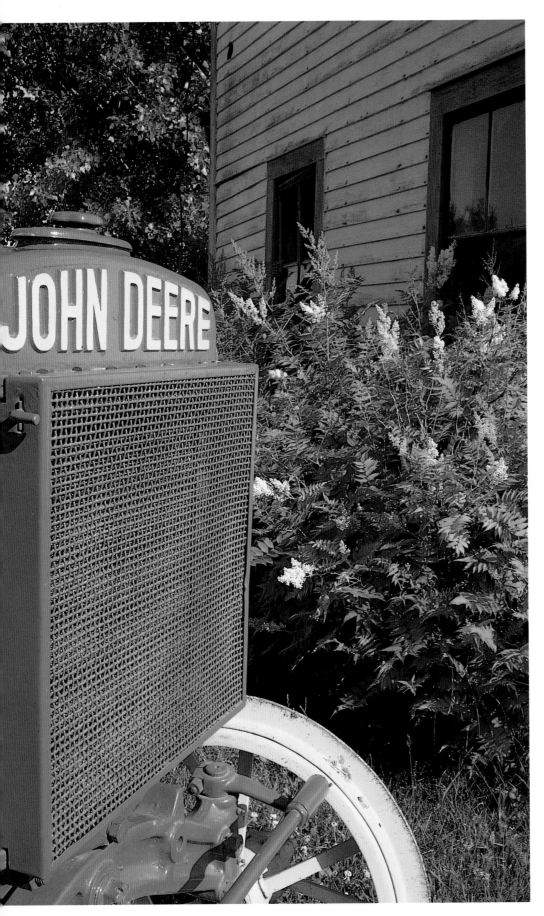

The box-like affair over the radiator of this John Deere Model C contained the radiator shutters. With the "thermocycle" (gravity) water circulation system, the use of a thermostat was not possible. Thus, to regulate coolant temperature, the operator hand-adjusted the shutters. With kerosene fuels, it was important to keep the temperature as high as possible without boiling.

to capitalize on the popularity of the name, and perhaps to get Henry Ford to pay them to use his own name. This tractor was so worthless that it soon died of its own accord.

At any rate, Henry's only son, Edsel, was now at an age where he wanted to become active in the business, so the new tractor company was opened as "Henry Ford and Son." The tractor was named the "Fordson," for short.

Enter The All-purpose Tractor

In 1921, a severe economic downturn surprised almost everyone. The agricultural industry was especially hard hit. Deere had scheduled 40 Waterloo Boys per day for the last half of 1921. In actual fact, they sold only 79 tractors for the whole year. If this was a problem for Deere, Ford had scheduled 3,000 Fordson tractors per day for 1921. By the time the seriousness of the recession was realized, Henry Ford and Son were awash in Fordsons! Henry knew what to do. He first cut the $785 price to $620. Other tractor makers followed suit, including Deere (dropping the Waterloo Boy to $890). So the irrepressible Ford further cut his price to $395. This was the end of the line for a large number of the independent tractor makers. Even the giant General Motors withdrew their tractor entry, the Samson. Ford managed to sell 35,000 Fordsons in 1921, and in 1922 sales were back to 67,000. And in 1923, over 100,000 were sold.

Only International Harvester had the strength to counter attack in 1921. Their crusty General Manager Alexander Legge exploded, over the phone, when told of Ford's final price cut: "What? What's that? How much? Two hundred and thirty dollars? Well I'll be . . . What'll we do about it? Do? Why, damn it all—meet him, of course! We're going to stay in the tractor business. Yes, cut two hundred and thirty dollars. Both models—yes, both. And say, listen, make it good! We'll throw in a plow as well!"

The competition that the Fordson stirred up provided the incentive to develop a machine that could do what the Fordson could not. The Fordson was not useful for cultivating crops. It did not have a driveshaft power take off, and therefore was not suitable for the new harvester implements. Most of all, while

Keller's beautifully restored Model C sets by the Haese Carriage House in Haese Memorial Village, Forest Junction, Wisconsin. Mr. F.G. Haese opened a general merchandise business here in 1888. It was later taken over by his son, Robert. Besides the store building, which included living quarters, there were several out-buildings appropriate to the times. These included the carriage house, a barn, a chicken coup, and storage buildings. The Haeses sold groceries, furniture, clothing, seeds, feed, lumber, and Oliver plows. They also operated the first gas station in the area.

it could replace some horses on a farm, it could not replace them all.

As early as 1910, Harvester engineers had talked to General Manager Legge about a more versatile tractor. The head of the Experimental Department at the time was a young engineer with an irrepressible spirit named Edward Johnston.

Johnston and his team, which included such geniuses as Bert R. Benjamin and C.W. Mott, had some ideas for improving the tractor's utility. Their first accomplishment was the invention of the rear driveshaft-type power takeoff (PTO). This was incorporated into their 8-16 tractor, and subsequently became standard equipment on the new 10-20.

The team also worked on and tested many variations on the all-purpose "Motor-Cultivator" theme. Some time during 1919 the name of their tractor was changed from "Motor-Cultivator" to "Farmall." As they went along, they kept General Manager Legge and Chairman McCormick informed, but no official corporate interest was shown.

In July of 1921, when the Fordson threatened the whole Interna-

Notice the different type of seat mounting on this rare side-steer tricycle 1929 GP. Most regular GPs use a post-type seat support. Also note the chain final drive housings. Among the John Deere tractors, only the GP and the Model D employed chain final drives. Prior to the time that metallurgy had progressed to where gear deflection under such high loads was no longer a problem, chain final drives were much in favor. This GP is Keller's, Serial Number 204213.

tional Harvester empire, Legge called in Johnston and ask him what had happened to the ten or so, all-purpose tractor designs. By then, Johnston and his team had focused on one type, and several prototypes of this design existed. Johnston insisted that this all-purpose "Farmall" could beat the Fordson in every way. When told this, Legge immediately ordered the construction of twenty more hand-built examples. He also ordered a full complement of implements to be built customized for the Farmall. Both were to be ready for thorough testing in 1922.

Legge and Johnston resisted the temptation to rush the Farmall into production despite the rising menace

of the Fordson. The engineers worked out design problems for both performance and mass production. In 1924, some 200 pre-production models were sold to customers. Harvester field men watched closely as the farmers put the new Farmall through its paces under actual conditions.

The Farmall sales exceeded all expectations in 1925. By 1926, the new Rock Island (Illinois) plant was in operation and Farmalls were rolling out the door. The Farmall then drove the lowly Fordson from the field. But even at its peak production, before the crash of '29, only about 24,000 Farmalls per year

During experiments with the John Deere Model C, the forerunner of the Model GP, one configuration tried was the tricycle layout. Later, when it was determined that the regular GP's arched wide-front axle, and its attendant 3-row equipment, were not accepted in some areas, a tricycle version of the GP was brought out. About Twenty-three of these were made in 1929 and 1930. The one shown, owned by the Kellers of Forest Junction, Wisconsin, is probably the only one that was not later returned to the factory to be modified into the GPWT (General Purpose, Wide-Tread) configuration and renumbered with a 400000 series serial number.

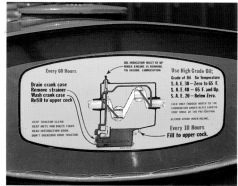

Lubrication requirements were visually augmented by this diagram that graced the end of the fuel tank on most of the older John Deere models. It was right in front of the driver where it couldn't be missed.

were built. This was a far cry from the 100,000 Fordsons built during Ford's peak years. By the end of the 1920s, International Harvester Company was clearly again at the top of the long-line farm implement industry. It enjoyed sales of three times that of its nearest competitor, Deere & Company, of Moline, Illinois.

Deere's first reaction to the Fordson challenge was to take a look at the Waterloo Boy in comparison to other tractors in the field. International Harvester had introduced a new 15-30 in 1921, and a 10-20 in 1922. Hart-Parr had come out with a new 12-25 and a 15-30 in 1918. All looked much more like a Fordson than like a Waterloo Boy! All were smaller, lighter, had automotive-type steering, and had the radiator/fan in front and an engine hood like a car. Even before Deere's acquisition, Waterloo Boy engineers had been working on a modernized version built after the fashion of the competition. Deere engineers quickly picked up on it and developed it into the first production two-cylinder tractor to be called a John Deere: the Model D. It was introduced in 1923. To say that the Model D was a success would be an understatement. It's thirty year production run is the longest of any tractor to date, and firmly established Deere as a maker of quality tractors.

The Advent of the GP

The Farmall differed radically from all other tractors. Its small front wheels were close together in order to run between two rows. Its rear axle did not run straight between the rear wheel hubs, but was connected down to the hubs through a large gear mesh. The result of this arrangement was a tractor with its rear axle built high, pro-

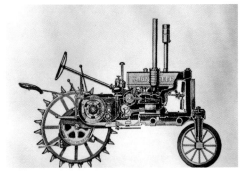

A cut-away shows the internal layout of the John Deere GP Wide-Tread. *Deere Archives*

The original GPWT (Wide-Tread) tractors had the same type of side steering as was used on the regular GPs. In 1931, the steering was converted to the overhead type, as shown here. This type of steering became almost universal for the various brands of row-crop tractors. The GPWT shown here has the "dished" potato wheels, which could be reversed for changing row spacing. *Deere Archives*

viding 30 inches of clearance above the ground. The larger-than-normal diameter rear wheels were wide enough apart to straddle the two rows that the front wheels ran between. It had a 20 horsepower engine and weighed about 4,000 pounds. Its main custom implement was a two-row cultivator

Many felt that Deere had finally gotten it right with the "over-the-top" steer GPWT. It was the most like the successful Farmall and Oliver all-purpose machines. The GPWT was only built one year (1933), and only 444 were built.

mounted to the front frame. This made power cultivation of crops such as corn and cotton practical (for the first time in a volume production tractor).

The new Farmall did not replace the standard tractor; the production of these continued to increase. By 1928, however, the Fordson's annual production was down to 12,500 and Henry Ford gave up, saying he needed the production space for his new Model A car. At International Harvester, the combination of their standard tread tractors and the new Farmall gave them a 70 percent share of the tractor market after the Fordson was gone. Deere & Company knew they had to react to Harvester's dominance of the field.

By the mid-twenties, John Deere had firmly established itself

as a viable tractor maker. Although it was experiencing fierce competition from Ford and International Harvester, the strongest competitor was still the horse. The powerful standard-tread Model D was generally considered a plowing tractor, or a prime mover engine for the thresher, jobs the steam tractor had long since taken over from the horse. But times were changing. At the time, most day to day farm work was done using a team of two horses. Thus, a need was recognized for a tractor smaller than the Model D for such work as could be done by a team, and because a tractor doesn't tire, it could actually replace four to six horses.

International Harvester was flooding the market with the new Farmall in 1926, billing it as a "general purpose" tractor. It could be used for planting, cultivating, and harvesting, as well as for plowing and driving the thresher. This was revolutionary, and a real challenge to the horse.

In response to the Farmall, John Deere brought out the 10hp (at the drawbar) Model GP (for "General Purpose"). The belt rating was 20 horsepower. The GP was introduced in 1928; the second production tractor to bear the John Deere

name. It had the same basic layout as the Model D, with wide-spread front wheels. The GP, however, had a high arched front axle which enabled it to straddle the center row and thereby cultivate not two rows, as the Farmall, but three rows at one time. A three-row planter was also developed. The GP was rated for a two-bottom plow.

The GP featured a mechanical implement power lift system, which was an industry first, plus individual rear wheel brakes. It also incorporated a 520rpm power take-off.

Like the Model D, and indeed all John Deere tractors until 1960, it used a two-cylinder engine similar to that of the Waterloo Boy. The GP's engine began life with 312ci, but after 1931, displacement was increased to 339ci. The GP engine was of the L-head type and engine speed was 950rpm. A 3-speed transmission was used. The basic weight of the Model GP was 3,600 pounds.

Although the GP continued in the line until 1935, its acceptance by farmers, especially in the South, and its performance in the field,

Keller's GPWT (General Purpose Wide-Tread) with over-the-top steering. Previous versions of the tricycle GP had an angled steering shaft. Some "side-steer" GPWT's were recalled to the factory and rebuilt to the over-the-top configuration.

was disappointing. Acceptance was low primarily because of the three-row concept. Farmers wanted two-row equipment in some areas, and four-row in others. Additionally, the $800 price tag was high for a 10/20 horsepower tractor, with the Farmall selling for around $600. The GP should have had more horsepower, but Deere engineers could not get the engine to come up to expectations until 1931, when the bore was increased a quarter of an inch. The rating was then upped to 16/24 horsepower.

The John Deere Model GP actually began life as the Model C in 1927 when twenty-five were built. Sixteen of these were rebuilt into an improved configuration. Sixty-nine more of this new configuration were also built, but more problems were encountered, so thirty-seven of these were recalled and modified. After 110 Model Cs were built, the designation was changed to GP. The designation was changed to better counter the "general purpose" image of the Farmall, and because C sounded too much like the designation of their other tractor, the D. One must remember the quality of the telephone system of the late twenties. The names "Powerfarmer" and "Farmrite" were considered but discarded.

During the experiments associated with the Model C, one configuration was tried which used a "tricycle" layout; that is, two front wheels close together and the rear wheels on a fifty-inch tread. As soon as it was recognized that the "three-row" layout of the standard GP was not being accepted in all quarters, a tricycle GP with this new tread arrangement was brought out. About twenty-three of these were interspersed in the GP production during late 1929 and early 1930. Two of these had special rear treads of sixty-eight inches to accommodate two standard potato rows.

Later in 1929, the GPWT, or GP Wide-Tread, was introduced. It had longer axles, giving it a seventy-six inch rear tread and allowing it to straddle two regular rows. In addition, some 203 were built with the special "potato" row axles. In 1931,

dished wheels were developed, allowing the standard Wide-Tread to be converted for potato rows and the "P" (for potato) series of GPs was eliminated.

One place in which the Farmall still held the advantage was in operator vision for cultivating. Therefore, in 1932, the hood of the GPWT was narrowed, and the steering was changed so that a shaft ran over the engine, like the Farmall, rather than along side the engine as on the other GPs.

The first John Deere orchard tractor was based on the GP. It had fender skirts covering the rear wheels down to below the hubs, and extending over the flywheel and belt pulley. This model, the "GPO," came out in 1930. Some of these were purchased by the Lindeman Company and were fitted with crawler tracks for use in the large, hilly apple orchards around Yakima, Washington.

In 1928, Charles Deere Wiman, great grandson of John Deere, became president of Deere & Company. William Butterworth was elevated to the new position of Chairman of the Board, partly because he had been elected president of the U.S. Chamber of Commerce, which required much of his time. Wiman was thus responsible during most of the travail of bringing the GP to fruition. And although the GP finally made a respectable showing in the Deere product line, Charles Wiman always remembered it as "an outstanding failure" and often commented: "Well do I recall how much tractor business was lost by our company due to the bad design of the GP line." Nevertheless, over 30,500 GPs were sold by the end of production in 1935.

John Deere Model GP

General Specification:	Wide-Front Version	
Years Produced:	1928-1935	
First Serial Number:	200211	
Last Serial Number:	230745	
Total Built:	30,534 appr., all types	
Price, New:	$800 (1928); $1,200 (1931)	
Horsepower (Max.)	Drawbar	PTO/Belt
5.75"x6.0"	18.7	24.7
6.0"x6.0"	26.2	29.6
Engine Displacement		
5.75"x6.0" Engine (to S/N 223802):	312ci	
6.0"x6.0" Engine (from S/N 223803):	339ci	
Engine Rated rpm: 950		
Wheels, Standard		
Rear:	42x10 inches	
Front:	24x6 inches	
Length (inches):	112	
Height to Radiator (inches):	56	
Weight (pounds):	3,600	
Transmission		
Speeds Forward:	3	

A 1933 John Deere GPWT with "over-the-top" steering, owned by Bruce and Walter Keller of Forest Junction, Wisconsin. This one is Serial Number 405135.

JOHN DEERE
GENERAL PURPOSE
REG. IN U.S. PAT. OFF.

EVERY 10 HOURS
FILTER AND WASH IN GASOLINE USING
DOWN MOTION. SWING VIGOROUSLY
TO GET OUT SURPLUS GASOLINE. SUBMERGE
FILTER 2 MINUTES IN NEW OIL. ALLOW
OIL TO DRAIN OFF AND REPLACE FILTER.

Chapter 4

A New Deal For Farmers

John Deere Models A and B

"With everything so quiet, it's hard to get any enthusiasm in work. It is depressing to learn so much about hard times, cutting expenses, etc. An experimental man needs enthusiasm to do good work. And I can see how this depression affects original thinking." Thus wrote Theophilus Brown in his diary in 1931. Theo Brown was head of Deere's experimental department, a Deere & Company board member, and a 1901 graduate of the Worcester Polytechnic Institute.

The 1920s was a decade of constant turmoil in the implement and tractor business. First it was the upheaval caused by the Fordson and the tractor price war. Next, it was the Farmall and the clear cut case for the horse-replacing all-purpose trac-

One of several variations on the logo theme that graced the early John Deere general purpose machines. This one is on Model B Serial Number 1000.

tor. In 1928, the Canadian giant Massey-Harris bought the J.I. Case Plow Works and established itself in Racine, Wisconsin. In the process, Massey-Harris acquired the rights to the competent Wallis tractor.

Case was not eliminated, however, as they retained the rights to the J.I. Case name, and immediately bought the Emerson-Brantingham Corporation. Emerson-Brantingham was an old-line implement maker in Rockford, Illinois, which had been in business since 1852. The history of Emerson-Brantingham included such steamer names as Geiser and Reeves. "Emerson-Brantingham" had been on a distinguished line of gas tractors, as well. Case merged Emerson-Brantingham with the J.I. Case Threshing Machine Company and called the resulting firm the J.I. Case Company, Inc.

Next, in 1929, the Oliver Chilled Plow Works, the Hart-Parr Company, the American Seeding Machinery Company, and the Nichols & Shepard Company

merged to form the Oliver Farm Equipment Company. Likewise, Minneapolis-Moline Power Implement Company was formed from of a conglomeration of individual companies that included the maker of the Twin City tractor. In addition, Allis Chalmers, a company that had been coming on strong, completed its line by adding the Monarch crawler tractor and the Advance-Rumely thresher. John Deere was also expanding, and completing its line by acquiring the Wagner-Langemo thresher and the Hoover potato harvester.

Thus, by 1929 there were seven major "long-line" implement companies vying for the business. They were ranked as follows:

- International Harvester   52%
- Deere & Company   21%
- J.I. Case   8%
- Oliver Farm Equipment   8%
- Minneapolis-Moline   4%
- Massey-Harris   4%
- Allis-Chalmers   3%

This rare ANH is owned by the Kellers of Forest Junction, Wisconsin. The 1938 model has a four-speed transmission and a 309ci engine.

Opposite page left, the Model B was introduced in 1935 as a smaller version of Deere's great Model A. This 1935 version of the Model B was rated at only 9.28 drawbar horsepower at the University of Nebraska tests. The last B, the 1952 model, was rated at 24.46 drawbar horsepower, showing how the model grew during its life.

Perfect restoration as is only befitting such a rare collector's item as this 1938 ANH. Only twenty-six were made!

The Wico magneto on an early unstyled Model A.

Interestingly, each one of these companies was engaged in a search for the perfect "All-Purpose," or "General Purpose" tractor.

After the tractor price war, business had been quite good for the implement makers, although Charles Deere Wiman still worried about Harvester's dominance. But it wasn't Harvester that was the unseen threat in the summer of 1929, but the twin specters of economic depression and drought. The market crash in October did not, at first, affect Deere or the other long-line companies (although Massey-Harris did show a loss for the year). By the summer of 1930, however, layoffs and factory closings were happening at Deere as well as the others. Still no one seemed to appreciate the catastrophe that was developing.

Overall industrial output was cut in half by 1933; unemployment soared. Prices, especially farm prices, plummeted. To add to this misery, severe droughts occurred in 1930 and 1934. Winds swept away the topsoil from Kansas and Oklahoma. To make matters worse for Deere, management had just before adopted a policy of financing the purchase of Deere equipment by the farmers. Now, the farmers who could were concentrating on subsistence farming; they had no cash to pay off equipment loans. Deere was in the ticklish spot of alienating (or bankrupting) their customers if they forced collection.

The John Deere B was essentially a scale model of the A, although there are subtle differences between the two in design details. The steering post and gear set shown here are on a 1935 B. It is somewhat different from the Model A post.

Would you believe...? This is the very first John Deere Model B tractor. Serial Number 1000. One of several "first editions" owned by the Kellers.

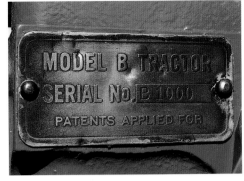

This brass tag is what every tractor collector dreams of finding on a relic behind someone's barn: the tag indicates this is the first of over 300,000 John Deere Model B tractors. It is, however, like most valuable antique tractors, already found. It belongs to the Kellers of Forest Junction, Wisconsin.

A 1936 "short-hood" Model B, Serial Number 18378, owned and restored by Lyle Pals of Egan, Illinois. Pals bought it from a neighbor who bought it new. Until Serial Number 42133 the Model B's frame was five inches shorter. After a gap in the numbering sequence to 42199 and beginning with Serial Number 42200, Bs are known as "long-hoods," or "long-frames."

It was within this forgoing scene that Deere President Charles Wiman made a fateful decision. He instructed Theo Brown, the research manager, to aggressively pursue the development of two new general purpose tractors. There was to be a 2-plow, and a 1-plow version. The idea was to replace the disappointing GP and to counter the successful Farmall and Oliver "row-crop" tractors. Although Wiman was forced to eliminate some non-machinery research, and to even close some experimental farms, it was his conviction that power farming was the wave of the future. It was his appreciation for machinery and his engineering training and interest that spurred the tractor program.

The year 1932 saw the election of Franklin Delano Roosevelt by a frustrated electorate, tired of Former-President Hoover's apparent "do-nothing" policy. Roosevelt considered his election a mandate to "do-something-even-if-wrong." His New Deal program changed the country to such an extent that the effects are still emerging 60 years later.

Nevertheless, the New Deal was good for the farmers of the Thirties. Just three months after Roosevelt took the oath of office, Congress passed his Agricultural Adjustment Act. In exchange for direct subsidy payments, farmers were to curtail production. Other New Deal legislation called for the distribution of farm surplus to those "on relief," soil conservation measures, farm credit, rural electrification, and re-settlement of inhabitants of uneconomical farms. Although some of these measures were later deemed unconstitutional, the farmers, and hence the farm machinery makers, began to prosper. By 1936 the sales of the long-line companies were almost what they had been in 1929.

Although outwardly remaining much the same over the years, the Model B engine grew in displacement from 149ci to 190ci over its lifetime. The engine shown is on B Serial Number 1000, the very first Model B.

Development of the Models A and B

In the depths of the Great Depression, Charles Wiman bet the company on the two new General Purpose tractors. The Model A came out first in April 1934; the B almost a year later in 1935. There were at least eight experimental tractors

Rubber tires were always an option for the John Deere B, introduced in 1935. This 1936 model is owned by Lyle Pals of Egan, Illinois. Lyle recalls when his dad first replaced the steel wheels with rubber on the old open fan-shaft Model A. Lyle, then a young teen, heard his father complain as Lyle drove through the farm yard, "Look Ma, he's got it in high already!"

built before settling on the configuration of the A. Six of these incorporated a new four-speed transmission. The other two used the traditional three-speed unit. These tractors were known respectively as Models AA-1 and AA-3. After thorough testing, the AA-1 configuration became the Model A. The Model B was essentially a two-thirds scale model of the A, incorporating all the same features.

The appearance of these two new models in the depth of the depression rocked the competition on their heels, and spoke volumes to the beleaguered farmers. The farmers, already in love with the rugged simplicity of Deere products, and the performance of Deere tractors on low-cost kerosene, also bet their farms on the new tractors. The fact that these two tractors "delivered the goods" for both the farmers and for John Deere accounts in part for their long-lived popularity. Like the lasting friendship of "foxhole buddies," those who struggled with new tractors in the early thirties were fully bonded with those machines when they worked well.

Company literature of the times stated that the Model A had the pulling power of a six-horse team, and had a daily work output greater than ten horses. The Model B was a 4/6 horse replacement. A 1939 option of a generator and lights made night work practical, further exacerbating the horse-tractor disparity.

This Model B sports a ring-type drawbar of the type used in the 1934-1936 time-frame.

By 1935 the power and weight of the GP were exceeding that of the new Model A. A new, smaller, more agile tractor was needed to compete with a team of horses. The Model B filled the niche not only because of its smaller size, but also because it cost less, and used less fuel than larger tractors, including the GP. Nebraska Tractor Test No. 232 showed the B producing a little over ten horsepower hours per gallon of low-cost kerosene; an improvement of about one horsepower hour per gallon over the GP.

In 1932, when Brown and his team began working on the new tractors, the general purpose, or "Row Crop" tractor had come into its own. By then, however, it was clear that there was a market for both row crop tractors as well as for standard tread tractors. Therefore, standard tread, or "regular" versions of both the A and B were introduced as the AR and BR. These were not considered to be "general purpose" tractors as they did not incorporate the implement lift, adjustable wheel tread, nor differential steering brakes. Orchard versions, the AO and the BO, were also available. The Lindeman Company, of Yakima, Washington, converted some 2,000 BO models to their Lindeman Crawler by adding Caterpillar-type tracks. Industrial wheel tractor versions of both the A and B tractors were also available as the AI and BI.

It had developed that the tricycle configuration was the conventional arrangement for general purpose machines, rather than the arched wide-front axle of the Deere Model GP. Except for certain specialized applications, the new tricycle GPs, as As and Bs were called, would vastly outsell the standard tread tractors. On the original configuration, the two front wheels were close together. By 1937, variations with only one front wheel, with adjustable wide-fronts, and extra high-clearance (hi-crop) versions of all front end-types were made available.

The Model A was introduced first simply because of the limitations of manpower and facilities.

A rare 1938 John Deere BWH (Model B, Wide wheel spacing, High crop clearance), one of only fifty made. The BWH was specially configured for corn, sugar cane, and cotton cultivation. This one, Serial Number 57718, is the favorite of owner Bruce Keller, Forest Junction, Wisconsin. The Keller family has one of the top five antique tractor collections in the world.

The early row-crop tractors had the words "John Deere" cast into the rear axle. It was one of some 300,000 Bs built until production was shifted to the Model 50 in 1952.

Besides designing and testing the new line, Theo Brown and his staff still had responsibility for the original Model GP, which continued in the Deere line until the B came out.

The Model B was originally available with pneumatic tires (the A was not), it also had a four-speed transmission, a PTO and a belt pulley. Its engine, a scaled version of that in the A, had enough power for

"WELL, SHEP, I suppose you think Joe could grease this a blame sight faster and better'n I can.

"An' you don't have to sit there lookin' like you're the only one that misses that kid. I expect he figures it's a lot more excitin' piloting a tank than riding this tractor, and he sure looked a lot snappier in his uniform than he did in a pair of overalls, but, shucks! . . . he'll be glad to get back one of these days.

"You know, Shep, it's kinda surprising how much less gas we use now that the kid ain't around to think up a thousand and one reasons why he should drive to town. Ma says the washing and ironing is a lot easier, too, but she don't seem to appreciate it much.

"We're pretty lucky back here, Shep. We ain't got any Germans or Japs takin' pot shots at us—not yet. But it ain't all easy sledding, neither. Humph!—no use thinkin' about what we're doin' back here, but if working and praying will do any good, Shep—an' it will—we'll have Joe back with us before too long.

"Go on! Git! Shep . . . you're takin' my mind off my work!"

*

Farm folk throughout our nation are carrying on courageously in the face of serious obstacles. Mentally awake—with hearts attuned to the great task before them—these defenders of the second line are meeting the need for the farm produce so important in the pursuit of the war and in the peace to come. In the same spirit, American industry has tuned its cadence to a martial tempo, speeding the production of war material.

Ours is a peace-loving nation. Our strength is built upon freedom of individual enterprise—on freedom from regimentation. It is to preserve and perpetuate these blessings that we enter whole-heartedly into a ruthless war—that we draw the double-edged sword of freedom and invoke a righteous wrath against the aggressor. And these blessings *will* survive, for an American people, aroused to the danger of domination, have rallied in defense of their liberties just as did their fore-bears a hundred and seventy-five years ago.

These things must survive the battle because, as a free-born people, we look forward beyond the strife and final victory to peace and the return to the American way of life.

We all await the day when machines will be used solely in peaceful pursuits. Meanwhile, we must keep our farm implements in good working condition, guarding zealously the performance of each. Your John Deere dealer will render invaluable aid in maintaining your farm equipment at greatest efficiency. Make his store your service headquarters.

JOHN DEERE

MOLINE, ILLINOIS

Are you ear-marking some of your War Bonds for farm equipment you will need after the war? Uncle Sam needs your dollars now—you'll find need for them later.

Right and below, the 1938 John Deere BWH. Still trying to be sure they got their share of the all-purpose tractor trade, John Deere emblazoned the hoods of the new Models A and B, when introduced in 1934 and 1935, with the words "General Purpose." International Harvester started the trend in 1926 when they introduced their eminently successful Farmall. The concept, signifying a machine that could plow, cultivate, and drive other implements via flat belt or power take off, had revolutionized the concept of the farm tractor. The concept also saved the tractor and implement makers from the overwhelming onslaught of the Fordson, which could not cultivate, and which had no PTO.

one 16-inch plow (the A was capable of pulling two fourteens).

What made the Models A and B so special? After all, the Farmall had been out for ten years by the time the A was introduced. These two GPs had two remarkable features that were industry firsts: fully adjustable rear wheel widths on splined axles, and hydraulic implement lifts. These alone were enough to insure the success of the A and B. In addition, a single-piece rear axle housing provided more crop clearance and allowed a center location for attachment of the drawbar, as well as a center location for the PTO.

Production of the Models A and B continued through 1952. Almost 300,000 Model As were built, and more than 300,000 Model Bs. These tractors were immensely profitable for both Deere and the farmers who bought them. Over the years there was a process of continual up-grade and improvement. One great line of demarcation occurred in 1938, however, when styling came to the John Deere tractor.

To be a farmer in that era, one had to be practical just to survive. Nevertheless, some tractor manufacturers were attempting to combine form and function as early as 1920 (the Peoria Tractor Company's "Streamline," for example). By 1935, many tractor makes had styled radiator grills.

The introduction in 1935 of the Oliver Hart-Parr 70 tractor marked one of the most profound turning points in the farm implement industry's direction. It reflected both the optimism of the improving econom-

ic situation and the increasing influence of the automobile on tractor design. From 1933, durable goods companies began to see that styling and product differentiation had a positive effect on sales. Up to the thirties, cars, for example, were quite a bit alike: boxy, 4-cylinders, clam fenders, exposed radiators. By the mid-thirties, styling was individualistic. Six-, eight-, twelve-, and even sixteen-cylinder engines had replaced the fours, and radiator grills were the hallmark of styling. The new Oliver 70, in 1935, was so carlike, that it immediately overshadowed the competition. It influenced tractor design from then on. It was styled! It was powered by a six-cylinder engine! It could be equipped with an electric starter and lights! Its high-compression engine was designed to run on 70 (hence the model designation) octane gasoline! It had an instrument panel and finger-tip controls! Advertising of the day showed "Sister" and "Bud" taking their turns at the wheel.

In other industrial areas, pleasing esthetic proportions were in vogue, from trucks to telephones, and some well-known designers were achieving a measure of prominence. One of these was Henry Dreyfuss of New York City. Charles Stone, who then headed Deere's manufacturing was approached by his engineers to allow them to contact Dreyfuss about tractor styling. Stone said he didn't think much of the idea but then added reluctantly, "The boys up here want it, so go ahead." The whimsical story is that in the fall of 1937, one of Stone's development engineers went unannounced to engage Dreyfuss for the task of styling the tractor line. The engineer showed up at Dreyfuss' New York office in a fur coat and a straw hat. This so impressed the designer with the potential for re-

designing a tractor that he returned that same day to Waterloo with the Deere engineer.

Dreyfuss made the deal with Deere officials, and within a month had a wooden mockup of a new version of the Model B ready for review. The functional beauty of it startled the Deere engineers. This was much more than a radiator grill addition. The styling was indeed functional. The striking new hood was slimmer, enhancing cultivator visibility, and the new radiator cover, more than just a grill, protected the cooling system from collecting debris.

In an incredibly short time, the Deere-Dreyfuss team brought both the A and B styled models out for the 1938 season. The acceptance by the customers led to a continuing styling improvement program that continues to this day. Completion of the initial "Styling" program continued for the next eleven years (due in part to the intervention of World War II) with the venerable AR and its orchard running mate, the AO, the last to receive the treatment in model year 1949. The BR and BO were discontinued 1947, so never received Dreyfuss styling.

International Harvester was not caught napping by the competition. Seeing the trend toward more functional and eye-pleasing design, Harvester engaged the services of Raymond Lowey; another noted industrial designer (who later gained worldwide renown with his rakish design of the 1953 Studebaker car line). Lowey was commissioned to overhaul the entire IHC product line from the company logo to product operator ergonomics. By late 1938, the same year that John Deere brought out "styled" tractors, Harvester introduced the new TD-18 crawler tractor. The TD-18 was undeniably

For its time, the John Deere Model AOS (Model A, Orchard, Streamlined) was a striking tractor. This example, owned by the Kellers of Forest Junction, Wisconsin, was manufactured January 21, 1937. Originally designated Serial Number 103, it was shipped to Windsor Locks, Connecticut. Later, it was returned to the factory for rebuild and was redesignated Serial Number 1319. It was then shipped to Traverse City, Michigan. It is one of only two AOS models with engine oil dipsticks.

striking in its new, bright-red, smoothly contoured sheet metal, hood, and grill. Just months later, a new lineup of wheel tractors was announced continuing the styling motif, and even carrying it farther through the application of contoured fenders and styled wheels. The 1939 Lowey Farmalls still look quite stylish today!

The Nebraska Tests Begin

Under the skin, the Model A remained much the same after styling for three years. For the B, however, engine displacement was increased from 149 to 175ci at this time. In 1941, the A received a displacement increase from 309 to 321ci, and the transmissions of both models went from four speeds to six. This transmis-

Most available mufflers for John Deere As are too tall to be correct. Lyle Pals disassembles mufflers such as this one, cuts off the excess, and welds them back together. Such are the lengths restorers will go to achieve originality.

sion change was first accomplished by employing a three-speed gear box and a high-low range auxiliary. Two shift levers were used. Later, a single-lever arrangement was substituted.

The Model A finished its career with this engine/transmission combination, but the B enjoyed one more displacement increase in 1947 to 190ci. Along with this change, both models went from a channel-iron frame to a pressed-steel frame.

This extremely rare John Deere Model AOS is displayed in the Haese Memorial Village, Forest Junction, Wisconsin. The AOS designation was given to differentiate between it and the previous orchard version of the Model A, the AO, which did not incorporate the flowing sheet metal to allow the tractor to slip through without snagging or damaging the trees.

1947 to 1952 Models A and B are known as "late-styled" versions.

Perhaps a word or two concerning tractor performance, and the measurement thereof, would be in order here. Early power farmers were more often than not the victims of over-sold, under-designed tractors. But because there were so many of them in those days, farmers had particular clout with the legislatures. They began to clamor for a national rating system for tractors, so that at least the power capability of a tractor could be understood. There had been competitive tractor trials in Winnipeg and at certain other cities in the U.S. and Canada that pointed out disparities between advertising claims and actual performance. These trials left a lot to be desired, as the tractors were

often heavily modified by the factory, and an army of mechanics and engineers kept them running long enough to compete. National legislation became bogged down in politics, however, and a reliable rating system never came to pass.

A Nebraska farmer, named Wilmot F. Crozier, who had also been a school teacher (to support the farm, he said), purchased a "Ford" tractor from the Minneapolis outfit not related to Henry Ford. The tractor was so unsatisfactory that he demanded the company replace it. They did, but the replacement was worse. Farmer Crozier then bought a Bull tractor. This too was completely unsatisfactory. Next, he bought a 1918 Rumely "Three-plow." The Rumely met, and

This late-styled Model AWH uses 12.4x42 rear tires.

The carburetor of Lyle Pals' 1949 AWH.

exceeded Crozier's expectations. Not only did it stand up to the strains of farming, he was able to regularly pull a five-bottom plow. Shortly afterward, Mr. Crozier was elected to the Nebraska legislature.

In 1919, Representative Crozier and Senator Charles Warner introduced legislature that resulted in the "Nebraska Test Law." The law required that any tractor sold in the state of Nebraska had to be certified by the state. The state was to test the tractors to see that they lived up to their advertised claims. The tests were to be conducted by the University of Nebraska, Agricultural Engineering Department. L.W. Chase and Claude Shedd devised the tests and the test equipment, which have since become standards for the world.

The first test was made in the fall of 1919 on a Twin City 12-20, but could not be completed because of snow fall. The first complete test was made in the spring of 1920. A certificate was issued for the Waterloo Boy Model N.

John Deere Model A

General Specification:	Row-Crop Version	
Years Produced:	1934-1952	
First Serial Number:	410008	
Last Serial Number:	703384	
Total Built:	300,000 (approx.), all types	
Price, New:	$2,400 (1952)	

Horsepower (Max.)	Drawbar	PTO/Belt
5.5"x6.5"	18.7	24.7
5.5"x6.75"(kero)	26.2	29.6
5.5"x6.75"(gas)	34.1	38.0

Engine Displacement:		
5.5"x6.5" Engine (to S/N 498999):	309ci	
5.5"x6.75" Engine (from S/N 499000):	321ci	

Engine Rated rpm:	975	

Wheels/Tires, Standard

	Wheels	Tires
Rear	50x6in	11.0x38
Front	24x4in	5.5x16

	Unstyled	1938-47	1947-52
Length (inches)	124.0	133.0	134.0
Height to Radiator (inches)	60.0	62.5	63.9
Weight (pounds)	3,525	3,783	4,909

Transmission		
Speeds Forward (early):	4	
(after S/N 499000):	6	

Nebraska tests soon became "gospel" for both buyers and sellers. Many manufacturers did not give their tractors ratings until the Nebraska tests were finished, so as not to be in disparity with the official numbers.

The Models G and H

As the decade of the thirties ended, the more progressive farmers generally had outgrown their horses. Now they were in the market for tractors that would handle larger implements, move them faster, and further multiply the efforts of manpower. They also saw the need for a small tractor, to replace one and two horses for small jobs.

Thus, the arrival of the big John Deere Model G in 1938 was appreciated by larger-acreage farmers who needed at least some row-crop capabilities. It was virtually the power equal of the D. The advent of the H in 1939 was welcomed by both large and small acreage farmers; it was the power equivalent of the original B. Both were general-purpose, row-crop configurations and were not available as standard-tread machines.

Production of the G actually began in May of 1937. It was billed as a full 3-plow tractor, meaning it could handle three 16 inch bottoms in most soils. It had essentially the same power as the D, but was about a half-ton lighter. Therefore, there was more power available to the drawbar, since was used to overcome the tractor's own weight.

Not long after its introduction, Deere began receiving complaints about the G overheating, especially

Like the monoliths of Easter Island, this early-styled B guards a hill side, awaiting the loving touch of the restorer. The true Deere aficionado would say, "add a little gas and give it a push; I'll bet she starts."

John Deere Model B

General Specification:	Row-Crop Version	
Years Produced:	1935-1952	
First Serial Number:	1000	
Last Serial Number:	310775	
Total Built:	300,000 appr., all types	
Price, New:	$1,900 (1952)	

Horsepower (Max.)	Drawbar	PTO/Belt
4.25x5.25in	11.8	16.0
4.50x5.50in	14.0	18.5
4.6 x5.50in (gas)	24.6	27.6
(dist.)	21.1	23.5

Engine Displacement		
4.25x5.25in Engine	(to S/N 59999) 309ci	
4.50x5.50in Engine	(to S/N 200999) 175ci	
4.69x5.50in Engine	(to S/N 310775) 190ci	

Engine Rated rpm
(to S/N 200999) 1,150
(to S/N 310775) 1,250

Wheels/Tires, Standard		
Wheels	Tires	
Rear 48x5.25 in	10.0x38	
Front	22x3.25 in	5.5x16

	Unstyled	1938-47	1947-52
Length (inches)	120.5	125.5	132.3
Height to Radiator (inches)	56.0	57.0	59.6
Weight (pounds)	2,760	2,880	4,000

Transmission		
Speeds Forward (early):	4	
(after S/N 499000):	6	

Lyle Pals's 1952 Late-styled Model BWH, Serial Number 289887. It has clam fenders and lights. The Model BWH is quite rare.

from farmers in warmer climates. Deere finally concluded their radiator sizing parameters did not extrapolate linearly, and that the radiator was indeed too small for the amount of heat being generated.

Accordingly, after Serial Number 4,251, the height of the radiator was increased. Those prior to that Serial are now known as "Low-Radiator Gs." The taller radiator interfered with the overhead steering shaft, so this radiator had a notch in the cast upper tank, which allowed passage of the shaft. Additional engine modifications were made at Serial

Number 7,100 in late 1938 to further improve cooling. These changes can be noted by the much increased size of the upper water pipe fitting on top of the engine.

The G was one of the last to receive Dreyfuss styling, in 1942. At the same time, its transmission was upgraded to six speeds and it was re-identified as the GM it was re-identified as the GM (for modernized) in order to get a price increase past the War Price Board. After the end of WWII, it again reverted to plain G, or New G.

The Unstyled G and the GM were available only as dual-front tricycle types. Post war (New G) versions were also available in single front wheel, wide front, and

Hi-Crop arrangements.

Besides the notched radiator, the unstyled G can be distinguished from its A stablemates in that the sides of the drawbar support are parallel on the G; rather than converging at the front as on the A. Unstyled As do not have cast shift guides, as do the Unstyled Gs, and the broad engine of the G required a bulge in the frame rails. Additionally, on the post 1947 Gs, the angle-iron frame was retained, rather than using the pressed-steel frame as did the A. Also, the Gs stacks were always side-by-side, rather than in-line as on Styled As.

From the '20s to the late '40s, marketing people and engineers at Deere saw their chief competition

John Deere Model G

General Specification:

Years Produced:	1938-1953		
First Serial Number:	1000		
Last Serial Number:	64530		
Total Built:	64,000 appr., all types		
Price, New:	$2,600 (1953)		

Horsepower (Max.)	Drawbar		PTO/Belt
	34.5		38.1

Engine Displacement
    6.12x7.0in Engine 412.5cid

Engine Rated rpm: 975

Wheels/Tires, Standard

	Wheels		Tires
Rear	51.5x7 in		12.0x38
Front	24x5 in		6.0x16

	Unstyled	GM	New G
Length (inches)	135.0	137.5	137.5
Height to Radiator (inches)	61.5	65.9	65.9
Weight (pounds)	4,400	5,624	5,624

Transmission	
Speeds Forward (early):	4
(after S/N 13000):	6

not so much from other tractor makers as much as from the lowly horse. Many farmers only had two or three teams, and many indeed only had one. It was the goal of the Deere designers, from the inception of the Model GP in 1928, to make a tractor that appealed to this large, low-end market.

"To meet the demands of small-acreage farmers everywhere for a tractor that will handle all power jobs at rock-bottom cost, and meet the demands of the large-acreage farmers who have always wanted and needed economical auxiliary power to handle lighter farm jobs, John Deere offers the new one-two plow Model H . . ." Thus reads the 1939 sales brochure introducing the new Model H.

To appeal to the target market, Deere engineers determined to lower the purchase price through simplified design, improved materials and reduced parts count. As with the other GPs in the line, the engineers counted on the two-cylinder engine design, balancing the engine power with the anticipated job. Through the use of low-cost distillate fuels, and through reduced power losses as a result of light-weight construction and by the use of large-diameter rubber tires, engineers intended to reduce operating costs.

The Model H was unique among the GP tractors, in that power was taken off the camshaft rather than the crankshaft. This was done for a number of reasons, all relating to the fact that the H engine was rated at 1,400rpm and could (with the governor override) be operated at up to 1,800rpm. By taking the power out through the camshaft, a 2:1 reduction had taken place and the speed

Author Robert N. Pripps with his 1948 late-styled Model B. The tractor was restored in 1992. The scene is the author's maple forest in north-central Wisconsin.

cut in half before coming out of the engine. This meant a simpler transmission and elimination of the bull-gears normally used to drive the rear axles. Also, at 1,400rpm, the belt pulley would have been too small in

The cows seem awed by the horsepower of this 1951 Styled G. Note the bulge in the frame side rails to make room for the G's 412.5ci engine. The ruggedness of the G, plus the size of its engine, makes it a favorite with the antique tractor pull hobbyist. Some reportedly get as much as 100 horsepower from the modified two-cylinder engine. The G shown is owned by Lyle Pals, of Egan, Illinois.

order to provide the desired maximum belt speed of approximately 3,200 feet per minute (fpm). By cutting the speed in half, the H used an oversized belt pulley (which improved belt traction) and still only provided a belt speed of 2,245 FPM. Because of the camshaft mesh, the belt pulley operated in the opposite direction from the conventional.

Elimination of the bull gears meant that the wheel brakes had to be directly on the axle shafts, rather than on the bull gearshafts, as was the usual Deere configuration. Internally-expanding

shoe-type brakes were provided.

There were four versions of the "H":

- Model H: Dual narrow front, row-crop.
- Model HN: The same as the H, but with a single front wheel. Designed for the California vegetable grower.
- Model HWH: Same as the H, but with 8-38 rear tires and an adjustable wide-front front axle to provide a minimum crop clearance of 21.4 inches.
- Model HNH: Same as the HWH, but with a single front wheel.

Wife object to your tractor collection? Jim Kenney of Streater, Illinois, solved the problem by getting one for wife Nancy. Nancy is shown here on her beautifully-restored John Deere H. *Author Collection*

There were three designations for the Model 320. The first 2,566 carried only the 320 designation. After this, the production was divided between the 320S version, such as the one shown, and a version with a lower stance designated the 320U. The original 320s were configured like the later 320S.

This late-styled John Deere Model B Row Crop has a mounted cord wood saw. Today, many collectors use their antique tractors for a variety of duties. Some even go so far as acquiring twenty or thirty acres to plant, cultivate, and harvest using their antique machinery. An unused antique tractor seems to deteriorate just as fast as one that is used. Besides, with a John Deere antique, you get to enjoy the sound as well! *Author Collection*

World War II and Its Aftermath

December 7, 1941, World War II came to America. Deere had already committed much of its production capacity to the war effort through its Canadian facilities. For U.S. forces, Deere became a subcontractor to the Cleveland Tractor Company in the construction of MG-1 military tractors. Other products included mobile laundry units, tail wheel assemblies, and munitions.

During the war years, Charles Wiman resigned the company's presidency and went into the U.S. Army's tank and combat vehicle group as a colonel in the Ordnance Corps. Later, he moved to a civilian job in the War Production Board. Burton Peek assumed the presidency on a war-duration basis. Late in 1944, however, because of ill-health, Wiman returned to his former job at Deere.

Nevertheless, despite his health problems, Wiman launched a period of expansion and reorganization that placed Deere & Company in good competitive stead for the Post-War boom. He directly encouraged revitalization of tractor development including a new line of tractors, the Model M, from the Dubuque facility. It was a good thing he did, as the specter of the Fordson was rising again like a phoenix; this time in the form of the Ford-Ferguson tractor.

John Deere Model H		
General Specification:		
Years Produced:	1939-1947	
First Serial Number:	1000	
Last Serial Number:	61116	
Total Built:	60,000 appr., all types	
Price, New:	$650 (1940)	
Horsepower (Max.)	Drawbar	PTO/Belt
	12.5	14.8
Engine Displacement:	99.7ci	
Engine Bore and Stroke:	3.56x5.0in	
Engine Rated rpm:	1,400	
Tires	Rear	8x32
	Front	4x15
Length (inches):	111.3	
Height to Radiator (inches):	52	
Weight (pounds):	3,035	
Transmission		
Speeds Forward:	3	

Chapter 5

Post-War Changes

Enter The Utility Tractor

"**Y**ou haven't got enough money to buy my patents," Harry Ferguson bluntly told Henry Ford, probably the richest man in the world in 1938.

"Well, you need me as much as I need you," responded Ford, "so what do you suggest?"

A 1939 Ford-Ferguson 9N, Serial Number 357, owned by Palmer Fossum of North-field, Minnesota. Fossum is only the third owner of the tractor. Even though the 9N was introduced to the public in June of 1939, more than 10,000 were delivered during the model year. *Author Collection*

Left, John Deere's answer to the Ford-Ferguson, the Model M. It was the first tractor produced in the new Dubuque tractor plant. Other than the previous small Models L and LA, it was the first Deere tractor with a driveshaft. The Model M was also the first Deere tractor to have the Touch-O-Matic hydraulic implement lift system. This nicely restored Model M is owned by Jim Kenney of Streater, Illinois. *Author Collection*

Ferguson's proposal was that Ford should build tractors incorporating Ferguson's patented hydraulic lift system. And he, Ferguson, would build implements for it and a dealer organization to sell and service it. With a handshake, the world's first "Utility Tractor" was launched. The result was the famous Ford-Ferguson 9N.

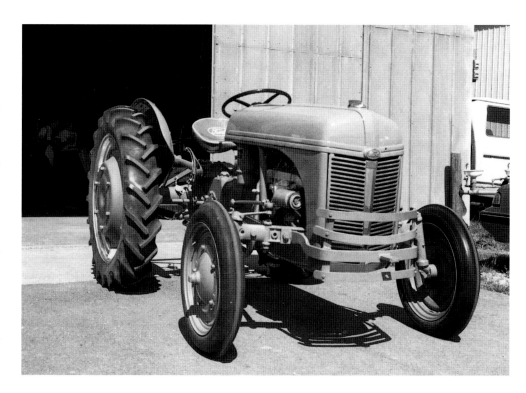

Ford-Ferguson 9N with wheel removed to show the load-transferring 3-point hitch. The plow is shown in the raised position. Draft loads tend to pull down on the rear wheels adding to the traction. The tractor was built by Ford Motor Company. It incorporated the Ferguson System's hydraulic 3-point hitch. This combination revolutionized the tractor business in 1939. *Author Collection*

Just what is a utility tractor? The definition has changed somewhat over the intervening years as tractors have changed. The first mention of such in R.B. Gray's *The Agricultural Tractor, 1855-1950,* concerns the 1918 Kardell Utility. Nothing more is recorded, other than the name and the fact that it was built in St. Louis, Missouri. The term, however, gradually came to be applied to the plethora of Ford-Ferguson look-alikes that developed in the 1950s as Ferguson's patents ran out; though seldom applied to the Ford-Ferguson itself.

By 1938, Ferguson, a somewhat aberrant genius, and his staff of geniuses, had spent seventeen years developing his system. The result of their efforts became known as the 3-point hitch with draft control. In this concept, the single upper link (sometimes called the "free-link") pushes forward on a hydraulic control valve in proportion to the rearward, or draft, load on the two other links. Once the hand-operated hydraulic control positions the implement to the desired depth setting, then the free-link manipulates

Harry Ferguson, left, and Henry Ford, at the press introduction of the 9N Ford-Ferguson tractor in 1939. Ferguson is pointing to the top, or "free," link of his patented 3-point hitch. Draft loads pushed forward on the free link, which was connected to a hydraulic servo valve, causing the hydraulics to raise or lower the implement in proportion to increasing or decreasing draft forces. *Author Collection*

The Ford 8N assembly line. At its peak, Ford was building over 400 of these tractors per day. The 8N (the "8" signifying 1948), was an update of the 9N, introduced in 1939. Ford and Ferguson had parted ways by then and were involved in a bitter law suit. Ferguson began building his own update of the 9N, the Ferguson TO-20. Thus began the proliferation of the squat utility tractor concept, which was to steer the industry away from the general-purpose row-crop configuration. *Author Collection*

At less than 2,500 pounds, the plow it carried (as well as several of the other implements) added almost twenty-five percent to the tractor's weight. Bear in mind that this weight is overhung behind the rear wheels, around which the tractor pivots when a brake is used for a sharp turn. When such a turn is abruptly halted, a roll coupling is imparted to the tractor tending to tip the tractor over sideways. Especially when the tractor's wheels drop into the furrow at the same time, this phenomenon can become quite hazardous. When this system was later applied to high center-of-gravity and tricycle tractors, they had to be much heavier in relation to their implements than the Ford-Ferguson.

Besides being squat and carrying mounted implements, the Ford-Ferguson defined the utility tractor in other ways as well. The operator sat low and well forward over the rear axle with his legs astride the transmission. No platform was used. With hydraulic controls, this much safer position was allowed since there was no need to reach back for implement handles. The front axle was similar to that of wide-front row-crops. It had downward extending king-pins, rather than being straight across as on the standard-tread machines. This feature gave the utility tractor the same crop clearance as wide-front row-

the hydraulics, raising or lowering the implement as required to keep draft load constant.

The effect of the Ferguson System on a tractor's "utility" was revolutionary. The tractor now carried its implements, rather than pulling them. It was now a simple matter to raise the implement at the end of a row, swing around to the next row, and drop it again. The system caused the weight of the implement, plus its draft and suction loads, to bear down on the rear

wheels, greatly improving the traction. Dramatically, the $600 Ford-Ferguson 9N, which made the scene in mid-1939, could plow as many acres in a day as the mighty John Deere G, which was $1,300. The Ferguson System made plowing such a simple task that it was demonstrated at the press introduction by an 8-year old boy!

The configuration of the Ford-Ferguson 9N was also the key to the Ferguson System's success. It was low and squat, and for good reason.

An unstyled B, a 520, and a Model 50 on display at the 1992 Central States Thresherman's Reunion in Pontiac, Illinois. *Author Collection*

crops. The rear axle of the utility tractor configuration generally did not incorporate any drop gearing. Wheel spacing was adjustable. Finally, the utility tractor was equally at home doing standard-tread tractor work or row crop work (up to

the limitation of clearance). It was also generally capable of doing orchard work as well.

Ford sold over 10,000 9Ns in the last half of 1939, over 35,000 in 1940, and over 40,000 in 1941. Yet most competitive marketing organizations thought it just a revived Fordson that would soon run its course. By the end of World War II, however, Deere management recognized that this was not the case.

Much to their chagrin, and that of other tractor manufacturers, the Ford-Ferguson was winning the hearts and minds of the under-100-acre farmer. The Ford-Ferguson was selling for about the same money as the John Deere H. The squat little Ford, however, could plow twelve acres while the H did seven.

From 1939 through 1947, Deere averaged about 25,000 tractors per year for the small-farm market. This

The start of the "Slow Race" at the 1992 Central States Thresherman's Reunion. Competing, left to right, a John Deere Model H; an Allis Chalmers Model G; a John Deere Model D; a John Deere Model M; and a John Deere Model 50. *Author Collection.*

number included Models B, L, LA, and H. In the same time, Ford-Ferguson sold an average 42,000 per year of their only model. Deere and other marketing organizations saw the beginning of the trend away from the tricycle front end.

The John Deere Model M

To counter Ford's inroad into the small farm marketplace, the John Deere Model M was born, replacing the L, LA, and the H. It was billed as a general-purpose utility tractor. The M came equipped with a gasoline-only, verti-cal, relatively high-speed (1,650rpm), two-cylinder engine—a departure from the customary horizontal transverse engine. It also had the Touch-O-Matic rear implement hydraulic lift. This was similar in function to the 3-point hitch. It did not, however, incorporate Draft-Control, as the situation with Ferguson's patents was still unclear.

The M's configuration was that of the Ford-Ferguson. With its verti-

The end of the "Slow Race." The John Deere Model 50 is the hands-down winner. The owner said he did nothing to make it especially slow, that's just the way it is. The John Deere H and the Allis G are battling it out for second place, with the G eventually getting the nod. The John Deere M is out of it, as is the 3-speed Model D, about 50 feet ahead when the operator killed the engine trying to make it run slower. *Author Collection.*

cal "in-line" engine, a driveshaft was required to bring the power back to the transmission. A foot-operated clutch was used. These features had been pioneered on Deere tractors by the diminutive garden-type Models L and LA which also had vertical, in-line two-cylinder engines. The Model M and its successors were built in Deere's Dubuque plant.

By the end of the 1947 model year, Henry Ford II had abrogated

the handshake agreement made by his grandfather and Harry Ferguson. He then began making an updated model called the 8N (for the year 1948). Ferguson, who had already begun making his own similar tractor in England (the TE-20), set up an American factory to make an Americanized version, the TO-20. TE-20s were imported until 1949 while the new factory was coming up to speed. So, with the 8N, the

John Deere Model M		
General Specification:		
Years Produced:	1947-1952	
First Serial Number:	10001	
Last Serial Number:	50580	
Total Built:	40,580	
Price, New:	$1,075 (1952)	
Horsepower (rated)	Drawbar	PTO/Belt
	14.65	18.23
Engine Displacement:	100.5ci	
Engine Bore and Stroke:	4.00x4.00in	
Engine Rated rpm:	1,650	
Tires	Rear	8x24
	Front	4.00x15
Length (inches):	110.0	
Height to Radiator (inches):	56	
Weight (pounds):	2,550	
Transmission		
Speeds Forward:	4	

TE-20 and the John Deere Model M, there were three bona fide "utility" tractors on the market in 1948. In 1951, Ferguson added an up-graded Model TO-30, Ford replaced the 8N with the Jubilee in 1953, and Oliver introduced the Model 55 in 1954. Other makers added rear hydraulic lifts to their regular tractors.

The M's configuration did not satisfy all of Deere's customers, however, so in traditional Deere fashion the MT was added to the line in 1949. The MT was essentially the same tractor, but could be equipped with an adjustable wide-front, dual tricycle front or single front wheel. Dual Touch-O-Matic was an added option, allowing independent control of right and left side implements.

While this series of unique and useful little tractors were extremely durable, productive, and popular, Ford still sold five times as many 8Ns between 1947 and 1952 as all of the variations of the M.

Postwar Expansion

In support of the war effort, Deere & Company produced 75mm cannon shells. To insure a continuing supply, the Army offered to share the cost of a new plant for their production. It was at this time that Charles Wiman returned from his stint in Washington D.C. to retake the reins of the company, full of enthusiasm for postwar prospects. It was under-

stood that this plant would be retained by Deere after the war. The company settled on Dubuque, Iowa, for this new plant. Dubuque was selected as being outside either the Moline or Waterloo labor markets, but yet close enough for ready control from Moline. Being on the Mississippi River also was a factor in choosing Dubuque.

Dubuque, then, became the home of Deere tractors with drive-shafts, such as the Model M and those of its family that followed. Note that the other Deere tractors, made at Waterloo, had transverse engines that were geared directly into the transmissions. This production arrangement was continued until 1960 when the two-cylinder engine was discontinued.

Chapter 6

The General Purpose Tractor Matures

The Numbered Series

"We see the limit here to the Rubber-tired tractor (45-50 drawbar horsepower)," stated Deere's vice president for product development, Charles Stone unequivocally, "after this, it has to be a crawler." 1951 saw an automobile horsepower race begin with the 180 horsepower Chrysler hemi V-8. A similar phenomenon was occurring in the tractor industry. Stone should have known better, though, as the Minneapolis-Moline Model G (1947) and the Massey-Harris 55 (1949) were the first production tractors to exceed 50 horsepower.

Left, the clutch-side of the 50. The "hubcap" covering the unit can be popped off with a screwdriver, exposing the adjusting castellated nuts. The clutch is a multiple-disk type.

The flywheel side of Ramminger's Model 60. On the opposite side of the engine is the clutch in about the same position. Deere heavily advertised the advantages of the accessibility of these two elements. The flywheel is used for manual starting and the clutch is readily disassembled for repair or replacement. Ramminger pointed out that it is the best policy to engage the clutch when the tractor is idling. One should never leave the transmission in gear with the clutch lever back. On their first John Deere tractor when Rich was a boy, they learned this the hard way and burned the clutch out in two weeks. His dad hung the plates on the wall as a reminder.

Previous page, Rich Ramminger's John Deere Model 50. Ramminger has a "matched set" with the 50 shown, and the Models 60 and 70 featured elsewhere in this book. Ramminger also owns an Oliver Super 99 GM; sometimes known as the "Bull Oliver."

What Stone missed, apparently, was the increased traction afforded by the load-transferring 3-point hitch. Today, of course, rubber-tired tractors are approaching 500 horsepower.

When the need for increased power was recognized at Deere, there were also powerful influences within the company to do away with the two-cylinder engine. These included Charles Deere Wiman. The new tractor group at Dubuque, who developed the vertical-engine Model M, had also been experimenting with four-cylinder engines for combines. Wiman favored capitalizing on their progress. Nevertheless, the pent-up demand following the war mandated caution. Tractor sales were

booming. Ultimately, however, there was not time to interrupt production long enough to change engines. Yet, the competition clearly demanded up-grading.

Therefore, after the 1952 model year, the complete line was revised and improved (except for the fairly-new Model R standard-tread diesel). Yet the existing configurations and the two-cylinder engine were retained. The new line of General Purpose tractors was announced as follows:

- The Model 40 replaced the M, which had replaced the H.
- The Model 50 replaced the B.
- The Model 60 replaced the A.
- The Model 70 replaced the G.

The Two-Numbered Series

Despite the dual tractor manufacturing complexes, Waterloo and Dubuque, the 1953 John Deere two-numbered tractors shared common features. Power was increased across the board, plus there were many improvements in styling and convenience. Most importantly, Deere's

answer to the 3-point hitch was universally available. Both the hydraulics and the PTO were now "live," that is, they were independent of the main clutch.

The Model 40 was first available in only a gasoline version, but later, the All-fuel version was added. The others were available in gasoline, All-fuel (for distillate, tractor fuel, or gasoline), and LPG versions. In 1953, a diesel version of the mighty Model 70 was unveiled.

The power increase in the non-diesel engines came mainly from a new duplex (2-barrel) carburetor feeding identical amounts of fuel to each cylinder; the moral equivalent of fuel injection. Revised combustion chambers, called "Cyclonic Fuel Induction," incorporated "raised eyebrows" around the intake valves. These caused swirling of the mixture for better combustion. Additionally, a manually operated manifold heat valve allowed adjusting intake heating according to outside air temperature. This feature,

The John Deere Model 50 was the successor to the venerable Model B. The 50 was built in year models 1952 through 1956. Like the Model 60, the 50 reverted to the angle-iron frame of the pre-1947 models, rather than the pressed-steel frame of the late-styled As and Bs. This one is owned by Rich Ramminger of Morrisonville, Wisconsin. Ramminger is also the owner of Morrisonville Power Equipment Company. This 1955 Model 50 appeared at the 1988 Two-cylinder Expo, and also in the book, *How Johnny Popper Replaced The Horse*. It was originally delivered to a farmer in Plain, Wisconsin. A machinery dealer bought it at an estate sale. Ramminger bought it from the dealer, red with rust. Ramminger then spent over $3,000, plus his and brother Roger's labor, in bringing it to this restored condition.

Rich Ramminger's 1956 Model 60 is shown at 82 year-old Walter Manthe's farm in Arlington, Wisconsin. Walter, who was born on the place, got his first tractor in 1942; a John Deere B. The 65-acre spread supported a family of four.

About 57,000 John Deere Model 60 Row-Crop tractors were built between 1952 and 1956. They originally sold for a little under $2,500. Not a bad price for a tractor with a basic weight of 5,300 pounds.

The Roll-O-Matic narrow front was a John Deere exclusive. The two wheels were geared together in such a way that when one went up, the other went down. This allowed the individual tire to step over an obstacle, such as a rock, raising the front of the tractor only half as much. The result was much easier riding and steering and as an added benefit, the system increased tire life.

The 70 Diesel was Deere's first row-crop diesel tractor. It came equipped with a V-4 pony-motor starter. Exhaust heat from the pony was routed through parts of the diesel to warm them up for starting. Shown is Ramminger's 1956 model shown on the Walter Manthe farm near Arlington, Wisconsin.

especially in the all-fuel and LPG versions, resulted in improved performance and reduced fuel consumption.

The changing of rear wheel spacing for the new models was improved with a rack-and-pinion adjusting mechanism. Also, new for the horizontal engine, a water

The Model 70 Diesel is the "no-neck" of the Deere row-crop line—big, strong, and born to pull! Yet, it set a record for the least fuel consumption on a pounds per horsepower hour basis at the University of Nebraska tests.

A Model 70 Hi-crop LP, one of only twenty-five made. This one is owned by Norman Smith of Carrolton, Illinois. The tractor originally sold for the price of a new Pontiac, but to get Smith's attention today, you'd have to be bringing the price of a new Jaguar or Porsche.

pump and thermostat were added. For the first time these tractors did not rely on the simple, effective, but old-fashioned thermosyphon cooling system. With this change came smaller, higher-temperature, pressurized radiators, using more steel and less copper (which was, because of the Korean Conflict, a military-critical material). Gone also were the manually operated radiator shutters.

With the introduction of the 50 and 60 tractors, the pressed-steel frame was replaced with the cast-steel frame of the type that was used before 1947. This was done, according to advertisements of the day, to provide increased strength for the variety of front-end arrangements while maintaining an equal front-end height. Other features of the new line included an improved seat, optional power steering (in 1954), a 12-volt electrical system, and lengthened clutch and throttle levers.

Although the competition was not standing still, Deere & Company was rapidly overtaking International Harvester as the number one equipment producer.

The Three-Numbered Twenty Series

By 1955, archrival International Harvester had restyled and renumbered their line of tractors. Not to be outdone, Deere in mid-1956, also introduced restyled and renumbered tractors. A number 20 was added to the first number of each series; thus

Lyle Pals bought this Model 70 Diesel, Serial Number 7036203, twice. The second time, he found it on a trailer heading for a scrap yard. Recognizing the serial, Lyle decided the faithful old 70 was too good a friend to see that happen. Since it had a cracked block, Lyle bought another 70 to get the engine, only to discover that the block in that one was cracked, too. Such are the tribulations of the restorer.

John Deere Model 40		
General Specifications:		
Years Produced:	1953-1956	
First Serial Number:	60,001	
Last Serial Number:	77,906	
Total Built:	33,000 Approx.	
Price, New:	$1,500 (1954)	
Horsepower (max., corrected)	Drawbar	PTO/Belt
Gasoline	22.4	24.9
Tractor Fuel	19.0	20.9
Engine Displacement:	100.5ci	
Engine Bore and Stroke:	4.00x4.00in	
Engine Rated rpm:	1,850	
Tires:	Rear	9x24
	Front	5.00x15
Length (inches):	114.3	
Height to Radiator (inches):	56	
Weight (pounds):	2,750	
Transmission		
Speeds Forward:	4	

the 40 became the 420, the 50 the 520, etc. At the same time the Model 320, a new small general purpose utility unit, was added.

The most striking feature of the new series was the yellow hood side panels, a change from the previous all-green sheet metal. The big news with the new series, however, was Custom Powr-Trol; Deere's version of Harry Ferguson's Draft Control. With Custom Powr-Trol a new position-responsive rock-shaft enabled the operator to preset working depth. He could then raise the implement for a turn at the row end, and then drop it to the same working depth as before. Also featured was Load-and-Depth Control (Draft Control). The patents Ferguson held were now up-for-grabs following his settlement with Ford. This feature automatically applied raise-pressure

John Deere Model 50

General Specifications:		
Years Produced:	1953-1956	
First Serial Number:	5000001	
Last Serial Number:	5033751	
Total Built:	33,000 Approx.	
Price, New:	$2,100 (1954)	
Horsepower (max., corrected)	Drawbar	PTO/Belt
Gasoline	27.5	31.0
Tractor Fuel	23.2	25.8
LPG	29.2	32.3
Engine Displacement:	190ci	
Engine Bore and Stroke:	4.6x5.50in	
Engine Rated rpm:	1,250	
Tires:	Rear	11.0x38
	Front	5.00x16
Length (inches):	132.75	
Height to Radiator (inches):	59.9	
Weight (pounds):	4,435	
Transmission Speeds Forward:	6	

John Deere Model 60

General Specifications:		
Years Produced:	1953-1956	
First Serial Number:	6000001	
Last Serial Number:	6063836	
Total Built:	57,300 Approx.	
Price, New:	$2,500 (1956)	
Horsepower (max., corrected)	Drawbar	PTO/Belt
Gasoline	36.9	41.6
Tractor Fuel	30.1	33.3
LPG	38.1	42.2
Engine Displacement:	321ci	
Engine Bore and Stroke:	5.50x6.75in	
Engine Rated rpm:	975	
Tires	Rear	11.0x38
	Front	6.00x16
Length (inches):	139.0	
Height to Radiator (inches):	65.6	
Weight (pounds):	5,300	
Transmission Speeds Forward:	6	

to lift the implement when tough soil conditions were encountered, thereby not only lessening the draft load, but also pulling down on the back wheels to improve traction. Once the hard-spot was passed, the system automatically returned the implement to its original depth.

Except for the diesel, the engines were all new. Power was increased eighteen to twenty-five percent. Displacement increased, speed increased and improved cylinder heads and pistons increased the power and reduced fuel consumption.

The science of ergonomics was used to increase the productivity of

A 1956 John Deere Model 70 diesel with pony-motor start. This one is owned by Rich Ramminger of Morrisonville, Wisconsin. Although it appears to be a fresh restoration, Ramminger did the work about ten years ago, and has worked the tractor about 150 hours since. Ramminger plowed with it during the spring of the year this picture was taken.

A row-crop utility version of the John Deere 420 tractor. Although the Dubuque line of vertical-engined two-cylinder tractors began life on the low end of Deere's horsepower spectrum with the Model M, power was up to 30hp on the PTO by the time the 420 came along. *Deere Archives*

John Deere Model 70		
General Specifications:		
Years Produced:	1953-1956	
First Serial Number:	7000001	
Last Serial Number:	7043757	
Total Built:	43,000 Approx.	
Price, New:	$2,800 (1955)	
Horsepower (max., corrected)	Drawbar	PTO/Belt
Gasoline	44.2	50.4
Tractor Fuel	41.0	45.0
LPG	46.1	52.0
Diesel	45.7	51.5
Engine Displacement		
Gasoline and LPG	379.5	
All-fuel	412.5	
Diesel	376.0	
Engine Rated rpm:	975; Diesel:	1,125
Tires	Rear	12.0x38
	Front	6.00x16
Length (inches):	134.6	
Height to Radiator (inches):	65.6	
Weight (pounds).(gasoline):	6,035	
Transmission		
Speeds Forward:	6	

the tractor by increasing the productivity of the operator. Therefore on the 20 Series, operator comfort and convenience features were added. A new more roomy, "stand-at-will" platform was added, the instruments were easier to read, the controls fell more naturally to hand, and the new Float-Ride seat, supported on an adjustable rubber torsion spring and a hydraulic shock absorber, was standard. Another new operator convenience was power adjustable rear wheel spacing on most models.

The new Model 320, just like the H of 1939, was "sold" to the small farm operator, the truck gardener, or the large-acreage farmer who needed an auxiliary tractor for light work. The 320 was built to handle two 12-inch bottom plows. For some reason, the 320 was never tested at the University of Nebraska.

Now, with all the variations: general purpose, standard tread, orchard, utility general purpose, high-crop; and some of these with a choice of four different fuel engines, the number of distinct tractor offerings was staggering. For the most part, the competition was overwhelmed.

The Three-Numbered Thirty Series

After the broad range of improvements incorporated into the 20 Series just two years earlier, you would think there would not be much left for a new model. Competition in the tractor business was so intense, however, that refinements in the line were mandated. The 238 horsepower Steiger was born in 1957, indicating the trend of the future. Case, Minneapolis-Moline and Oliver had also introduced new, capable diesels in 1957. New automatic transmissions were coming in, such as the Case-O-Matic, and Ford's Select-O-Speed, as well as torque-amplifier step-down shifters on several competing brands; and the Oliver 995 had a torque converter.

John Deere, for the "30" series, concentrated on styling, safety and comfort. New standard-equipment flat-topped fenders, with hand holds, protected the operator from mud and dust, and from accidental

The instrument panel of a pony motor-start Model 70 Diesel has functions for both the pony motor and the diesel itself. By 1953, when the Model 70 came out, instrument panels were much more complete than in the early days of general purpose tractors.

John Deere Model 420

General Specification:

Years Produced:	1956-1958	
First Serial Number:	80001	
Last Serial Number:	136868	
Total Built:	55,000 Approx.	
Price, New:	$2,300 (1958)	
Horsepower (max., corrected)	Drawbar	PTO/Belt
Gasoline	27.1	29.2
Tractor Fuel	21.9	23.5
LPG	28.0	30.0
Engine Displacement:	113ci	
Engine Bore and Stroke:	4.25x4.00in	
Engine Rated rpm:	1,850	
Tires	Rear	9-24
	Front	5.00x15
Length (inches):	119.3 (RCU)	
Height to Radiator (inches):	56	
Weight (pounds):	3,250	
Transmission		
Speeds Forward:	4 (5 optional)	

contact with the tires. Besides the hand-holds, a convenient step in front of the axle made mounting and dismounting safer and easier. The fenders also incorporated a new lighting system for improved night work. A new angled instrument panel featured instruments clustered around the steering column, which now projected upward at a more convenient angle. A 24-volt electric starting option was available in place of the V-4 pony motor on the new 730 diesel. And finally, all models had new quieter "Oval-Tone" mufflers.

A 420H (High-Crop) tractor operates with a sprayer in an alfalfa field. The 420 employed a vertical two-cylinder engine. Like other Deere tractors with vertical engines, it was made in the Dubuque plant. *Deere Archives*

The view from above shows the rugged lines of this 1956 Model 70 Diesel. Starting power was provided by an 18.8ci V-4 pony motor. The basic weight of the Model 70 was over 6,500 pounds. With ballast, that weight can double.

Orv Rothgarn has owned this 520 for about thirteen years. He's used it in planting and cultivating, and has done nothing to it as yet in the way of restoration. The tach shows 5585 hours.

The last new John Deere two-cylinder tractor added to the line appeared in 1959. It was the Model 435 Diesel. This version of the 430 series was powered by a two-cylinder version of the General Motors two-cycle supercharged diesel. This was the first John Deere tractor introduced after the adoption of industry PTO standards; as such, it was available with either a 1,000 or a 540rpm PTO. The 435 was available in only the row-crop utility configuration.

These were truly the ultimate in two-cylinder tractors! Because power did not change for the new models, they were not tested at Nebraska.

The End of the Reign

Early in 1953, after the success of the Two-Numbered Series was assured, Deere management again turned their thoughts to tractor engines with more than two cylinders. The handwriting, they realized, was on the wall: despite their market niche, and all the touted advantages of the two-cylinder engine, its limits had been reached. The question was not whether, but when, for the larger tractors. Another question was whether to switch only the diesels, or to change the entire line at one time.

With all the secrecy of the Manhattan Project, select engineers were

---

John Deere Model 520

General Specification:		
Years Produced:	1956-1958	
First Serial Number:	5200000	
Last Serial Number:	5213189	
Total Built:	13,000 Approx.	
Price, New:	$2,300 (1958)	
Horsepower (max., corrected)	Drawbar	PTO/Belt
Gasoline	34.3	38.6
Tractor Fuel	24.8	26.6
LPG	34.2	38.1
Engine Displacement:	190ci	
Engine Bore and Stroke:	4.69x5.50in	
Engine Rated rpm:	1,325	
Tires	Rear	12.4x36
	Front	5.50x16
Length (inches):	132.75	
Height to Radiator (inches):	59.9	
Weight (pounds):	4,960	
Transmission		
Speeds Forward:	6	

Left, Orv Rothgarn's Model 520. The 520 was introduced in 1956 and production continued into 1958. It was advertised at 26 drawbar horsepower and 32 PTO horsepower.

A typical setting for the John Deere 620 Row Crop tractor. This one is pulling a Model 494 planter with a dry fertilizer attachment. The 620 was made between 1956 and 1958. *Deere Archives*

The row crop version of the 720 was the most common. This one is shown with a Model 666 plow. *Deere Archives*

pulled from their assignments and sent to a remote site. What followed was one of the best-kept non-governmental corporate undercover operations in history. The Deere "Butcher Shop Boys" (they were set up in a former grocery store building) were assigned the task of designing a "New Generation" of tractors. These tractors were to have all-new multi-cylinder engines. They were to be ready for introduction in 1960. There was no concession to retain the two-cylinder for smaller tractors, although, strangely, it was retained in several industrial wheeled tractors and crawlers through 1964. Also, the Model 730 was built for export in Waterloo until early 1961, and was also built in Argentina throughout the 1960s.

With the decision to replace the two-cylinder also came end the reign of Charles Deere Wiman. In 1954 he learned he had a terminal illness and only had months to live. As head of the company since the days of the GP in 1928, Wiman's last major responsibility was to oversee the selection of his replacement. The company's predisposition to Deere family members was upwards in his mind, but such lineal descent was not considered mandatory by the Board. Nevertheless, William Hewitt, Wiman's son-

John Deere Model 620

General Specification:		
Years Produced:	1956-1958	
First Serial Number:	6200000	
Last Serial Number:	6222686	
Total Built:	22,600 Approx.	
Price, New:	$3,000 (1956)	
Horsepower (max., corrected)	Drawbar	PTO/Belt
Gasoline	44.2	48.7
Tractor Fuel	32.7	35.7
LPG	45.8	50.3
Engine Bore and Stroke:	5.50x6.75in	
Engine Rated rpm:	1,125	
Tires	Rear	12.4x38
	Front	6.00x16
Length (inches):	135.25	
Height to Radiator	(inches): 66.0	
Weight (pounds):	5,900	
Transmission Speeds Forward:	6	

The mighty 720S LP. With a 361ci two-cylinder engine, operating on LPG, it could produce a maximum of 60 PTO horsepower. Of the 3,000 720Ss built, very few had the LP option, and are now much sought after by collectors. *Author Collection*

in-law, was selected. On May 12, 1955, Charles Deere Wiman died.

Fortune Magazine ran an article on the leadership transition at Deere. Mr. Hewitt's attributes for the position, the article pointed out, were more real than hereditary. He was young (just 40), but experienced in the business; he had begun his career with Ford-Ferguson and had then served in a branch office of Deere & Company before marrying Patricia Wiman. He was a graduate of the University of California at Berkeley, (except for Wiman, college graduates were not common in Deere management at that time). And he had had a distinguished Navy tour during World War II, rising to the rank of Lieutenant Commander. The Fortune article went on to say that Hewitt's associates within Deere & Company regarded him highly for his friendly personality, leadership, and coolness under pressure. William A. Hewitt assumed the chairmanship of Deere in 1955. August 30, 1960, with hoopla rivaled only by the Super Bowl, the "New Generation" John Deere tractors were unveiled in Dallas. They were an undeniable success for both Deere & Company and for the world's farmers.

John Deere Model 720

General Specification:		
Years Produced:	1956-1958	
First Serial Number:	7200000	
Last Serial Number:	7229002	
Total Built:	29,000 Approx.	
Price, New:	$3,700 (1958)	
Horsepower (max., corrected)	Drawbar	PTO/Belt
Gasoline	53.0	59.1
Tractor Fuel	41.3	45.3
LPG	54.2	59.6
Diesel	53.7	58.8
Engine Displacement		
Gasoline and LPG:	360.5	
All-fuel:	360.5	
Diesel:	376.0	
Engine Rated rpm:	1,125	
Tires	Rear	12.0x38
	Front	6.00x16
Length (inches):	134.6	
Height to Radiator (inches):	65.6	
Weight (pounds).(gasoline):	6,790	
Transmission		
Speeds Forward:	6	

The John Deere Model 320 was introduced as part of the 20 Series in 1956. It
was rated as a one-or two plow tractor.
This one is equipped with the later angled
steering wheel, instead of the vertical
wheel of the original 320s.

John Deere Model 435

General Specification:

Years Produced:	1959-1960	
First Serial Number:	435001	
Last Serial Number:	439626	
Total Built:	4,500 Approx.	
Price, New:	$3,000 (1960)	

Horsepower (max., corrected)	Drawbar	PTO/Belt
	27.6	32.9

Engine Displacement:	106ci	
Engine Bore and Stroke:	4.87x4.50in	
Engine Rated rpm:	1,850	

Tires	Rear	13.6x28
	Front	6.00x16

Length (inches);	119.3	
Height to Radiator (inches):	56	
Weight (pounds):	4,000	

Transmission	
Speeds Forward:	4 (5 optional)
Direction reverser optional	

Certainly one of the neatest collector tractors of all time, this Model 320 represents the best of the later two-cylinders in a small package. Nevertheless, the weight of this diminutive machine exceeded 2,700 pounds.

The Model 320 is fairly rare with only about 3,000 built between 1956 and 1958. It had the 100.5ci engine of the Model 40, rather than the new 113.5ci engine of the 420. The price difference of only about $400 caused most farmers to opt for the capability of the larger engine.

John Deere Model 320

General Specification:
Years Produced:	1956-1958
First Serial Number:	320001
Last Serial Number:	325518
Total Built:	3,083 Approx.
Price, New:	$1,900 (1958)

Horsepower (max., corrected)	Drawbar	PTO/Belt
Gasoline	22.4	24.9

Engine Displacement:	100.5ci
Engine Bore and Stroke:	4.00x4.00in
Engine Rated rpm:	1,850

Tires	Rear	9-24
	Front	5.00x15

Length (inches):	119.3 (RCU)
Height to Radiator (inches):	50
Weight (pounds):	2,750

Transmission	
Speeds Forward:	4

John Deere Model 330

General Specification:
Years Produced:	1958-1960
First Serial Number:	330001
Last Serial Number:	331091
Total Built:	1,000 Approx.
Price, New:	$2,200 (1960)

Horsepower (max., corrected)	Drawbar	PTO/Belt
Gasoline	22.4	24.9

Engine Displacement:	100.5ci
Engine Bore and Stroke:	4.00x4.00in
Engine Rated rpm:	1,500

Tires	Rear	9-24
	Front	5.00x15

Length (inches):	119.3 (RCU)
Height to Radiator (inches):	50
Weight (pounds):	2,750

Transmission	
Speeds Forward:	4

Above, powering a mower and a hay conditioner were normal tasks for this John Deere Model 330 tractor. It was essentially the same as the previous 320, but the steering wheel was placed at a more convenient angle. *Deere Archives*

A Model 430W (Row-Crop Utility) with mower and hay conditioner. Almost 6000 of this version were delivered between 1958 and 1960. *Deere Archives*

The diminutive John Deere Model 320 tractor with a Model 23B planter. Using the same engine as the earlier M Series tractors, the 320 was rated at 22 horsepower. Only a few over 3,000 320s were built. *Deere Archives*

John Deere Model 530

General Specification:		
Years Produced:	1958-1960	
First Serial Number:	5300000	
Last Serial Number:	5309814	
Total Built:	9,800 Approx.	
Price, New:	$2,400 (1960)	

Horsepower (max., corrected)	Drawbar	PTO/Belt
Gasoline	34.3	38.6
Tractor Fuel	24.8	26.6
LPG	34.2	38.1

Engine Displacement:	190ci	
Engine Bore and Stroke.:	4.69x5.50in	
Engine Rated rpm:	1,325	

Tires	Rear	12.4x36
	Front	5.50x16

Length (inches):	132.75	
Height to Radiator (inches):	59.9	
Weight (pounds):	4,960	

Transmission		
Speeds Forward:	6	

John Deere Model 630

General Specification:		
Years Produced:	1958-1960	
First Serial Number:	6300000	
Last Serial Number:	6317201	
Total Built:	18,000 Approx.	
Price, New:	$3,300 (1958)	

Horsepower (max., corrected)	Drawbar	PTO/Belt
Gasoline	44.2	48.7
Tractor Fuel	32.7	35.7
LPG	45.8	50.3

Engine Displacement:	321ci	
Engine Bore and Stroke:	5.50x6.75in	
Engine Rated rpm:	1,125	

Tires	Rear	12.4x38
	Front	6.00x16

Length (inches):	135.25	
Height to Radiator (inches):	66.0	
Weight (pounds):	5,900	

Transmission		
Speeds Forward:	6	

The 430 also came in a LP model. This one is shown with a 5-foot disk at a Deere experimental farm. *Deere Archives*

A John Deere Model 430 Row-Crop Utility tractor with a 4640 cultivator. *Deere Archives*

John Deere Model 430

General Specification
Years Produced:	1958-1960	
First Serial Number:	140001	
Last Serial Number:	161096	
Total Built:	12,680 Approx.	
Price, New:	$2,500 (1960)	

Horsepower (max., corrected)	Drawbar	PTO/Belt
Gasoline	27.1	29.2
Tractor Fuel	21.9	23.5
LPG	28.0	30.0

Engine Displacement:	113ci	
Engine Bore and Stroke:	4.25x4.00in	
Engine Rated rpm:	1,850	

Tires	Rear	9-24
	Front	5.00x15

Length (inches):	119.3 (RCU)	
Height to Radiator (inches):	56	
Weight (pounds):	3,250	

Transmission
Speeds Forward: 4 (5 optional)
Direction reverser optional

John Deere Model 730

General Specification:
Years Produced:	1958-1960
First Serial Number:	7300000
Last Serial Number:	7330358
Total Built:	30,000 Approx.
Price, New:	$3,700 (1960)

Horsepower (max., corrected)	Drawbar	PTO/Belt
Gasoline	53.0	59.1
Tractor Fuel	41.3	45.3
LPG	54.2	59.6
Diesel	53.7	58.8

Engine Displacement	
Gasoline and LPG:	360.5
All-fuel:	360.5
Diesel:	376.0
Engine Rated rpm:	1,125

Tires	Rear	12.0x38
	Front	6.00x16

Length (inches):	134.6
Height to Radiator (inches):	65.6
Weight (pounds).(gasoline):	6,790

Transmission
Speeds Forward: 6

Lyle Pals' 530 is serial number 530930, a 1958 model. Note the big "Oval-Tone" muffler which characterized the 30 series tractors.

Lyle Pals' 530 has the Custom Powr-Trol load compensating 3-point hitch. It also has dished rear wheel weights, Deere part number F 1478 L and R.

The well-worn clutch housing of this Model 630 attests to many hours of use. The brake-pad mechanism is for stopping the down-stream half of the clutch from rotating by its own flywheel effect to enable the shifting of gears.

Although over thirty years old, this 630 is still much in demand by farmers for routine farm chores. A new 40-50 horsepower tractor would cost three to four times as much as a good refurbished 630. Plus, with the 630, you get the distinctive sound of the two-cylinder engine.

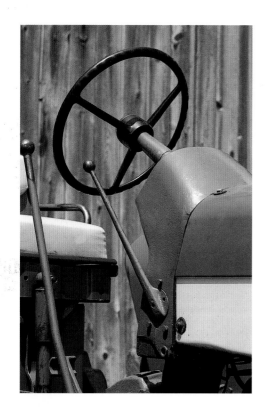

Left, the 30 Series boasted convenient controls. Shown is the "office" of a 630. The throttle lever is on the side of the cowling; the other, longer lever is the clutch.

Right, Orv Rothgarn, of Owatonna, Minnesota, is a typical John Deere collector. He has twenty-three John Deere tractors, including this 630, and 300 model, or toy tractors. He does some farming and landscaping (using two Ford Ns and a John Deere M), and is a retired lathe supervisor at the Owatonna Tool Company.

Lyle Pals' 1959 Model 730 Electric-start Diesel. Originally sold to Melvin Hagemann of Bailyville, Illinois, Pals is the third owner.

The culmination of the line, the Model 730 was the ultimate two-cylinder row-crop. Most of the 30,000, or so, built between 1958 and 1961 are still at work.

The "Float-Ride" seat of this Model 730 can be adjusted to the weight of the operator.

The GM diesel engine powering the John Deere 435 tractor is a two-cycle two-cylinder unit with a roots-type blower. Produced only in 1959 and only in the Row-Crop Utility version, the 435 is fairly rare for such a late year model (less than 5000 were built). Capable of a maximum PTO horsepower of 32.9, according to tests at the University of Nebraska, the Model 435 was the first John Deere to adopt the 1000rpm PTO speed standard. Owner Lyle Pals says he uses ether for starting even in the summer.

Right, this placard on the "Float-Ride" seat of a John Deere 730 explains the proper settings for different driver weight categories.

The dual lights in each fender greatly enhanced night operations for this Model 730. The flat-top fenders protected the operator from contact with the tire and from dust and mud. Note the hydraulic snubber on the front of the "Float-Ride" seat.

The last of the two-cylinders, the Model 435. Produced only in 1959, the 435 employed a supercharged General Motors 2-53 two-cycle diesel engine. This one, Serial Number 436200, is owned by Lyle Pals, of Egan, Illinois. Lyle says you drive it like you want to kill it, in reference to the requirement to keep the rpm up so that the supercharger does its job. Also, since it is a two-cycle, it sounds like its going twice as fast as it actually is.

The last two-cylinder tractor model to be added to the line, the Model 435 Diesel. This one is owned by Lyle Pals, of Eagen, Illinois. The 435 was powered by a GM 2-53 two-cycle supercharged engine. Introduced for the 1959 model year, it was discontinued after one year when the "New Generation" tractors came out in 1960. *Author Collection.*

Chapter 7

The Two-cylinder Engine

Origins

It was in the Eighteenth Century when steam power was first applied to transportation. A Frenchman named Cugnot is said to have made the first self-propelled vehicle in 1769. Farm steam engines followed the invention of the thresher in the early 1800s. At first they were steam power units only, with no self-moving capabilities. The self-propelling feature, and the ability to pull loads began to appear in the late 1850s. By 1880, the steam traction engine was a mature device which found routine use in plowing, land clearing, and belt-powering a variety of farm implements. By the start of the Twentieth Century there were 31 steam engine manufacturers producing around 5,000 engines per year.

The first internal combustion engines, like the first steam engines, pumped water with the vacuum created in the cylinder as heat dissipated. Abbé Hautefeuille of France

invented such an engine in 1678, using gunpowder to create the heat.

In the earliest internal combustion engines, an "explosive" mixture was set off above the piston, which was at the top of its stroke. There was no attempt to first compress the mixture. This, of course, is like the steam engine, where compression is done in the boiler, and the cylinder is merely an expander. In both types of engines it is the heat that does the work. Heat raises the pressure to move the piston within the cylinder.

Frenchman Beau de Rochas first came up with the idea of compressing the combustible mixture in the cylinder before ignition, but it was up to Nikolaus Otto to develop an engine that had compression, expansion, exhaust, and intake cycles. Thus came into being the four-cycle, or Otto-cycle engine in about 1876.

Two factors delayed the acceptance of the four-cycle engine. Most early experimenters could not ac-

cept the perceived disadvantage of only one power stroke for every two revolutions. Furthermore, Otto had the concept fairly well tied up with patents. By the year 1890, these two factors were largely being ignored, and the four-cycle engine rapidly gained universal acceptance.

Early gas engines, as these internal combustion power plants were called in those days, were generally one cylinder affairs. Progress in carburetion occurred rapidly, but ignition systems were problematic. Initially, a pilot-light type of ignition was tried, through which the pre-pressurized fuel-air mixture was passed on its way into the combustion chamber. Next, heated ceramic "glow-plugs" were used. These were followed by "low-tension," or low-voltage spark switches in the com-

Although not a general purpose tractor, this John Deere 820 standard tread clearly shows the new yellow and green paint scheme introduced with the "Twenty" series tractors in 1956.

JOHN DEERE DIE

bustion chamber. Finally, the high-tension system, with its attendant magneto and spark plugs, made its way onto the scene.

One may now wonder at the crude technology of the early machines. Keep in mind that the construction of the Daimler engine, the first production four-cycle engine, began in 1885. It was twenty-nine years later in 1914 when L.W. Witry put the first 4-cycle horizontal twin-cylinder engine on the Waterloo Boy tractor. Daimler, an associate of Otto, was a German pioneer. In those days, everything about engines was new; ignition systems, spark plugs, carburetors, valves, lubrication, and the like; all had to be invented.

In August of 1897, Louis W. Witry joined the Waterloo Gasoline Engine Company as shop manager and engineer. In May 1930, Mr. Witry recorded his recollections of the early days of the company and the people associated with it. His history is summarized in the following paragraphs.

According to Witry, John Froelich, the father of the Waterloo Boy tractor, had entered the custom threshing business in 1888 when he was 39 years old. Froelich purchased a Case steam traction engine and threshing machine from Case's traveler, S.G. Stewart, who was from Waterloo. In the off-season, Froelich occupied himself as a well driller.

In 1890, Froelich bought a 4.5 horsepower single cylinder Charter gas engine to power his well rig. After two years experience with the gasoline well rig and four years with the steam threshing rig, the idea came to him to make a gasoline-powered threshing rig. The idea was prompted, to a large extent, by the difficulty he had obtaining fuel for the steamer.

It was at this time that Froelich saw an engine advertisement by the Van Duzen Company of Cincinnati, Ohio. Van Duzen specialized in the larger single-cylinder farm gas engines. After some correspondence, Froelich made a trip to Cincinnati. Here he purchased a 20 horsepower vertical engine with a bore and stroke of 14 inches each. He had the engine shipped to his home town of Froelich, Iowa (which had been named for his father).

Back in Iowa, Froelich engaged a blacksmith to help him mount the engine on a chassis he had purchased from the Robinson Company, a maker of steam engines. The result was a 4-wheel, mid-engine, rear wheel drive machine with one speed forward and one in reverse which was capable of traveling at a rate of two miles per hour. The operator's platform was in front. It had provisions on the end of the transverse crankshaft for a belt pulley and was equipped with a fly-ball speed governor.

The machine seemed to operate reliably, so Froelich again contacted Stewart, the Case salesman, and purchased a new 40- inch thresher. Froelich then tested out the new rig by threshing a setting near Froelich, Iowa, in the fall of 1892. Again, the machine operated reliably. Later that same year, he took it on a 72,000 bushel custom threshing run. Stewart witnessed the operation with much enthusiasm, and later returned to Waterloo, Iowa, where he described the results to some of his friends. The friends wanted to see more, so in the winter of 1892, they invited Froelich to bring his tractor to Waterloo.

Froelich demonstrated his machine to the Waterloo group, and showed them the records of the 72,000 bushel threshing run. They were impressed. They then began negotiations with Froelich to manufacture the tractor in Waterloo. On January 10, 1893, The Waterloo Gasoline Traction Engine Company was organized with Mr. Froelich as president.

Four tractors were built along the lines of the original Froelich design. Two of these were sold to customers, but without Froelich's mechanical touch, the customers couldn't keep them operating and returned them to the factory for refund.

Meanwhile, in order to generate some cash flow, Mr. Froelich engaged Sam Shoop, whom he had met at the Charter Engine Company, to help him build a copy of the Charter engine he had used on the well rig. This, and several other size engines, sold fairly well.

Gas engine sales were not sufficient, however, to keep the young company afloat. Therefore, reorganization was undertaken to get a fresh infusion of cash. The new investors installed a new president and changed the name to Waterloo Gasoline Engine Company, dropping the "Traction" term. It was at this time that Froelich left the company. Twelve sizes of single-cylinder engines, with horsepowers ranging from 1.5 to 32, were made by the new company.

After the turn of the century, the merger-mania caught the Waterloo Gasoline Engine Company and they joined with the Davis Engine Company to form the Waterloo Motor Works. It was their intention to manufacture the 3-cylinder Duryea automobile. Before production started, however, the Waterloo Gasoline Engine Company stockholders decided to withdraw from the merger and continue as before.

In 1905, the Waterloo Gasoline Engine Company redesigned its entire line, making the engines simpler and lighter. The line was reduced to six, rather than twelve, models. It was at this point that the name

"Waterloo Boy" was applied to the engines. The company also experimented with automobile manufacture, building a car with a two-cylinder horizontally opposed engine. Six were sold to local purchasers.

In 1912, Witry designed a two-cylinder horizontally opposed engine after the fashion of the automobile engine of 1905. This was installed in a 3-wheel tractor chassis. After experimenting with this arrangement for a while, it was decided to change to a 4-wheel arrangement. Called the L-A, only about twenty of these tractors were sold.

Early in 1914, a horizontal twin (two cylinders side-by-side) was designed. This engine had a 5.5 inch bore and a stroke of 7 inches. The cylinders and head were integrally cast. The valves were in cages at the ends of the cylinders, similar to those of the Buick Automobile of the time.

The side-by-side arrangement was chosen, rather than horizontally-opposed, since this arrangement was finding such favor in the industry at that time. Machines by such companies as Nichols and Shepard, Hart-Parr, International Harvester, Rumely, Case, and Aultman-Taylor used what was then known as a horizontal-twin. Even Henry Ford used this arrangement in his first cars. Crankshaft throws were staggered (except for the International Harvester Titan and the Ford car) to provide dynamic balance without massive counterweights. Now the power strokes were not 360 degrees of crankshaft rotation apart, as with the two-cylinder horizontally opposed or with the two-cycle types; now they were 180 degrees apart, then 540, 180, 540, etc. In subsequent John Deere years, when all else had gone to four-or six-cylinder engines, this peculiar firing sequence, and its distinctive exhaust note, gave rise to the popular cognomen, "Poppin' Johnny" for John Deere tractors.

Thus, the famous John Deere two-cylinder engine came into being. It was soon converted to burn low-cost kerosene, which also was to become a John Deere standard. The cylinders and valves close to each other lent themselves well to the vaporizer-type intake system, which uses exhaust heat to help vaporize the fuel.

The long stroke, big bore engine was well suited to tractor duty, producing a goodly amount of torque, and a flat torque curve. Initially, operating speeds were low, but in later years they eased upward, although they were always much lower than other tractor engines of similar horsepower.

The End of the Two-cylinder Era

The two-cylinder engine was known for its simplicity, long life, and fuel economy; factors that are always requirements of a tractor engine. Eventually, however, as the 1960s approached, John Deere management realized that the two-cylinder configuration was restricting design configurations. The advantages of cross-engine mounting: that is, straight spur gearing and the belt-pulley directly on the end of the crankshaft, no longer applied. Also, kerosene vaporizer manifolds and the like had been replaced by the diesel. Though the two-cylinder made a good diesel, the configuration offered no advantages. Further, much of the future of Deere's business would be in self-propelled combines and similar machines, and in individual diesel engine sales. Here the large and heavy two-cylinder was at a disadvantage against the high-speed four-cylinder diesel. And finally, design limits were being reached as far as increasing horsepower was concerned,

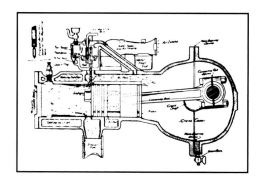

The internal arrangement of a typical two-cycle engine of the 1920s. *Deere Archives*

and Deere management could predict horsepower doubling and even tripling in the next decade. The largest version of the two-cylinder, the diesel used in the 820/830 tractors, had an eight inch stroke and a displacement of 471.5 cubic inches. It had a maximum operating speed of 1,125rpm and produced about seventy horsepower. A modern seventy horsepower John Deere four-cylinder diesel, the one used in the Model 2630 tractor, operates at 2,500rpm; displaces 276 cubic inches and has a five inch stroke. While the maximum power fuel consumption of these two engines is similar, the four-cylinder model exhibits much better part-load fuel consumption. Thus, with the introduction of the Model 435 diesel tractor in 1959, the last of the two-cylinders was born (which, interestingly, was a two-cycle, made by GM). In 1960, after nearly half a century, two-cylinder farm tractors were terminated in favor of the new three-, four-, and six-cylinder models.

The correct term should be "essentially terminated," as two-cylinder model 730s were built for export throughout 1961. Also 730s were built in Argentina until 1970. In addition, the vertical Dubuque two-cylinder was used in various applications as well as in industrial crawlers for several more years after 1960.

Chapter 8

Deere & Company Today

The Pursuit of Excellence

"Deere's best years are yet ahead," said William Hewitt as he approached the mandatory retirement age of 67, which he himself had established. Deere & Company was then one the world's preeminent industrial concerns. It still is. Having passed its 150th birthday a few years back, it is also one of the world's oldest.

But Deere is unique in another way. It has been well documented by corporate analysts for business publications the world over that there is an "attitude" throughout Deere. It's an attitude that borders on the nostalgic. From the ma-

The Deere & Company Headquarters in Moline, Illinois, is an architectural masterpiece. It is located on a rolling 1,000 acre site overlooking the Rock River valley. The site is about seventy miles down river from the place where John Deere started the business. Called The Administrative Center, it was designed by famous architect Eero Saarinen. *Author Collection*

hogany offices to the production floor, there is a universal respect for the past. Deere men and women believe in their company, not so much because it's their company, but because they feel it deserves it! This respect for the past is reflected in their concern for the future; in maintaining the traditional qualities of product and service. Any shortcoming in the way each does his or her daily job is like a breach of trust; a failure to live up to the tradition. This attitude of regard for tradition and an expectation of quality in product and service has also found its way out of the company to its customers. The usual Deere customer is as loyal to the company as any employee or stockholder. And that's good for business! Since Hewitt's retirement in 1982, the company has no longer been managed by a Deere family member. Nonetheless, there has been a succession of able chief executives that have carried on the tra-

ditions. The company's reputation for well-engineered products and superb service is as high as ever. Because Deere has routinely plowed a greater portion of their profits into development and research than most such companies, new products are technically advanced and well-proven before being released to the farmers. In fact, much work is done on products and projects that the farmer might never see. In the Research Center, for example, is a test bed for testing the effects of various soils on implements and for traction. There is also a cab simulator, rivaling an aircraft flight simulator, that can be programmed to give an operator the exact sensations encountered in operating, for example, a combine.

It's a little known fact that Deere & Company held the Western Hemisphere rights to the Wankel rotary engine for fifteen years. (Japan's Mazda having the Eastern Hemisphere rights). Deere's interest in this engine stemmed from concerns similar to those causing the transition from the two-cylinder engine: weight and fuel consumption. In this case, it was not so much the amount of fuel as the type of fuel. The rotary engine, as developed by Deere, incorporated "stratified charge" fuel induction, which allowed it to burn just about any combustible liquid without adjustment. It was the "fuel crisis" of 1973 that prompted this interest. In those fuel crisis years, farmers and truckers competed for scarce diesel fuel. The idea was for the farmer to be able to burn diesel, gasoline, furnace oil, or even home-made alcohol in the event of another such fuel crunch. In recent years, developments in conventional multi-fuel engines reduced Deere's interest in the rotary. Because of its high power-to-weight ratio, it was deemed more appropriate for aircraft, and the rights have been sold off to a company developing the engine for aircraft use.

The Headquarters Facility

Anyone interested in agriculture would definitely enjoy a visit to the Deere & Company Administrative Center. The Center is located in Moline, Illinois, on a 1,000 acre site overlooking the Rock River Valley. The site is about 70 miles down river from Grand Detour, Illinois, where John Deere started the business in 1837.

Just as Dreyfuss styling brought technical credit to Deere tractors in 1938, so William Hewitt recognized that architectural excellence in the headquarters facility would ultimately be reflected in product quality. Since it opened in 1964, the Administrative Center, designed by the late Eero Saarinen, has won a number of awards for excellence and innovation.

The Administrative Center consists of a main office building, a 400-seat auditorium, a product display building, and the West Office Building. Space is provided for about 2,000 employees. The main office building sits across a wooded ravine with the product display and auditorium buildings to the east. The West Office Building is on a plateau to the west. Both are connected to the main office building by glass bridges. The buildings are surrounded by beautiful landscaping with lakes and sculpture. Inside is a collection of art, sculpture, and antiques, both in the office areas and on the display floor.

The display floor always houses some of the most perfectly-restored antique John Deere tractors to be seen anywhere. Some are on loan from collectors and some are company owned. These beautiful historic tractors take their places among the new agricultural and industrial equipment, as well as the lawn and garden variety. Tours are available which include a presentation in the auditorium and the display floor is always open during business hours.

Architect Saarinen said of the facility he designed, "We tried to get into these buildings the character of John Deere products, the Company, the customers it serves, and the friendly informal attitude of its personnel." I think it's fair to say he accomplished his goal and captured the essence of the mystique that is John Deere. It may no longer be a "family" business in the true sense, but John Deere's legacy lives on in the company that "gave to the world the steel plow."

Sources and Recommended Reading

The following books offered essential background on the origins and history of Deere & Company, and about the tractors and equipment of the times. These make good reading and good library additions for any tractor buff. Most are available from Motorbooks International Publishers & Wholesalers, P.O. Box 2, 729 Prospect Avenue, Osceola, Wisconsin 54020 USA.

The Agricultural Tractor 1855-1950, by R.B. Gray, Society of Agricultural Engineers; an outstanding and complete photo history of the origin and development of the tractor.

The American Farm Tractor, by Randy Leffingwell, Motorbooks International; a full-color hardback history of all the great American tractor makes.

The Century of the Reaper, by Cyrus McCormick, Houghton Mifflin Company; a first hand account of the Harvester and Tractor Wars by the grandson of the inventor.

Classic American Farm Tractors, by Andrew Morland and Nick Baldwin, Osprey: a superb color documentary of some of the great old tractors.

Encyclopedia of American Farm Tractors, by C.H. Wendel, Crestline; notes and data on all the old (and some obscure) tractors.

Farm Tractors 1926-1956, Randy Stephens, Editor, Intertec Publishing; a compilation of pages from *The Cooperative Tractor Catalog* and the *Red Tractor Book*.

Farm Tractors 1950-1975, by Lester Larsen; The American Society of Agricultural Engineers.

Fordson, Farmall and Poppin' Johnny, by Robert C. Williams, University of Illinois Press; a history of the farm tractor and its impact on America.

Ford Tractors, by Robert N. Pripps and Andrew Morland, Motorbooks International; a full-color history of the Fordson, Ford-Ferguson, Ferguson, and Ford tractors, covering the influence these historic tractors had on the state of the art of tractor design.

Great Tractors, by Michael Williams and Andrew Morland, Blandford Press; describes in words and pictures tractors that were milestones in history.

Henry Ford and Grass-roots America, by Reynold M. Wik, The University of Michigan Press; recounts the era of the Tin Lizzie and the Fordson.

Harvest Triumphant, by Merrill Denison, WM. Collins Sons & Company LTD; the story of human achievement in the development of agricultural tools, especially those in Canada, and the rise to prominence of Massey-Harris-Ferguson (now known as the Verity Corporation). Rich in the romance of farm life in the last century and covering the early days of the Industrial Revolution.

How Johnny Popper Replaced the Horse, by Donald S. Huber and Ralph C. Hughes, Deere & Company; the history of the two-cylinder tractor from the perspective of Deere & Company.

How to Restore Your Farm Tractor, by Robert N. Pripps, Motorbooks International; follows two tractors through professional restoration. Includes tips and techniques, commentary and photos.

John Deere's Company, by Wayne G. Broehl, Jr., Doubleday and Company; a scholarly tome on the history of Deere & Company and its times.

John Deere Two-Cylinder Tractor Buyer's Guide, by Robert N. Pripps, Motorbooks International; a model-by-model guide to all the Johnny Poppers and Waterloo Boys from 1914 to 1960 indicating their characteristics and collectability.

John Deere Tractors, Big Green Machines in Review, by Henry Rasmussen, Motorbooks International.

John Deere Tractors and Equipment, Volumes One and Two, by Don MacMillan, American Society of Agricultural Engineers; all the details on not only tractors, but other Deere-made equipment.

Nebraska Tractor Tests Since 1920, C.H. Wendell, Crestline Publishing; consolidated descriptions of all the tractor tests conducted by the University of Nebraska. A "must" for any old- tractor enthusiast!

Traction Engines, by Andrew Morland, Osprey; descriptions and color photos of most of the great old steamers.

Two-Cylinder Collector Series, Volumes I and II, Published by The Two-Cylinder Club. A collection of articles on historic John Deere tractors and implements and on the company itself.

150 Years of International Harvester, by C.H. Wendel, Crestline Publishing; a complete photo-documented product history of International Harvester.

Other books with great photos by Andrew Morland in Motorbooks International's Color History Series:
Allis-Chalmers Tractors, by C.H. Wendel
Farmall Tractors 1924-1956, by Robert N. Pripps
Ford Tractors 1914-1954, by Robert N. Pripps
Massey Tractors, by C.H. Wendel
Minneapolis-Moline Tractors 1870-1969, by C.H. Wendel
Oliver-Cockshutt Tractors 1929-1962, by Robert N. Pripps
Threshers, by Robert N. Pripps

Appendix 2

Clubs, Newsletters & Magazines

Magazines and Newsletters providing a wealth of information and lore about individual brands of antique farm tractors and equipment have been on the scene for some time. More are springing up each year, so the following list is far from complete. Many of these publications come with collector club membership.

Name	Editor	Address
Antique Caterpillar Machinery Owners Club	Marv Fery	10816 Monitor-McKee Road, N.E. Woodburn OR 97071
Antique Power	Patrick Ertel	PO Box 838 Yellow Springs, OH 45387

Name	Editor	Address
Belt Pulley Antique Tractors	Kurt Aumann	PO Box 83 Nokomis, IL 62075
Engineers and Engines (Steam and IC Tractors)	Donald Knowles	1118 N. Raynor Ave. Joliet, IL 60435
Gas Engine Magazine	Linda Sharron	PO Box 328 Lancaster, PA 17603
Golden Arrow (Cockshutt and Co-op)	John Kasmiski	N7209 State Hwy 67 Mayville, WI 53050
Green Magazine (John Deere)	R. & C. Hain	RR 1, Bee, NE 68314
M-M Corresponder (Minn-Moline)	Roger Mohr	Rt 1, Box 153, Vail, IA 51465
Farm Antique News (Tractors and Antiques)	Gary Van Hoozer	PO Box 96 Tarkio, MO 64491
Ferguson Club Journal	Ken Goodwin	Denehurst, Rosehill Road Market Drapton TF9 2JU England
Fordson Club News	Tom Brent	Box 150 Dewdney, B.C. VOM 1HO Canada
9N-2N-8N Newsletter (Ford)	G.W. Rinaldi	PO Box 235 Chelsea, VT 05038-0235
Hart-Parr/Oliver *Collector*	Kurt Aumann	PO Box 687 Charles City, IA 50616
Iron Men Album (Steam)	Gerald Lestz	PO Box 328 Lancaster, PA 17603
Old Abe's News (Case)	David T. Erb	Rt 2, Box 2427, Vinton, OH 45686

Name	Editor	Address
Old Allis News (Allis Chalmers)	Nan Jones	10925 Love Rd, Belleview, MI 49021
Oliver Collector's News	Dennis Gerszewski	Rt 1, Manvel, ND 58256-0044
Plug 'N Points (Antique Trucks)	Tom Brownell	RR 14 Box 468 Jonesboro, TN 37659
Prairie Gold Rush (Minn.-Moline)	R. Baumgartner	Rt 1, Walnut, IL 61376
Red Power (Int. Harvester)	Daryl Miller	Box 277, Battle Creek, IA 51006
Two-Cylinder Clubs Worldwide (John Deere)	Jack Cherry	PO Box 219 Grundy Center, IA 50638
The Tractor Magazine Antique Tractors	Steve Sharp	PO Box 174 Spencer, NE 68777
Wild Harvest (Massey-Harris, Ferguson)	Keith Oltrogge	1010 S Powell, Box 529, Denver, IA 50622

For a directory of Engine and Threshing Shows, Stemgas Publishing Company issues an annual directory. Their address is:

P.O. Box 328
Lancaster, Pennsylvania 17603
717-392-0733

The cost of the directory has been $6.00. It lists shows in virtually every area of the country. Stemgas also publishes *Gas Engine Magazine* and *Iron-men Album*; magazines for the enthusiast.

Restoration Specialists and Parts Suppliers

Tom Detwiler Sales and Service
S3266 Hwy. 13 South
Spencer, WI 54479
715-659-4252

Travis Jorde
935 9th Ave, NE
Rochester, MN 55904

Brandon Pfieffer
7810 Upper Mt. Vernon Road
Mt. Vernon, IN 47620

K. Johnson
6530 Maple Grove Road
Cloquet, MN 55720

Antique Tractor Restoration
Huntley, Illinois
708-669-3560

Wengers, Incorporated
251 S. Race Street
Meyerstown, PA 17067
717-866-2135

K & K Antique Tractors
RR 3 box 384X
Shelbyville, IN 46176
317-398-3733

Polacek Implement
Phillips, Wisconsin 54555
715-339-3323

Steiner Tractor Parts, Inc.
G-10096 S. Saginaw
Holly, MI 48442
313-695-1919

Machinery Hill
Phillips, WI 54555
715-339-3788

Appendix 4

Competitive Analyses

Notes on abbreviations used in tables:

Fuel: K = Kerosene
Dis. = Distillate
D = Diesel
G = Gasoline

Belt hp: From Test D. If the generator, hydraulic pump, etc., were not standard equipment, they were removed for these tests.

Drawbar hp: Taken from Test H data, it is based on rated drawbar pull and speed. The difference between this and PTO HP is due to slippage, and to the power required to move the tractor itself. The heavier the tractor, the less the slippage, but the more power required to move the tractor. Factory engineers looked for the ideal compromise.

Pull: Test G. The maximum drawbar pull in pounds.

Fuel Cons.:   The rate of fuel consumption in horsepower hours per gallon taken from Test C conditions. The higher the number, the better.

Weight: The weight of the tractor plus ballast in pounds. Ballast was often added for Test G and other heavy pulling tests, and then removed for other tests to improve performance.

Wheels: Steel or Rubber.

Row Crop Tractors
1934-1936

	John Deere A	Farmall F-20	A-C WC	Oliver 70	Massey Chlngr	MM JT
Engine displ.	309	221	201	201	248	196
Rated rpm	975	1200	1300	1500	1200	1275

Weight	4059	4500	3792	3500	4200	3880
Belt hp	23.6	22.2	21.5	25.3	26.2	21.9
Drawbar hp	18.7	15.4	12.1	17.0	16.3	14.8
Max. Pull	2923	2334		3120	2883	2787
Fuel Cons.	10.5	10.5	10.2	11.1	10.1	10.5
Trans. Speeds	4	4	4	4	4	4
Fuel Type	K	K	K	G	Dis.	Dis.
Wheel Type	S	S	R	S	S	S
Test Number	222	221	223	252	265	233

1947-1952

	John Deere A	Farmall M	Oliver 77	MM Z	A-C WD
Engine displ.	321	248	194	206	201
Rated rpm	975	1450	1600	1500	1400
Weight	5228	6770	8012	5810	6057
Belt hp	33.8	31.3	33.0	31.6	30.6
Drawbar hp	26.7	24.9	25.8	25.2	23.6
Max. Pull	4034	4365	4714	3498	4304
Fuel Cons.	11.4	12.5	11.7	10.7	11.8
Trans. Speeds	6	5	6	5	4
Fuel Type	G	Dis.	G	G	G
Wheel Type	R	R	R	R	R
Test Number	384	327	425	438	440

Row-Crop Tractors
1935-1937

	John Deere B	Farmall F-12	Fordson A'Around	Case RC	MM ZT
Engine displ.	149	113	267	132	186
Rated rpm	1150	1400	1100	1425	1500
Weight	3275	3280	4020	3350	4280
Belt hp	14.3	14.6	20.3	17.6	23.6
Drawbar hp	9.8	10.1	11.9	11.6	16.0
Max. Pull	1728	1870	1409	2103	3262
Fuel Cons.	10.2	9.5	7.7	9.7	10.1
Trans. Speeds	4	3	3	3	5
Fuel Type	K	K	K	G	Dis.
Wheel Type	S	S	S	R	R
Test Number	232	212	282	251	290

1947-1952

	John Deere B	Farmall Super C	Oliver 66D	MM R	Massey 30 RT
Engine displ.	190	123	129	165	162
Rated rpm	1250	1650	1600	1500	1500
Weight	4400	5041	5717	4920	5265
Belt hp	24.5	20.8	22.5	23.8	30.1
Drawbar hp	19.1	16.3	17.7	18.3	20.6
Max. Pull	3353	N/A	3571	2801	3273
Fuel Cons.	11.8	10.8	14.2	10.1	11.1
Trans. Speeds	6	4	6	4	5
Fuel Type	G	G	D	G	G
Wheel Type	R	R	R	R	R
Test Number	380	458	467	468	409

Utility Tractors
1947-1954

	John Deere M	Ford 8N	Ferguson TE-20	Oliver 55	Ferguson TE-30
Engine displ.	100.5ci	120	120	144	129
Rated rpm	1,650	1,750	1,750	2,000	1,750
Weight Tested	2,695	4,043	4,268	5,501	4,211
Max. pto hp	19.5	26.2	24.0	34.4	29.3
Max.Drawbar hp	17.5 est.	20.8	22.6	29.6	24.4
Fuel Cons. *	11.1	10.1	10.3	10.1	10.0
Trans. Speeds	4	4	4	6	4
Fuel Type	G	G	G	G	G
Test Number	387	443	392	524	466

*10 hour run at rated load.

1953-1956

	John Deere 40	John Deere 50	John Deere 60	John Deere 70
Engine displ.	100.5ci	190	321	380
Rated rpm	1850	1250	975	975
Weight Tested	4,569	5,433	7,405	8,677
Max. pto hp	23.5	28.9	38.6	45.9
Rated db hp	17.4	20.9	28.0	33.6
Fuel Cons. *	9.4	10.5	10.2	10.3
Trans. Speeds	4	6	6	6
Fuel Type	G	G	G	G
Test Number	503	486	472	493

	Farmall Super M	Ford Jubilee	Case SC	Massey Pacer	Farmall Super H
Engine displ.	264ci	134	165	91	164
Rated rpm	1,450	2,000	1,600	1,800	1,650
Weight Tested	8,929	4,389	6,213	3,469	6,713
Max. pto hp	43.9	30.2	23.7	17.9	31.3
Rated db hp	33.3	20.2	18.5	13.0	23.5
Fuel Cons. *	10.3	10.1	9.4	9.3	10.3
Trans. Speeds	5	4	4	3	5
Fuel Type	G	G	TracFuel	G	G
Test Number	475	494	497	531	492

* 10 hour test @ rated Drawbar power, horsepower hours per gal.

1956-1958

	John Deere 420	John Deere 520	John Deere 620	John Deere 720
Engine displ.	113ci	190	303	376
Rated rpm	1850	1325	1125	1125
Weight Tested	5781	6505	8655	9237
Max. pto hp	27.3	36.1	44.3	56.7
Rated db hp	20.8	26.1	33.6	40.4
Fuel Cons. *	9.7	11.1	11.3	16.6
Trans. Speeds	4	6	6	6
Fuel Type	G	G	G	D
Test Number	599	597	598	594

	Farmall 300	Ford 960	MM 455	Oliver Sup 88	Farmall 400
Engine displ.	169ci	172	206	265	281
Rated rpm	1750	2200	1550	1600	1450
Weight Tested	8257	6156	6423	9446	9263
Max. pto hp	36.0	44.1	40.0	54.9	48.8
Rated db hp	27.0	30.7	31.2	37.9	34.7
Fuel Cons. *	9.6	10.3	10.6	13.4	12.8
Trans. Speeds	5	5	10	6	10
Fuel Type	G	G	G	D	D
Test Number	538	569	579	527	608

* 10 hour test @ rated Drawbar power, horsepower hours per gal.

GREAT AMERICAN
TRACTORS

FARMALL TRACTORS

Text by Robert N. Pripps
Photos by Andrew Morland

To Seth and Tyler Pripps, my nine-year-old grandsons (cousins)—good little guys who already appreciate old tractors

Acknowledgments

My thanks to:

Roger Grozinger of Rusch Equipment Company, Freeport, Illinois, who supplied serial number details and other information about Farmalls. Rusch Equipment is a Case-International dealer.

Austin G. Hurst of Lafayette, California, a private-practice psychiatrist, farm toy collector, and Farmall enthusiast, for technical help and advice with the manuscript for this book.

Andrew Morland, photographer, and Michael Dregni, editor in chief, Motorbooks International Publishing. Without their applied expertise, this book would not have been produced.
Robert N. Pripps

Preface

"Loyalty" is a word not so much in vogue today as it was before the second half of the twentieth century. Loyalties to one's faith, country, flag, political party, and mate were then taken for granted. Today, such fidelity to per-

The Farmall H was equipped with a 152ci engine, with a rated operating speed of 1650rpm. A five-speed transmission was standard. In Nebraska Test Number 333, the H (with gasoline fuel) developed 24.3 belt and 19.8 drawbar horsepower. While most Farmall Hs were sold on rubber, this 1940 example, owned by John and Mary Lou Poch of New Holstein, Wisconsin, has the optional steel.

sons, places, or things is derogatorily referred to as "blind allegiance." Thus, it puzzles some of the younger set when their elders retain brand loyalty for cars, trucks, and tractors.

This devotion is particularly true for tractors, and those who used Farmalls were among the most fanatical. The reasons for this fierce allegiance are many and may be hard to understand if you haven't been there. In the following pages, we will focus on both the times that spawned the Farmall and the tractor's attributes. We may not be able to make a fan out of you, if you're not already one, but we can, perhaps, shed some light on why Farmall fans are so loyal to the mighty Farmall.

Turbulent Times in the Tractor Business

"What? What's that? How much? Two-hundred-and-thirty dollars? Well, I'll be . . . What'll we do about it? Do? Why damn it all, meet him, of course! We're going to stay in the tractor business. Yes, cut two-hundred-and-thirty dollars. Both models. Yes, both. And, say, listen, make it good! We'll throw in a plow as well."

That is half of a 1922 telephone conversation between International Harvester's Chicago and Springfield, Ohio, offices. The words are those of Alexander Legge, the company's gritty general manager, as recorded by Cyrus McCormick III in his book *The Century of the Reaper*. The occasion was a salvo fired by Henry Ford in the great tractor war of the twenties. He had just announced a price cut to $395 for the Fordson tractor.

McCormick's grandfather had countered the loss of his reaper patent protection by branching out into other implement areas. His heirs likewise recovered their loss of supremacy in the binder and harvester arenas at the time of consolidation into International Harvester by branching out into tractors. Wrote McCormick, "The harvester war of the Eighteen-Nineties was cruel, disastrous to the weaker

Introduced in 1939, the Farmall H was originally sold with steel wheels for about $750. Some opted for rubber front tires and steel rears, for a price of about $775. Full rubber raised the price to about $950.

combatants, and yet it was inspiring in the way its testing brought out the finer qualities of men. But in the first twenty International years, competition had perhaps become routine. Henry Ford's presence in the implement province and the new type of competition he soon introduced returned the industry for a time to the atmosphere of battle."

Since its formation in 1902 until after World War I, International Harvester Company had been under constant legal attack. This was an era when trust busting was a fashionable thing for politicians and lawyers to be engaged in, and some considered the merging of several companies to form International Harvester to be a patent attempt to eliminate competition. Several states, at least for a short time, forbade International Harvester to do business within their borders. All this culminated in about 1918 with the sale of three of the companies comprising International Harvester and the elimination of dual (McCormick and Deering) dealerships. Having survived all that, McCormick's heirs now found themselves under a strong, competitive attack.

By the end of World War I, International Harvester's "full-line" competitors were proving increasingly able, especially in the tractor market. Chief competitors included Massey-Harris, Case, and Deere, just entering the tractor fray in 1919 with the purchase of the Waterloo Boy outfit. There were also many short-line, or tractor-only,

competitors, including in 1917 one Henry Ford of automobile fame.

Ford was raised on a farm and empathized with the hard-working, under-paid, and mostly unappreciated farmer. He was concerned especially for the eastern and midwestern small farmer trying to wrest a living often from fewer than 80 acres. Ford, who never cared much for horses stated, "The burden of farming must be lifted from flesh and blood and placed on steel and motors."

Ford intended his tractor to do for the farmer what his Model T car had done—that is, free him from bondage to the horse. The tractor was to be made by a separate company from the car company (which was then stockholder-owned) called Henry Ford and Son. The "Son" part was to signify the inclusion of his young son, Edsel. The tractor, therefore, was to be named the "Fordson."

Thanks to the postwar economic depression, Ford soon found himself with more tractors than he could sell, and so he started cutting prices to move inventory. The early twenties market continued to shrink, further exacerbating the then-industry-wide overproduction problem. Other producers, eager to maintain market share, also cut prices, and soon found themselves em-

A slightly scaled-down version of the mighty Farmall M was the Farmall H. The H used a 152ci engine, rather than the 248ci engine of the M. Wheelbases and frame mountings were the same, however, allowing the use of the same mounted implements. Standard rear tires were 10x36; fronts were 5.50x16. The H could comfortably handle a 22in threshing machine.

broiled in a good old-fashioned price war.

The tractor price war had three prominent effects. First, many farmers took advantage of the below-cost prices to get into power farming. Second, substantial companies were eliminated from the tractor market when they could not get their prices down sufficiently to compete—mainly the short-line companies specializing in larger,

heavier tractors. Finally, the survivors were forced to copy Ford's production-line methods and to redesign their products to be more appealing to the myriad of smaller farmers.

In 1920, *Farm Machinery and Equipment* magazine listed 166 tractor companies, which produced slightly more than 200,000 tractors. That year, Ford produced 54,000 Fordsons in Dearborn and 43,000 in Cork, Ireland. Obviously, Ford was the competition, and only International Harvester had the strength to take him on.

The Fordson had been launched in late 1917. At first, the industry didn't take it seriously. One Philip C. Rose, writer of the *Black Book*, dismissed the Fordson as inconsequential, saying that the other tractor manufacturers need not worry about Ford. "His machine," Rose said of Ford's Fordson, "will not stand up; that he will find in short order."

The tractor "gurus" of the time disdained the Fordson for several reasons. First, Ford's claim to fame was the Model T car. While the Model T did put America on wheels, it also spawned a whole new lingo of expletives. About the kindest thing to be said about the "Tin Lizzie" was that it was cheap. One thing the tractor gurus missed, however, was that the Model T really did quite well on the semi-improved rural roads, and it soon was a favorite of the beleaguered small farmer. In addition, because of Ford's apparent concern for the "little guy" (as demonstrated by his five-dollar-a-day pay for assembly-line work), many people lauded Henry Ford as a kind of saint.

Second, the Fordson was ridiculously small and light. At 2700lb, it was dwarfed by other new tractors of the times, such as the 6000lb Waterloo Boy or the 8700lb IHC Titan.

Finally, Ford was not in the farm implement business. The most prosperous tractor suppliers also made such equipment as threshers, spreaders, mowers, and the like.

What the tractor gurus failed to anticipate was that Ford would distribute the tractors through his extensive automobile dealer network. He issued quotas for each; even big city dealers had to take their share, doing anything to get rid of them.

Furthermore, World War I had just begun, and even though Ford was a pacifist, he generously made a gift of the patent rights to the Fordson to the British Board of Agriculture. He also agreed to set up a factory to produce them in Cork, Ireland, and, in 1918, shipped 6,000 Fordsons to Great Britain to help alleviate the wartime food shortage.

It was these, 6,000 exported Fordsons that brought the tractor its credibility. In these days before Nebraska Tractor Tests, there was not much a farmer could do to assure himself of a tractor's viability. In Great Britain, in addition to the Fordson, several other makes of tractors were pressed into service. Objective comparisons could be made. The British County War Agricultural Committees hired drivers and paid for repairs and fuel, and kept records of acres plowed per hour and of associated costs. According to Michael Williams, in his book *Ford and Fordson Tractors*, the Fordson could plow more acres per hour than either the Titan or the Waterloo Boy, and do it at less cost for fuel and repairs.

Now Fordson production took off. Production numbers for the two plants

in Dearborn and Cork topped 90,000 in 1920, more than most tractor models saw as a lifetime run. By 1921, however, the postwar depression caused sales to drop to fewer than 37,000. Henry Ford's tractor "engine" was running, though, and a way had to be found to move more tractors. Thus, the prices were cut throughout the year from $700 to $625, and finally down to $395: Ford was testing the elasticity of demand. In any case, Fordsons sold. The year 1922 saw production back to around the 70,000-unit level, and in 1923, to more than 100,000.

International Harvester first countered with the 10-20 McCormick-Deering in 1922, a smaller version of the 15-30 introduced in 1921. Others, such as Case and John Deere, brought out new, smaller, lighter, less-expensive models as well. Nevertheless, Ford carried more than 60 percent of the market. Competition from the Fordson eliminated many companies from the field over the next several years, including the mighty General Motors' entry, the Samson.

By 1929, the great tractor war was over. Of the 166 listed for 1920, there were only forty-seven tractor manufacturers left, and they were still producing just slightly more than 200,000 units. By then, both the Fordson and the Model T were also gone from the scene. Henry Ford said he stopped production of the Fordson because he needed the space to begin construction of the new Model A car, brought out in 1928 to replace the Model T. But the facts are that the Fordson, as well as the Model T, had been overtaken by determined competition: In the case of the Model T, it was the Chevrolet automobile, and in the case of the Fordson, it was the Farmall tractor, introduced by International Harvester in 1924.

Chapter 1

In the Beginning

During the early part of the nineteenth century, transportation, communication, power for manufacturing, and financial facilities were nothing at all like we enjoy today. It was a time of dramatic change, a time now known as the Industrial Revolution, fueled by the appearance of several interrelated inventions. George Stephenson in Great Britain and Robert Fulton in America showed the world how to use the power of steam for transportation. Samuel Morse invented the telegraph; Eli Whitney, the cotton gin; Elias Howe, the sewing machine; Henry Bessemer, the steel-making process; Cyrus McCormick, the reaper; and John Pope, the threshing machine. None of these inventions by themselves would have amounted to much. But together, they synergistically facilitated each other's development—and

The Farmall M, introduced in August of 1939, was without a doubt International Harvester's most famous tractor. More than 288,000 were sold before production ended in 1952. Configurations included various high-crop and wide-front versions; shown here is a 1940 vintage M on full steel. The most powerful member of the Farmall clan, the mighty M was a three- or four-bottom plow tractor. In most cases, the smooth four-cylinder power of the M could handle a 30in thresher. Although most Farmall Ms were delivered with rubber tires, this 1940 example is on full steel, a popular option in those days.

ultimately led to the birth of machinery factories.

Work became less labor-intensive as industry was taken out of the home workshop and transferred to these factories. Automation replaced handwork in every area of life. Skilled specialists managed the great new enterprises, and marketing became national, rather than local and regional.

Especially in agriculture, invention sparked further invention, as farmers modified existing or developed new machines to make their lives easier. In this way, International Harvester was formed mainly out of Cyrus McCormick's and William Deering's implement companies, companies that resulted from efforts to invent and perfect new grain-harvesting machinery.

It is mind-boggling to consider the physical labor needed to produce a loaf of bread at any time before the turn of the nineteenth century. First, the soil was tilled with a primitive plow or spade, and then, the seed was sown by hand. Next, the grain was cut by sickle or scythe. Finally, the grain was threshed from the stalk with a flail, and the chaff and straw were winnowed from the grain—a laborious process indeed. All this had to be done before the grain could be milled into flour for baking. There had to be an easier way.

As early as the first century A.D., attempts were made to mechanize the task of collecting, or reaping, grain. These early efforts took the form of

machine consisting of two serrated cutter bars, one on top of the other and oscillating in opposite directions. Projecting fingers in front of the cutter bars were used to hold the stalks against the cutters. Salmon's machine also used a "divider" bar, which separated the stand to be cut from that to be left for the next pass.

The Pioneers

Cyrus Hall McCormick was born to Robert and Mary Ann McCormick on February 15, 1809. Robert was by then a fairly wealthy Virginia farmer, with more than 500 acres of land. His estate had its own grist mill, sawmill, smelter, distillery, and blacksmith shop. An imaginative man with mechanical ingenuity, Robert tinkered with the invention of a mechanical reaper as early as 1809, but success was to wait for his son. Robert did succeed, as did his British counterparts, in making a workable grain cutter, but, as with the British machines, it left the grain stalks too tangled for binding. Son Cyrus was no doubt party to these endeavors as he was growing up and, in July 1831, demonstrated the first truly successful reaping machine.

The McCormick reaper used a sickle bar after the fashion of the Salmon cutter, with the fingers projecting out front to hold the stalks at the moment of cutting. It had the sweep reel of the British Ogle and Bell machines and it used the divider of the Salmon machine. McCormick's device had three unique features: a platform onto which the grain fell, to then be raked off onto the ground in bunches suitable for bundling; the horse, and hence the line of draft, placed off to one side, thereby allowing the horse to walk in the stubble of the swath already cut, rather than trample the standing grain; and one main wheel, which operated the cutter and carried the machine, mounted directly behind the horse in the line of draft. Two men and a horse with a McCormick reaper could harvest about an acre per hour.

McCormick sold a few reapers along the lines of his first model, but

The Farmall M used a large 248ci four-cylinder overhead-valve engine, operating at 1450rpm. Bore and stroke were 3.88x 5.25in. The standard rear tires were 11.25x36; the fronts were 6.50x16. Weights of up to 7000lb with ballast were common.

head-strippers: usually a box on wheels or runners and pushed by oxen into the standing grain. The leading upper edge of the box was a metal bar with sharp, tapered slots. As the contraption advanced, the stalks entered the slots and the "ears" were stripped and fell into the box behind. At least that is what happened in theory. The fact that these stripping harvesters did little to replace the scythe, or even the reaping hook, is testimony to their inefficiency.

An Englishman by the name of Salmon did, however, invent a mowing

farmers were not clamoring for them. Most considered them to be curiosities. American farms of the 1830s were not sufficiently developed to be free of stumps, humps, and rocks, and farmers were skeptical of the machine's ability to work under these conditions. McCormick also found some of the reticence encountered by his British counterparts—that is, a resentment by farm laborers who thought that these machines would throw them out of work.

Besides the lack of a market for reapers, Cyrus McCormick and his

father found their interests diverted to other pursuits at this time. They were involved in other farm inventions and manufacturing activities—one of which was the McCormick cast-iron plow, which sold well before the steel plow was invented. And while their interests were elsewhere, a Mr. Obed Hussey secured, in 1833, the first US patent for a reaping machine.

The Hussey patent jolted Cyrus's attention back to reapers. He immediately filed for his own patent, which was granted in 1834. Thus began a bitter conflict that lasted for years.

A McCormick BWD6 with owner Churchill and his dog Flick at the great Dorset Steam Fair near Blandford, England. In 1954, the BMD was replaced by the BWD6. Possibly for marketing reasons, they were not described as "Standards." The International Harvester Company in Great Britain expanded its production facilities into the old Jowett car and van works at Idle, Bradford.

Hussey's reaper was somewhat different from McCormick's in that it had two drive wheels, plus smaller wheels to carry the cutter; it used no reel, and side delivery was not provided. The binder had to keep up with the machine so that the sheaves would be out of the way before it came around again. The main advantage of the Hussey reaper was the open-top guard finger bar that allowed chaff and other debris to exit, instead of plugging up and jamming the cutter.

The War of the Reapers

By 1840, McCormick was beginning to enter the market in earnest. Due to some unfortunate changes, the popularity of the Hussey reaper was beginning to wane. Feeling the pressure of competition, Hussey challenged McCormick to a field trial, and by 1843, Hussey and McCormick agreed to a public contest, to be held in the James River area of Virginia. Each machine was to harvest similar plots of the same field; the first one done was the winner. In two events, McCormick's reaper finished first, partly because of mechanical problems with the Hussey machine and partly due to the more difficult binding configuration wherein the binders had to keep up with the machine.

Hussey continued to challenge McCormick in the field and in the courtroom until his death in 1860 in a railroad accident. Unfortunately for both men, their patents expired at just about the same time that mechanical reaping was gaining wide acceptance with farmers. Mechanical reaping really caught on when the self-raker came on the market. Later, came the self-tying binders that made all the old reapers obsolete.

Severe competition continued throughout the rest of the nineteenth century as each of the major concerns tried to be the first to acquire the manufacturing rights to promising new inventions. Armies of machinery agents tromped across rural America searching for customers to fight over—with the salesmen sometimes coming to blows. Advertising and promotional budgets soared. And when a sale was made, the salesman feted the customer lavishly. Often, the farmer's entire family would be invited to town to take delivery of the machine, and then honored with a grand restaurant meal. On one occasion, a McCormick agent had several machines to deliver on a certain day. He hired three bands, had floats made, and had a parade, with the customers riding in fancy carriages.

The McCormick Harvesting Machine Company

By 1847, the McCormick Harvesting Machine Company of Walnut Grove Farm, Virginia, had already been in business for more than seven years. Like both John Deere and J. I. Case, Cyrus McCormick recognized that the market for grain harvesting equipment was farther west and decided to move his operations to the frontier town of Chicago. On August 30, 1847, McCormick entered into a partnership with C. M. Gray of Chicago. While McCormick was away from Chicago, Gray sold half of his half-interest in the new company to Messrs. Ogden and Jones. Needless to say, McCormick was upset over the arrangement and took Gray to court. While the matter was awaiting decision, Gray sold the remaining portion of his interest to Ogden. Thus, in 1848, the business was renamed McCormick, Ogden and Company, with Jones still a junior partner. By September of the next year, Ogden and Jones sold their interests to McCormick for $65,000.

To help him run his burgeoning business, Cyrus invited his brothers, Leander and William, to come to Chicago. Things went well until William died in 1865, and acrimony arose over the distribution of his estate. Cyrus and Leander did not get along well from then on. In 1879, the partnership was converted into a corporation, with Cyrus holding three-fourths of the stock and Leander, the balance.

Next page
John Poch's Farmall 450 has the optional torque amplifier, which has ten forward speeds and two reverse, rather than the standard five and one. This tractor also has the optional adjustable wide front. John has fabricated a three-point hitch for it. It has no muffler so John can fit it into his garage. The Farmall 450 diesel is essentially the same as the 400, except for a 281ci four-cylinder engine instead of the 264ci.

Harvester War

In *The Century of the Reaper*, a McCormick agent recounts this tale of an incredible scrap over the sale of a binder late in the 1880s.

"A dealer telegraphed me, saying the Champion outfit was trying to break up a sale he had made of an eight-foot binder. They had pulled their machine onto the farm and challenged the farmer to a competition.

"When I got there, the farmer was having trouble with our machine, and the Champion boys were giving him plenty of poison about it and me. I got the machine fixed so that it worked satisfactorily.

"Meanwhile, Champion had notified every farmer around to come see them beat the McCormick binder in a contest set for the next day, thus hoping to get them to cancel any orders for McCormick machines.

"I got up at three o'clock in the morning and drove out to the farm and woke the farmer up. He put on his pants and came out to the barn where I gave him such a sales talk that he was absolutely convinced the McCormick was the best machine.

"A big crowd of machine men had come to the hotel that night. The Deering men said they would join the contest and show us both up. The next morning there were at least a hundred and fifty farmers there. The Deering outfit was the first to start. They had a new machine, all decorated with flags, and four big gray horses. But when the first bundle of tangled barley came through it choked and they were done.

"The farmer, driving our binder, was having no trouble, but I caught a Champion man trying to put a handful of straw in our elevator chains to foul them. I grabbed him by the neck and he fell down in the stubble. Then the whole Champion crew started after me, but somebody got between us. They started to abuse the farmer, a big powerful man, and he struck the Champion dealer. The farmer's old father stopped the fight, but the whole competition broke up into a row. Finally, Champion left in disgrace without having driven us from the field."

Farmall Super M production ran from 1952 to 1954, replacing the M, which itself replaced the F-30 in 1939. The engine of the Super M displaced 264ci, up from 248ci for the M and down from 284ci for the F-30.

Cyrus H. McCormick died in 1884, after witnessing the great revolution in mechanized agriculture, after acquiring great wealth, and after seeing his

reaper company grow to become the largest of its kind. His widow and his son, Cyrus Jr., bought out Leander's interest in 1890. By this time, however, the company's preeminence in the field was being seriously challenged, because McCormick had been too slow in picking up promising new invention rights—the slowness due in the most part to the bickering between the brothers.

Deering Company

William Deering was one of those to capitalize on McCormick's slowness. McCormick had been in the reaper business for about forty years when Deering, then forty-four years old, bought into the rights to the Marsh harvester.

Before entering the implement business, Deering had made a substantial fortune in the wholesale dry goods business in Maine. In 1870, he made his way to Chicago to invest in some land, but happened to call on an acquaintance named Elijah Gammon, a retired Methodist preacher, who had become a partner in the firm that was attempting to manufacture the Marsh harvester. Gammon persuaded Deering to look no further for investments, but to put his money into the harvester company. When, two years later, the books showed that Deering had doubled his money, he asked to be taken into the business as a partner. By the next year, poor health caused Gammon to call for Deering to move to Chicago and take over management of the business. In 1880, Gammon sold out to Deering.

The idea of amalgamation, wrote Cyrus Hall McCormick III, was first broached between McCormick, Sr., and Deering before the former's death in 1884. Nothing came of it, however, because the temperaments of those first-generation harvester men were too individualistic. After the death of C. H. McCormick, Sr., the records are full of accounts of meetings called to consider merger, meetings that included other smaller implement companies. The smaller companies recognized that the kind of competition that had flourished would be ruinous for all concerned, and so wanted, at least, an understanding on pricing.

The American Harvester Company

By 1890, McCormick and Deering were the commanding leaders in the harvesting industry. Deering, by now getting on in years, encouraged consolidation. In the fall of 1890, the McCormicks, the Deerings, and eighteen other competitors met in Chicago to attempt the industry's first amalgamation. What emerged was an industrial giant, the American Harvester Company. The six chief shareholders elected themselves directors, with Cyrus McCormick, Jr., as president and the aging Deering as chairman.

The American Harvester Company was doomed from the start. At that time, all the harvesting companies bought their knives and cutters from the Akron, Ohio, firm Whitman, Barnes Company. Its president, Colonel A. L. Conger, conceived the idea for the American Harvester Company in such a way that guaranteed the preservation of his own little concern. For several years before the grand Chicago merger meeting, on sales trips, Colonel Conger enthusiastically discussed the idea with all his customers. His mistake was in encouraging the smaller entrepreneurs to establish the economic valuation of their own companies, without benefit of formal appraisal, and these were the values attributed when the consolidation occurred.

While the valuation of the new company was high, banks saw through the scheme and refused to lend working capital. McCormick and Deering also balked at supplying the funding for what they saw as weaker competitors—and the short-lived American Harvester Company foundered. The government was also threatening involvement under the newly passed Sherman Antitrust Act, as it clearly saw the consolidation as restraint of trade.

For the next decade, the industry vacillated between merger and ruinous competition. Deering proposed, in 1897, to sell out to Cyrus McCormick, Jr., but McCormick was unable to raise the cash. Vigorous competition resumed, with Deering continuing to gain on McCormick's leadership.

The International Harvester Company

The years 1896 and 1897 saw a severe recession in American business, due in large extent to over-saturation of markets through devastating price wars. Companies reacted by merging to eliminate competition as the economy recovered. Between 1898 and 1902, 212 consolidations occurred, almost twice the number from the preceding nine years.

The two harvesting dynasties now became serious about getting together. Deering proposed a two-step merger: Each family should buy minority interest in the other firm, and then, together, they would acquire three other competitors, Plano Manufacturing of Chicago; Warder, Bushnell & Glessner of Springfield, Ohio; and Milwaukee Harvester Company of Milwaukee, Wisconsin.

The McCormicks, still the strongest, balked at any suggestion of loss of control. The merger efforts almost stalled until George W. Perkins, a J. P. Morgan partner and adviser to the McCormicks, proposed a ten-year stock trust. The trust would hold all of the stock of the new International Harvester Company, with Perkins, McCormick, and Charles Deering (William's son) serving as trustees.

Thus, after more than ten years of cat-and-mouse play, on July 28, 1902, International Harvester Company was born. The name, picked by George Perkins, was selected to reflect its global scope. Harvester, as it came to be called, controlled 85 percent of US harvester production and boasted assets of $110 million (a staggering amount in 1902). Included were malleable iron works, twine factories, timberland and sawmills, hemp properties, coal and iron mines, and the Illinois Northern Railway—plus the plants in Chicago, Milwaukee, and Springfield.

The stockholders of the new concern had every reason to be confident, and they were not disappointed. Although profit margins were small at first, the company's monopolistic position, its reputation for producing good equipment, and its strong dealer network assured success. There were still many serious internal struggles, however. It was fortunate that Perkins was able to override the petty squabbles between the McCormick and the Deering factions. He became disgusted with Harvester's "millionaire officers" who refused to work or follow orders, and was finally able to promote from within Clarence Funk to general manager, a capable professional executive with ties to neither family.

After the voting trust set up by Perkins expired, the McCormicks borrowed $5 million from John D. Rockefeller to regain control. Rather than reinstate their rather inept management, however, the McCormick family kept Perkin's idea of professional management. Their first move after regaining control was to fire Funk and replace him with a McCormick loyalist, Alexander Legge.

The talented Legge, who had worked himself up from a position in a field office collecting bad debts from farmers, was one of the key players in the events that followed. It was his vision that resulted in the Farmall tractor—the tractor that saved the company during the great tractor war of the twenties.

The End of American Harvester Company

The American Harvester Company died in January 1891. Just before it breathed its last, C. H. McCormick, Jr., and William Deering went to New York to consult with the financiers, who were unwilling to get involved. The two machinery tycoons were sharing a parlor suite. Late at night, as McCormick sat alone pondering the situation, the door of Deering's room opened. Clad only in his nightshirt, the old gentleman walked in and stood before the glowing fireplace, his hands clasped behind his back and his face grave with concern.

"McCormick," he said at last. "Are these other fellows trying to make the two of us carry water for them?"

"It looks that way to me," replied McCormick.

"All right, let's go home and call it off."

"I agree," said McCormick, and both went to bed.

(from *The Century of the Reaper*)

Chapter 2

Birth of the Farmall

In 1769, James Watt of Great Britain obtained a patent on a steam engine that used a separate condenser, thus recovering much of the water. This device made the steam engine practical for propelling ships and trains. Watt, therefore, is generally credited with inventing the steam engine, although expansion engines date back to more than 100 years before the birth of Christ.

The steam traction engine was the first step in power farming. One of the first more-or-less successful of these was the Fawkes Steam Plow, made in 1858. Others followed in short order, but all were big, heavy, and expensive, suitable for only the largest farms.

Then in 1876, Nikolaus August Otto invented the four-stroke-cycle internal-combustion engine—no small task, considering that spark plugs, carburetors, and ignition systems had not yet been created. Such pioneers as Daimler, Benz, Duryea, Olds, and Ford soon took the "Otto Cycle" engine out of the novelty realm. Powered buggies of all sorts began to appear.

The first successful Otto Cycle-powered traction engine was built by John Froelich of Froelich, Iowa, in 1892. It could be considered a hybrid because Froelich used a Robinson steam engine frame and running gear upon which he mounted a Van Duzen one-cylinder engine. The machine had an operator's platform in front and a steering wheel, and could propel itself backward and forward. The 20hp en-

gine was operated on gasoline, a fuel that a short time before had been considered a hazardous by-product of the lubricating oil business.

During the 1892 harvest season, Froelich used the machine in a fifty-day custom threshing operation. He both pulled and powered a Case 40x58 thresher, harvesting approximately 72,000 bushels of small grain. A year later, Froelich was instrumental in forming the Waterloo Gasoline Traction Engine Company of Waterloo, Iowa. This company went on to produce the Waterloo Boy tractor, the forerunner of the John Deere line.

Early efforts of the Waterloo Gasoline Traction Engine Company did not, however, produce a commercially viable tractor. That honor goes to two men of Charles City, Iowa: Charles Hart and Charles Parr. As a youth, Hart, who grew up near Charles City, dreamed of motorized farming, and methodically began achieving his goal. As a young man, he enrolled in Iowa

For its production timeframe (1952–1954), the Super M was in the "big league" as far as power was concerned. The big league for row-crop tractors in those days was the more than 40hp class. In its Nebraska tests, the various M versions averaged 45 maximum belt horsepower. In its class were the Allis Chalmers WD-45 (45hp), the Cockshutt 50 (50hp), the John Deere 70 (46hp), the Massey-Harris 44 (45hp), and the Oliver Super 88 (54hp). Dan Langy of Lena, Illinois, operates this 1952 example.

FARMALL Plowing and Belt Work Simply Can't Be Surpassed!

THERE is enthusiasm for the work of the FARMALL wherever this perfected tractor appears. On all crops, on all jobs in field and barnyard, it shows the power farmer *something new in handling and efficiency*.

Plowing is one of its strongest suits. The FARMALL owner goes out to tackle that once-dreaded job with interest and good humor. He has learned that FARMALL and its plow will move handily and rapidly over the fields and leave well-turned furrows behind, in ideal shape for the operations and the crops to follow.

On belt work it is the same. We have dozens of positive letters from owners.

D. M. Hastings of Atlanta, Ga., writes, "You deserve a pat on the back for the FARMALL. Please do not thank me for this as it is well deserved." He has used his FARMALL on every kind of work including many belt jobs.

Remember that the Harvester engineers devoted several years to working out this *all-purpose, all-crop, all-year design*. They tried out thoroughly *every* type of design. When FARMALL was *right for all drawbar, belt and power take-off work* they offered it to the farmer. The FARMALL is *the one all-purpose tractor that plants and cultivates, too*. It is the feature of power farming today.

Begin by asking the McCormick-Deering dealer where you can see a FARMALL on the job

INTERNATIONAL HARVESTER COMPANY
of America
(Incorporated)
606 So. Michigan Ave.   Chicago, Illinois

... And next spring your FARMALL will be all ready to go at the PLANTING and CULTIVATING jobs. It's that kind of a tractor!

This early, 1927 Farmall advertisement stressed that the Farmall was an all-purpose tractor.

State College of Agriculture and Mechanical Arts. He soon discovered that the professors did not share his enthusiasm for power farming, and transferred to the University of Wisconsin, where he not only found a more congenial faculty, but also met another talented engineering student, Charles Parr, who soon joined him in his mechanized farming dream.

While still students, they formed the Hart-Parr Gasoline Engine Company, and began manufacturing engines for sale. Upon graduation, they moved their operations to Charles City and began work on the traction engine. In 1902, they completed their first unit, one that from the outset was designed for drawbar work. Consequently, the transmission and drivetrain were extremely rugged.

By 1907, one-third of all tractors (about 600) at work in the United States were Hart-Parrs. In fact, a Hart-Parr employee is credited with coining the word "tractor," saying that "traction engine" seemed too cumbersome for use in advertising.

International Harvester Tractors

The William Deering Company made its first gasoline engine in 1891, a 6hp two-cylinder device. Also available were 12hp and 16hp versions, which were used on self-propelled corn pickers and mowers.

McCormick's first venture into the engine business was in 1897 with a two-cylinder engine installed on a running gear. It used a two-speed transmission, with reverse.

After International Harvester was formed in 1902, interest in and work on tractors accelerated. Harvester was among the first of the long-line implement companies to offer a tractor, the first of which was introduced in 1906.

Early design was faulty. A single-cylinder engine was mounted on rollers so that it could be moved back and forth to engage a friction drive. The engine had an open crankcase and used spray-tank cooling. This tractor was initially built in Upper Sandusky, Ohio, but the plant soon moved, first to Akron and then to Milwaukee.

With the second move, the friction drive was replaced by a clutch and gearbox. By 1910, International Harvester overtook Hart-Parr and became the nation's leading tractor producer. Only a few thousand tractors were produced each year in the whole country: they were expensive, being essentially shop-built, and were extremely large. Also, only a small market existed at the time, as most farmers could neither use nor afford such monstrosities.

Nevertheless, other farm equipment suppliers jumped on the slow-moving tractor bandwagon, and soon overproduction swamped the market.

The office of the 1913 45hp Titan.

Other names—Rumely, Avery, J. I. Case, Aultman-Taylor, and Minneapolis—soon graced internal-combustion tractors. Smaller companies with good ideas also entered the fray. In 1910, Harvester added its Mogul to the lineup. Most of these tractors reflected the heritage of the steam engine; some even looked like steamers. Their average weight was more than 500lb per engine horsepower.

The Tractor Takes On the Horse

The giant tractors built before 1915, both steam- and gasoline-powered, were built for two purposes: driving the ever-larger threshing machines and busting the virgin prairie sod in the Canadian and US Great Plains. Farm publications and Department of Agriculture studies touted the advantages of power farming. All recognized the problem: the tractor would only be viable for the average farmer when it could replace horses.

Records indicate that some families in those days actually subsisted on farms of fewer than forty acres. The farther west one went, the larger the farms were, on average. Even in the 1940s, most farms east of the Mississippi River were fewer than 100 acres. Required horsepower averaged about one horse, ox, or mule for every fifteen acres under cultivation. And the animal ate the produce of at least three acres.

There were at least perceived advantages to animal power over the tractor. Animals provided fertilizer and hides for leather; bones and hoofs were also used. And there was an affectionate bond between it and the farmer; the hours of toiling together and in sharing in the harvest resulted in a bonding between human and animal that tran-

Power farming was not for the faint of heart—or those with a small wallet. This mammoth J. I. Case steam engine plowing a demonstration plot pulling a twelve-bottom plow was typical of power farming at the turn of the century.

An International Harvester Mogul 10-20 tractor on display at the Living History Antique Equipment Show in Franklin Grove, Illinois. The Mogul 10-20 was manufactured between 1916 and 1919. Mogul tractors were sold by McCormick dealers; more than 8,900 were built. It had a single-cylinder engine with a bore and stroke of 8.50x12.00in. A two-speed transmission was featured, along with a roller-chain final drive. The engine operated on kerosene, with water injection available for hard pulls and hot days. The engine was started on gasoline. Three needle valves, convenient to the driver, controlled the flow of gasoline, kerosene, and water.

A McCormick-Deering 15-30 Gear Drive Tractor pulls a self-powered McCormick-Deering combine through a Kansas wheatfield in the 1920s. The 15-30 was the first International tractor with a one-piece cast-iron frame, introduced in 1921. Smithsonian Institution

scended that which a person might have for a pet. Following World War I, animal advocates derided and denounced the concept of the horseless farm, solemnly predicting various evils that would befall the nation.

There was one big advantage to horse power over horsepower: with the horse, there were no new models and no new ways to learn. As a person grew up on a farm, they learned without any special training how to handle the draft animals. With the tractor, he or she had to "learn to drive." A whole new technology had to be learned, and with the rapid pace of progress, the goal of mastering it kept moving out ahead. The farmer before the 1930s saw the time it would take to learn to use this

laborsaving device and scoffed at it as, rather, a labor-causing device.

Smaller and Lighter Tractors

After 1912, to appeal to the smaller farmer, tractor designers sought to make smaller, lighter, and cheaper tractors—machinery versatile enough to replace the horse in at least some farm tasks, reducing the total number required on the farm.

The next year, the Bull Tractor Company introduced a 12hp single-wheel-drive tractor, selling for around $400. This trim, agile little device rattled the industry as it out-maneuvered the doddering behemoths it competed against. While it was never mechanically sound, it did sweep the

A 1913 45hp Titan by International Harvester. The Titan brand tractors were made for sale by Deering dealers. Titan was an appropriate name for this 21,000lb monster. It readily handled a 14in ten-bottom plow. At the Winnipeg Competition, it demonstrated a 2.54 acres-per-hour plowing rate. The unusual two-cylinder engine was started by compressed air and drove its own compressor. The engine was unusual in that the side-by-side pistons operated together on the same crank throw, rather than opposite, as do most other two-cylinder engines. Being a four-stroke engine, this gave even firing, once per revolution. This Titan is owned by the American Thresherman's Association and was displayed at the Central States Thresherman's Reunion near Pontiac, Illinois.

This prewar Farmall ad uses the cartoon approach. Note in the third box the reference to the fact that the "team is getting old. . . ." The horse was a major competitor to the Farmall in 1941.

field of customers, being first in sales (displacing International Harvester) by 1914. Its popularity did not last long, but it did spawn a subsidiary much in evidence today: Toro, the lawn, garden, and golf course equipment maker.

With the advent of smaller, lighter tractors, the farmer received an additional benefit: the farmer could convert horse-drawn implements to tractor use, thereby saving considerably on cost. Many of these implements did not fully use the tractor's capability, and others were simply not strong enough to stand up, but the transition to power farming was being made.

The rapid rise of the automobile also affected the tractor industry as advances brought by large production trickled down. Automobile use proliferated tenfold between 1910 and 1925. As farmers availed themselves of the benefits of the automobile, they also became more comfortable with the tractor—especially a smaller tractor that had features and controls similar to those of the car.

Persistent borrowing of automobile technology indicated to many that the tractor had more in common with the automobile than with other implements such as plows and threshers. Therefore, it did not take a great leap of faith to believe rumors as early as 1914 that Henry Ford was about to get into the tractor business.

Ford had been experimenting with "automobile plows" as early as 1906. One effect of the Ford rumors was that a group of Minneapolis entrepreneurs, which included a man by the name of Ford, organized the Ford Tractor Company, attempting to capitalize on the magic name. Although this outfit did actually make and sell a few tractors, their efforts, like their tractors, were short-lived.

The Minneapolis Ford tractor had less of an impact on power farming than did a spate of Model T Ford car-to-tractor conversion kits available at the time. C. H. Wendel lists forty-five such kit manufacturers, as of 1919, in his book *Encyclopedia of American Farm Tractors.*

These kits, which were advertised as being easy to install and remove, usually included large lugged wheels to be mounted on a frame extension with chain reduction drives from the regular axles. Costing around $200, these kits did fill the bill for many a two- to three-horse farmer, but their usefulness was definitely limited. The Model T itself, however, did quite well under these trying circumstances, further endearing it to the hapless small farmer. Henry Ford must have relished the publicity garnered for his Model T, and in no way discouraged the kit-makers.

The Advent of the Fordson

With the impeccable timing, the Fordson burst on the scene on October

8, 1917. Although fewer than 300 were made that year, the concept of the light, small, mass-produced, and inexpensive tractor was realized.

The timing was right because of the civil and social turmoil then boiling up in Europe and soon to involve America. American farmers saw an increase in produce prices as much of Europe was taken out of production because of the war. The war also required the services of farmhands and horses. Both draftees and draft animals went off to war in record numbers, leaving the farmers with little choice but to use the laborsaving tractor.

European governments sought large-scale shipments of American tractors to stave off food shortages; this is when Henry Ford committed much of the 1918 Fordson production to Great

Britain. There is no question that the Fordson had Harvester on the ropes in 1922, but when the going got tough, Harvester's management brought in a tough engineer.

Enter Edward A. Johnston

The competition the Fordson stirred up provided the incentive to develop a machine that could do what the Fordson could not. The Fordson was not useful for cultivating such crops as corn and cotton; it did not have a driveshaft power takeoff and, therefore was not suitable for the new harvesting implements; and, most of all, it could replace some horses on a farm, but not all of them.

As early as 1910, Harvester engineers had talked to General Manager Alexander Legge about a more ver-

A 1929 Farmall Regular, Serial Number T70344, owned by John and Mary Lou Poch, of New Holstein, Wisconsin. The Farmall pioneered the configuration of the dual-narrow-front, row-crop tractor, with the steering rod over the top of the engine. The steering rod engages the vertical steering post through a gear mesh. The Farmall also pioneered frame mounting points for mounted implements.

satile tractor. The head of the Experimental Department at the time was a young engineer with an irrepressible spirit named Edward A. Johnston.

Johnston had started with the McCormick outfit during the harvester war of the 1890s. He had been instrumental in keeping McCormick's products competitive with patents covering mowers, knotters, binders, headers,

155

Previous page
The classic Farmall styling, by famous industrial designer Raymond Loewy, remained in production between 1939 and 1957. This example, a 1952 Super M, shows the timeless beauty of form and function.

and the like. Johnston's activities with motor vehicles began with a machine he made for himself before the turn of the century, which he dubbed the "Auto Buggy." For many years, he used it to commute between his home and the plant. In the early 1900s, Cyrus McCormick became interested in the Auto Buggy and commissioned Johnston to make one after the fashion of a farm wagon, capable of hauling a ton of cargo. This machine appeared on the market in 1906 and was the forerunner of the International truck.

Farmall F-12 production began in 1932, but only twenty-five were built that year. More than 123,000 were built before production ended in 1937.

Johnston and his team, which included such geniuses as Bert R. Benjamin and C. W. Mott, had some ideas for improving the tractor's utility—including the development of an all-purpose tractor. As development progressed, they kept General Manager Legge and Chairman McCormick informed, but the company expressed no official interest.

That changed in July 1921, when the Fordson threatened the whole International Harvester empire. Legge called in Johnston and asked him what had happened to the ten, or so, all-purpose tractor designs. By then, John-

ston and his team had focused on one type, of which several prototypes existed. Johnston insisted that this all-purpose "Farmall" could beat the Fordson in every way. When told this, Legge immediately ordered the construction of twenty more hand-built examples. He also ordered a full complement of implements to be customized for the Farmall. Both were to be ready for thorough testing in 1922.

Legge and Johnston resisted the temptation to rush the Farmall into production despite the rising menace of the Fordson. The engineers worked out design problems for both performance and mass production. Numerous patents were obtained. A third generation of test prototypes was built and tested. In 1924, 200 preproduction models were sold. Harvester field representatives watched closely as farmers put the new Farmall through its paces under actual conditions. Feedback to the design team resulted in a few more changes to the tractor and implements and in many new implements. Estimates acquired by the field representatives indicated a sixfold reduction in planting, tilling, and harvesting costs versus horse farming.

Farmall sales exceeded expectations in 1925. By 1926, the new Rock Island, Illinois, plant was in operation and Farmalls were rolling out the door. The Farmall then drove the lowly Fordson from the field.

Even at its peak production, before the crash of 1929, only about 24,000 Farmalls were built each year, a far cry from the 100,000 Fordsons built during Ford's peak years. By the end of the 1920s, International Harvester Company was clearly again at the top of the long-line farm implement industry. It enjoyed sales three times that of its nearest competitor, Deere & Company of Moline, Illinois.

The introduction of the Farmall was an enormous triumph for Harvester not only because of its victory over the Fordson. It also overcame sticky resistance to the concept of the all-purpose tractor both within the company and in the industry at large. When the first Farmall rolled out, there was no advertising blitz, no ceremony, not even a press conference. Harvester management was so cautious that initially sales were to be made only in Texas to prevent corporate embarrassment if they were not successful. An article in the March 1931 issue of *Agricultural Engineering* recounts the situation: "No development in the industry was regarded with more distrust and wholesale opposition than the suggested general-purpose tractor. . . . The opposition came more from farm implement manufacturers' home organizations than from the field, and those organizations certainly deserve credit for their relentless efforts to have this type of tractor released for experimental development. . . ."

When the Farmall appeared, it seemed top-heavy and fragile-looking compared to standard-tread tractors of its day. The Farmall and its imitators sold so well that they changed the concept of the conventional tractor to that of the row-crop configuration. This remained so into the 1960s when chemical herbicides replaced the need for crop cultivators and wide-fronts again became popular. With the current interest in ecological safeguards, the tractor cultivator may again be used to fight weeds.

To say that the Farmall was a success would be an understatement. The farmers loved this tractor. Most, however, hedged their bets and kept their horses for another season. Few did after the first year. Sales of the new tractor, while not disappointing, were low because farmers did not have the necessary cash. Lack of real faith in the Farmall by company management also left the production facilities somewhat strained and prevented lowering of the price through the full impact of true mass production. Nevertheless, the Farmall assembled well, worked well on the farm, sold well, and made a profit for the stockholders.

The surviving competitors quickly joined the all-purpose tractor field, but International Harvester enjoyed unchallenged tractor leadership until, in 1939, Henry Ford again redefined the word "tractor" with the introduction of the Ford-Ferguson 9N.

Chapter 3

Development of the Farmall Tractor

The configuration of the new Farmall tractor is generally credited to Bert R. Benjamin. In 1921, when International Harvester General Manager Alexander Legge commissioned the all-purpose tractor, Benjamin was superintendent of the McCormick Works' Experimental Division.

Harvester engineers had been experimenting with various tractor and motor cultivator configurations since 1910. Other tractor makers were struggling with unconventional approaches to the problem of replacing the horse. Many unusual configurations (which now seem ridiculous) were built, tested, and even sold.

After the appearance of the Fordson, especially, a great amount of actual tractor field data was made available to designers. The Fordson more-or-less established the configuration of the "conventional" tractor. Many new tractors of the early twenties resembled the Fordson, at least externally. These included the McCormick-Deering 15-30 and 10-20, the General Motors Samson, and the John Deere Model D.

Despite its prominence, Farmall designers avoided being influenced by

Mary Lou Poch, New Holstein, Wisconsin, sits aboard her pride and joy: a 1936 Farmall F-12. Mary Lou is a secretary at Tecumseh Motors. She and husband John are working toward a collection of twenty-five classic tractors. Mary Lou's F-12 has the optional fenders, which cost the original owner about $12 extra.

the Fordson except in the areas of the lighter weight and lower cost. There were, however, several other designs and innovations that swayed all future tractor configurations—especially those of the Farmall.

The International Harvester Motor Cultivator

Between 1915 and 1918, Harvester's experimental engineers worked on a device for powered cultivation of such crops as corn and cotton. Ed Johnston and colleague C. W. Mott in 1916 filed for a patent for a specialized machine that "pushed" a two-row cultivator.

The device, called a "Motor Cultivator," had an unusual configuration. A four-cylinder engine rode directly above a pair of drive wheels positioned closely together and connected by a vertical driveshaft. This rear-drive element swiveled on the frame, around the driveshaft, for steering. The driver sat in front of the engine and had a steering wheel and levers for selecting forward and reverse. In front of the operator, cultivator shovels were mounted between a pair of non-steerable, wide-stance front wheels. About 300 Motor Cultivators were sold in 1917 and 1918, but the idea did not catch on and production ended in 1918.

Harvester learned several things from the Motor Cultivator: that good visibility was needed for cultivator work and that multiple-row cultivation worked. Experience with the rear-

Although its production was limited by the failure of its parent company, the Moline Universal was really the first all-purpose tractor. This example is on display in the Smithsonian Institution. Smithsonian Institution

wheel steering arrangement proved that it was not such a good idea. Rearwheel steering is like a rudder on a boat: it swings the rear in the opposite direction from the desired course. On the Motor Cultivator, at least some of the shovels were mounted behind the front wheels. These shovels swung with the rear wheels toward the crops the farmer needed to avoid, rather than away from them, as steering corrections were made.

The Moline Universal

Introduced in 1917, the Moline Universal was an unusual contraption, even by the standards of those days. It was, however, the world's first successful all-purpose tractor.

The Universal's dominant feature was a pair of large drive wheels in the front, which provided the tractive effort and steering. Dolly wheels in the back were only used when no implement was installed; each implement had its own system for carrying the back end. The operator sat at the extreme rear, where he or she had a fairly good view of the implement ahead.

Other unique features of the Universal included adjustable drive wheel height, to keep the tractor level when one wheel was in a furrow; power lift; electric lights and starter; and an enclosed drivetrain and radiator.

The Universal was a success, but its parent company could not withstand the onslaught of the Fordson. The Universal was discontinued, and the

concept of the all-purpose tractor almost died as the Moline Plow Company struggled for its life.

Harvester's engineers adapted the longitudinal engine configuration and enclosed radiator, and learned the importance of engine air filtration—without an air filter, the life of the engine was short.

The Power Takeoff

One of International Harvester Company's initial responses to the competition of the Fordson was the development of the rear driveshaft-type power takeoff (PTO). In 1918, it came attached to a new small tractor, known as the 8-16. The 8-16 borrowed much of its configuration from the International truck line. The drive housing ended up with a 1.125in splined shaft sticking out. This was an idea from the fertile mind of Ed Johnston, who had seen a similar thing in France more than ten years earlier.

A French tractor experimenter by the name of Gougis was having trouble with a McCormick binder because of

John Poch's 1940 Farmall H on full steel. John has had the H for about nine years. It had been sold new on steel, but the original wheels had been cut off and converted to rubber. John had already purchased a full set of appropriate vintage steel wheels before he had the tractor. When he found the tractor, the engine was stuck but the sheet metal was good. To make the H more typical of the period, John removed the starter, lights, and generator.

This 1956 Prairie Farmer *ad touts the Fast Hitch and the Torque Amplifier. The Torque Amplifier, standard on the 300 and 400 models, provided a real competitive advantage over the rival John Deere 60 and 70. Note the short muffler used originally on both Farmall models.*

wet, slippery ground. The bullwheel, which drove the binder mechanism, did not have sufficient traction, and in frustration, Gougis adapted a tumbling-rod drive between his tractor's engine and the binder, eliminating the bullwheel drive. Although crude, he saved his wheat harvest. Ed Johnston happened to be in International Har-

vester's Paris office when news of this event arrived. He visited Gougis, and did not forget what he saw.

To justify the splined extension shaft sticking out of the back of the 8-16, Johnston and his team immediately began inventing the PTO Binder. The binder was useful only if used with the 8-16. It's not clear whether the binder sold the 8-16, or vice versa. Nevertheless, considering the times, both were quite successful. PTOs were incorporated into the next Harvester tractors, and became standard equipment on the 10-20.

By 1922, it was recognized that an all-purpose tractor had to do more than just plow, cultivate, and provide belt power. To truly replace the horse, the tractor had to be able to apply its horsepower directly to implements such as this binder.

Available Implements

With the development of new PTO equipment came a new basis of designing a tractor's productivity output and configuration: the tools it had to work with. While the long-line implement makers offered equipment compatible with their tractors, farmers often did not use them, trying instead to modify horse-drawn implements. Not only was this less than satisfactory because of the difference in the horsepower applied, but another factor was now appearing: to be cost-effective, the tractor had to be laborsaving, as well. It was not feasible to have an implement operator as well as the tractor driver. What had to be developed were implements that could be controlled from the tractor seat, implements that would do the jobs of horse-drawn implements, but faster and better, and implements that would harness the tractor's power to do jobs the horse had not done.

For example, plows could be made to run deeper, improving the soil's fertility and tilth for alfalfa and similar crops. The tractor farmer soon found he or she was receiving real dividends.

The Farmall designers knew they had to envision new tools from the outset, thus developing beet pullers, corn binders and pickers, planters, spreaders, and haying equipment. Because the tractor's configuration was so different, many of these implements had to be custom-designed.

Evolution of the Configuration

After years of development and several prototype configurations, when the Farmall emerged in its final form it sold so well that the factory couldn't fill orders quickly enough and the Farmall soon engendered imitators. The conventional tractor configuration was eventually altered to be the Farmall type, rather than the standard-tread Fordson type.

The Farmall's two outstanding features were that it was tall and narrow. Actually, it was spindly, and looked like a milk stool or a three-legged spider. Its height enabled it to go over row crops such as corn, and its narrow front aided visibility. The tricycle front wheel arrangement allowed it to move between the rows and facilitated tight turns. Originally, the two wheels were set closely together vertically, but were later angled out at the top to prevent shimmy and to make steering easier.

Although the Farmall looked spindly, it was not as light as it looked. It was more than 1000lb heavier than a Fordson, and the weight was as far aft and as low as possible for good traction and stability.

With the proper implements, the Farmall "could perform all the farm tasks except milking," as Cyrus Hall McCormick III wrote in *The Century of the Reaper.* It could comfortably handle a two-bottom plow with 14in bottoms, it could drive a 22in thresher if the bundles weren't thrown in too quickly, it could cultivate four rows, it could drive PTO binders and mowers, and it could do other routine pulling and powering tasks around the farm.

Farmall Development

The Farmall was a far cry from the Motor Cultivator of 1918, but the heritage was obvious. Under the ominous clouds of Fordson market domination

in 1921, Ed Johnston was not given much time to marshal a defense. By then, the rear drive and pivoting engine of the Motor Cultivator had been changed. The engine was now fixed to the frame, with a drive arrangement to the front wheels. Steering was still at the back.

A late 1945 Farmall advertisement advocates the Farmall System, perhaps a veiled counter to the successful Ferguson System.

By 1920, the Motor Cultivator was unofficially known as the Farmall, and important changes had been made. The

The Farmall Regular is shown in this 1930 ad, which stresses that "Farmall" is an International Harvester name—an apparent attempt to thwart another brand's attempts to get in on the concept. Names such as "All-crop," "General Purpose," and "All-around" were proliferating; some unscrupulous salesmen were even referring to their row-crop tractors as "Farmalls."

transverse engine mounting had been changed to longitudinal, and the tractor was made reversible. For some applications, the driver sat facing the drive wheels; for others, the driver faced the close-set steering wheels. In this later direction, the machine began to take on the Farmall look. This is where Johnston found things when he called on Bert Benjamin to pull together, as rapidly as possible, an all-purpose Farmall.

Benjamin first eliminated the reversible seating with its vertical steering-wheel post. He substituted over-the-engine steering using a front wheel pivot and gearbox from an old IHC Mogul. He included detachable, front-mounted cultivator gangs.

By 1923, the configuration of the Farmall was fixed and a corporate naming committee officially gave the tractor the "Farmall" name and registered it as a trademark. Twenty-two copies of the 1923 version were made and sent to various places for testing—interestingly, places where the McCormick-Deering 10-20 was not selling well anyway, as management did not want farmers delaying purchases to wait for the Farmall.

Field engineers accompanied the tractors, and various implements—plows, harrows, planters, and cultivators—were tried. Later in the year, such items as crop dusters and mowers were added. Then came hillers, middle breakers, and PTO harvesters.

Also integral to the 1923 version was a unique cable-and-pulley affair that automatically applied one brake when the steering wheel was turned to its limit. Always a problem with tricycle tractors, the steering moment arm cannot be made as long as the designer would like without making the tractor too long. Bert Benjamin elected to use this mechanism, which came to be called the "triple control," and to keep the Farmall as short as possible.

Against the better judgment of many in Harvester marketing, the company decided on a production run of 200 Farmalls for 1924; the Marketing Department predicted that the new tractor would take sales away from the proven 10-20. Nevertheless, the price was set arbitrarily at a low $825, which was about the same as the 10-20 at that time.

Several improvements were made to the 1924 Farmall model. The rear axle housing was made heavier, as were the rear wheel hubs, transmission case, and drawbar. The frame was also strengthened and made from box-section steel, rather than channel steel.

The 1924 model used a tall air intake stack at the left side of the engine. A flannel cloth covered the intake in the first effort to get cleaner air for the engine. Beginning in 1925, an oil-bath air cleaner was mounted in front of the radiator.

For 1925, the price was raised to a more realistic $925. A total of 837 were built, with only minor changes in configuration from the 1924 model. To help placate the marketing staff and to avoid conflict with the McCormick-Deering 10-20, the Farmall did not receive a horsepower rating. In September 1925, however, the tractor was tested at the University of Nebraska (Test Number 117), so horsepower figures were soon well known.

Although the Farmall's engine displacement was 221ci versus 284ci for the 10-20, the power was almost the

The Farmall 300 was produced from 1954 to 1956. This 1956 model is owned by Austin Hurst of Lafayette, California.

same at 20hp. The reason for this was that the Farmall engine had a rated speed of 1200rpm, rather than the 1000rpm of the 10-20. Fuel for both was kerosene. As tested, the Farmall was almost 100lb heavier than the 10-20.

An experimental version of the Farmall from 1920.

The Nebraska Test report indicated that the 1925 version of the Farmall ran a total of thirty-nine hours during the rigorous testing, requiring neither repairs nor adjustments. It was an impressive debut for the world's first all-purpose row-crop tractor.

Full-Scale Production Begins

The Rock Island, Illinois, plant was ready to begin mass production of the Farmall in 1926. Alexander Legge purchased and then refurbished this structure, which ironically had been the former factory for the Moline Universal. It went on-line in time for 4,418 Farmalls to be completed that year. There was no longer any doubt about the acceptance of the all-purpose tractor. No longer was there any concern for hurting 10-20 sales. The problem

An experimental version of the Farmall from 1921.

now was producing enough Farmalls to meet demand.

The Farmall's configuration did not change much after 1925 until variations were introduced in 1931. A "Fairway" model—with special steel wheels customized for intended duties on golf courses and airports—was offered in addition to the regular Farmall.

By 1930, 200 Farmalls were being produced every day, for a grand total of 100,000 for that year. The team at International Harvester had beaten off the Fordson challenge and in the process changed farming just as surely as did the Fordson. While many horses were still providing farm power through World War II, the appearance of the Farmall spelled the end of horse farming. From 1926 on, it was more the result of an individual's economic situation that kept the horse in use; many farmers simply did not have the cash or credit to replace old Dobbin.

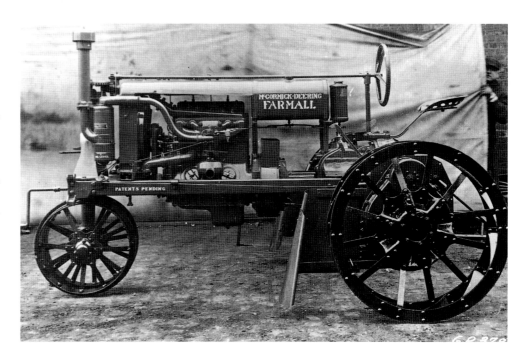

A "studio" photograph of the first production Farmall, 1924.

A Farmall 350 with a pull-type combine in tow. International Harvester power steering was an option on the 350. This Farmall is pictured at the Franklin Grove, Illinois, Living History Show in 1992.

20th Birthday

OF THE FARMALL
and the Farmall System of Farming

The Original Farmall - Born in 1923

FOR TWENTY YEARS the Farmall IDEA has been the foundation for *all* experiments in general-purpose tractor design....

TODAY 4 sizes of modern FARMALLS—the sturdy "A" and "B", and the big powerful "H" and "M"—with special machines and tools for every crop, operation, and season, lead the way in the battle for food.

★

FOOD fights for FREEDOM
and the
FARMALL fights for FOOD

★

In 1923 came FARMALL, the first true all-purpose tractor . . . the farm power unit designed from the soil up . . . the tractor that *started from the implement end*.

Harvester built it, based on EXPERIENCE—and that made SENSE!

After 1923, the call for farm power really swept the nation. It was Farmall that made the old dream of horseless farming come true. Here was the tractor that did almost everything. From every state came comments like these: "Not a horse or hired man on my place"... "At least ⅓ cheaper to farm this new way"..."My Farmall works in crooked rows where a snake would get lost"..."My two boys, 13 and 11, do anything that I can do with it."

Pretty soon there were a hundred thousand, and then a half-million Farmalls. Today there are more Farmalls producing food on American farms than all other makes of general-purpose tractors *combined*.

When war struck our nation, a Farmall army, with an infinite number of working tools, went into battle. The greatest food crisis in our history was at every farm gate—and the *Farmall System* was ready!

✳   ✳   ✳

So we mark the 20th Birthday of this most popular of all tractors. There's a proud record of progress between the old "Original" of 1923 and the streamlined red Farmalls of today—endless improvements in power and machines. Today millions know that Farmall is the ideal power for any farm, whatever the size. Farmall showed the way, and *will* show the way when the boys get home from war.

Farmall and Harvester are pledged to the faithful service of that great American institution—the family farm.

INTERNATIONAL HARVESTER COMPANY
180 N. Michigan Ave., Chicago 1, Ill.

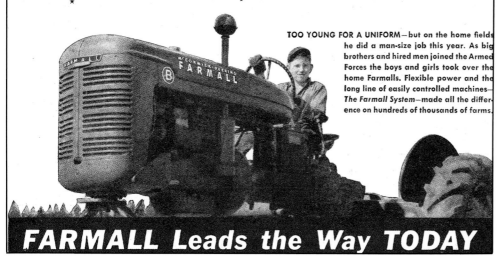

TOO YOUNG FOR A UNIFORM—but on the home fields he did a man-size job this year. As big brothers and hired men joined the Armed Forces the boys and girls took over the home Farmalls. Flexible power and the long line of easily controlled machines—*The Farmall System*—made all the difference on hundreds of thousands of farms.

FARMALL Leads the Way TODAY

This wartime ad commemorates the twentieth Farmall birthday. The ad also commends youngsters for taking over farming duties when the men went to war. As the ad states, "Too young for a uniform—but on the home fields he did a man-size job this year."

A 1940 Farmall H on full steel, owned by John and Mary Lou Poch of New Holstein, Wisconsin. Although most of the H series tractors were sold on rubber, steel was an option until after World War II.

This 1934 Farmall F-20, owned by Steve Wade of Plainwell, Michigan, is equipped with an auxiliary road gear that gives a top speed of 18mph. This photograph was taken at the Prairieville Old-Fashioned Farms Days. Rubber tires were optional on the Farmall from 1933. The Farmall F-20 had adjustable rear wheel spacing. The wheels could be set at either 74in or 83in. Special narrow- and wide-front versions were also available: 57in or 77-in for the narrow, and 68in or 96in for the wide. Both versions were available with an adjustable wide-front axle.

A wide-front Farmall Model H, built in 1944. This is the same model and year tractor that the author drove as a 12-year-old lad in northern Wisconsin, working for a neighboring farmer. Such a striking piece of new machinery during the depths of the war years made a lasting impression on many. The tractor shown here, however, was photographed in the wet fields of Dorset, in photographer Andrew Morland's native England.

By 1956, when this 300 was new, there was not much call for belt pulleys; this live PTO, however, got a real workout. Owner Austin Hurst tells of mowing a great deal of acreage with a fast-hitch pitmanless mower—using fourth gear!

Chapter 4

Characteristics
of the Farmall Models

F Series

Until 1936, all Farmalls were painted Battleship Gray. For the 1936 year model, the color Farmall Red was introduced. All the F Series, except some F-12s and F-14s (which were gasoline only), were started on gasoline and, after the manifold got hot, were operated on kerosene.

Farmall Regular

The McCormick-Deering Farmall, introduced in 1924, defined the row-crop tractor design. It was also the first of the all-purpose or general-purpose tractors, a concept that greatly broadened the usefulness of the farm tractor and affected the form of other configurations, as well.

Until the Farmall, farm tractors had gradually evolved from a modified steam traction engine into a foreshort-

This 1929 Farmall Regular is owned by Bill Rollinger of Pecatonica, Illinois. Son Jason is on the tractor, and son Billy rides the sickle-bar mower. Rollinger, a heavy construction equipment buyer, is an avid Farmall collector and an active participant in the Stephenson County Antique Engine Club Show in Freeport, Illinois. The Regular had a three-speed transmission and an all-gear final drive. Its four-cylinder engine produced 18hp at the belt in the University of Nebraska rated load test. Before other Farmall models were introduced in 1931, this tractor was simply known as the Farmall. When the others came out with F-number designations, it became conventional to refer to these earlier undesignated ones as Regulars.

ened highway truck arrangement. The rear wheels were larger than the front ones to carry the great weight over soft ground and to increase traction. Front wheels were smaller to facilitate a shorter turning radius without interfering with the frame and to cut costs. The front axle passed under the front of the tractor with kingpins on either end; crop clearance was thus dictated by the diameter of the front wheels. No attempt was made to raise the clearance, as no one except Farmall designer Bert Benjamin believed a full-sized tractor could be an effective cultivator.

Benjamin had experience with an experimental tractor configured to operate in either direction depending on the task assigned. This led him to the tricycle layout of the Farmall, with its two front wheels close together. The front wheels, being under the nose of the tractor, could pivot 90deg without interfering with the structure, and they could move between two crop rows, so as not to interfere with the taller crops. They dictated the height of the main body of the tractor.

To allow for reasonably sized rear wheels, drop gearing was used at the end of each rear drive axle. This caused the high torque to be developed as far down the geartrain as possible, reducing the loading on upstream gears and bearings.

Early in his experimenting with the tricycle configuration, Benjamin learned what anyone who has driven tricycle tractors knows: the steering

No attempt was made to muffle the exhaust of the Farmall Regular. Before 1931, there wasn't enough power to spare on muffling sound. Note the close proximity to the brass carburetor to help vaporize the kerosene. The Farmall series, except for the Cub, always used overhead-valve engines. Note also the removable port covers to facilitate bearing adjustment.

loses authority at high cramp angles. To overcome this, he incorporated an automatic, cable-actuated, individual rear wheel brake system. While this may seem overly complicated today, at the time it was not.

In 1924, many Farmall drivers had not previously driven a motor vehicle, let alone one with a four-row cultivator. At the end of the row, the farmer had to make a turn in minimum space, manually raise and lower the cultivator, adjust the throttle, and work the clutch. Automatic braking eased the workload at a critical time. The idea of putting both brake pedals on the right side near the right foot would not be implemented in the Farmall until 1939.

The new Farmall also featured a steering rod running over the top of the longitudinally installed four-cylinder, overhead-valve engine. The steering rod engaged a gearbox at the front, mounted on top of the steering post; this configuration became the norm for the industry, worldwide. The Farmall used a three-speed transmission, and also pioneered the use of implement mounting holes in the frame members on the forward part of the tractor.

The tractor was known as the McCormick-Deering Farmall until 1931 when the Model F-30 came out. After that, Farmalls built between 1924 and 1932—before its replacement, the F-20, was introduced—came to be known as the Farmall Regular.

A second version for industrial and golf course applications, the Fairway, was built until 1933. It featured special steel 40x16 rear wheels and 25x8 front wheels.

Farmall F-30

The first variation on Bert Benjamin's theme was the more powerful F-30. The Regular was considered a two-plow tractor, and the new F-30 was a three-plow model. It was designed for the larger farms in row-crop country where the big, standard-tread machines had already been in use. The idea was not so much to eliminate horses as to replace conventional competitive tractors. By 1931, there were a plethora of Farmall copies available from other manufacturers, so by introducing a second size of tractor, McCormick-Deering was turning up the competitive wick.

At 147in long, the new F-30 was 2ft longer than the Regular. It was also almost a ton heavier.

The engine for the F-30 was based on the successful engine in the 10-20

A Farmall Regular is put to the belt at the Midwest Thresherman's Reunion near Pontiac, Illinois. Note the cable along the frame rail which actuated the brake to assist the front wheels in steering.

Production of the F-30 began in late 1931. It was the first variation on Bert R. Benjamin's theme, although the changes are hard to distinguish visually. The F-30 was longer and, at 5,300lb, much heavier than the 4000lb Regular. Production ended in 1939, but as with the F-20, tractors were completed from available parts and sold well into 1940. This example is owned by Bill Rollinger of Pecatonica, Illinois.

Power for the Farmall F-20 came from a four-cylinder overhead-valve engine with a bore and stroke of 3.75x5.00in. Rated operating speed was 1200rpm. This power allowed the F-20 to pull two 14in bottoms. Thus equipped, the F-20 could plow about seven acres in a 10hr day on about 10gal of fuel.

conventional tractor. Otherwise, the F-30 kept the same configuration as the Regular. Remaining the same were the steering and brake arrangement, the engine placement and the three-speed transmission, thermo-syphon cooling, splash lubrication, and all-gear drive.

The McCormick-Deering W-30 was a standard-tread version of the Farmall F-30 introduced in 1932.

F-20

McCORMICK-DEERING
FARMALL
MADE BY
INTERNATIONAL HARVESTER COMPANY
CHICAGO
U. S. A.

GASOLINE

DISENGAGE CLUTCH
BEFORE SHIFTING
PULLEY CLUTCH LEVER

ALWAYS CLOSE NEEDLE VALVES
BEFORE SWITCHING FROM ONE
FUEL TO ANOTHER—WHEN BOTH
VALVES ARE OPEN AT ONE TIME
THE FUELS WILL MIX—THIS
MAKES IT IMPOSSIBLE TO START

DO NOT ATTEMPT TO PULL WHEN DRAWBAR IS OUT
ALL HITCHES MUST BE ATTACHED TO DRAWBAR

FARMALL
REG. U. S. PAT. OFF. JULY 17, 1923

A 1939 Farmall F-20 with owner Larry Gloyd aboard. This tractor was photographed on Independence Day at Gloyd's estate in the country outside Rockford, Illinois. Larry, who is CEO of CLARCOR, uses the tractor almost exclusively to give his grandchildren rides. He has owned the tractor for about four years.

Previous page
The Farmall F-20. During 1932, the Regular was replaced by the F-20. Among the improvements was a four-speed transmission, instead of three; a 15 percent power increase through a half-inch increase in the bore; and a reduction in the belt pulley speed to bring belt speed to the new industry standard of 2395ft per minute. Farmalls were gray until 1936, when the color was changed to the now-familiar red. The Farmall's configuration is credited to International Harvester Engineer Bert R. Benjamin, whose efforts saved the company during the great tractor war of the twenties. This F-20 is owned by Steve Wade of Plainwell, Michigan.

By 1934, variations included a wide-front axle arrangement and conventional tread versions known as the W-30 and I-30. In 1936, pneumatic tires and electrical lighting became options. With factory rubber tires, a high-speed fourth gear was installed. Late 1938 saw the availability of power lift.

Farmall F-20

During 1932, the Farmall Regular was updated and given the designation F-20. The engine cylinder bore was increased 0.50in to produce about 15 percent more power. To improve steering authority, length was increased from 123in to 140in. A four-speed transmission was added. The speed of the belt pulley was reduced from 690rpm to 650rpm to produce a belt speed close to the industry standard of 2395ft per

minute. The weight also increased because of these changes. The F-20 can generally be distinguished from the Regular by a shorter air intake stack.

Additional power made the F-20 capable of handling a 14in two-bottom plow. Thus equipped, it could plow about seven acres in a ten-hour day. The F-20 could handle a 22in threshing machine under most conditions.

The F-20 was available in regular and narrow versions, each of which had two optional rear wheel treads. The regular version rear wheels could be set at either 74in or 83in; the narrow version could be set at either 57in or 77in. By 1935, the narrow version could be ordered with a wide-front axle. In 1938, a wide version that could reach a 96in width was offered. An adjustable wide-front axle was available with that

version. A single-wheel front end was also an option instead of dual narrow wheels that year.

Production of the F-20 ended in 1939, although tractors were available from stock during part of 1940. Almost 150,000 were built, shattering all previous McCormick-Deering model production records.

Farmall F-12

Also introduced in 1932, the diminutive F-12 first appeared in late fall and only twenty-five were built that year. The F-12 was listed as a one-plow tractor, capable of pulling a 16in bottom. A PTO was included as standard equipment, as was, in 1934, fully adjustable rear wheel spacing.

The F-12 was originally equipped with a Waukesha engine, which was

The 1939 Farmall F-20 featured individual left and right foot-operated brakes, both on the right side of the platform. Production of the F-20 ended in 1939, although they were made from parts and sold into 1940. The F-20 was replaced on the International Harvester assembly line at Rock Island, Illinois, by the styled Farmall H. Almost 150,000 Farmall F-20s were built between 1932 and 1939, greatly exceeding the production volume of any previous International Harvester tractor. Although the F-20 was slightly longer and heavier than its predecessor, the Farmall Regular, there was really very little design change in Bert R. Benjamin's original concept between 1924 and 1939.

The Farmall F-12 featured a four-cylinder overhead-valve engine with a 3.00x4.00in bore and stroke. Displacement was 113ci, and rated operating speed was 1400rpm. The F-12 was available in either gasoline or kerosene versions. A McCormick carburetor was used. The diminutive F-12 was built between 1932 and 1938. Originally, it was available only in the single front wheel version, but soon dual-narrow-front, standard-tread, industrial, and orchard versions were also available. Note that there is very little camber angle on the front wheels. This is also the case with all the unstyled Farmalls.

soon replaced with one of Harvester's own, available in either gasoline or kerosene version. The early F-12s were equipped with a single front wheel.

Dual and wide fronts were offered later.

The F-12 could be adjusted to as narrow as 44.5in, approximately the width of a horse. This made it ideal for the truck gardener, who was used to one-horse specialized implements. With its standard PTO, the F-12 could handle a 10ft binder or a 6ft mounted mower. The 7ft turning radius of the F-12 allowed for neat mowing in a square pattern. Front-mounted equipment included cultivators, hay sweeps, and side-disk plows. The F-12 was available on factory rubber from its first full year of production.

Production of the F-12 ended in 1938. It was built in a standard-tread W-12 version, an I-12 industrial version, an O-12 orchard version, and a Fairway version for golf courses and airports.

Farmall F-14

Production of the F-12 ended in 1938 after more than 123,000 F-12s had been built. It was replaced by the almost-identical F-14. The only observable difference was that the engine was rated at 1650rpm, rather than 1400rpm. This change gave the F-14 about 14 percent more horsepower, enough to handle two 14in plow bottoms. It was available in either gasoline or kerosene burning versions and on either rubber or steel; wheel weights were optional equipment when rubber tires were used.

As with the F-12, there were standard-tread, Orchard, Fairway, and Industrial versions of the Farmall F-14. The serial numbering system for the F-14 began with 124000. A gap of several hundred numbers was left,

The right side of the Farmall F-12 engine showing the McCormick-built magneto. University of Nebraska Test Number 212, in 1933, indicated that the F-12 was capable of a maximum of 16.2 belt horsepower and 11.7 drawbar horsepower. It was capable of exerting a pull of more than 1800lb. Gasoline was the fuel used in Test Number 212. Similar results were recorded in Test Number 220 with kerosene fuel.

This 1939 Farmall F-14 with dual front wheels is owned by Bill Rollinger of Pecatonica, Illinois. The F-14 succeeded the F-12 in 1938. It was produced only in 19338 and 1939, with fewer than 30,000 being built. The F-14 was virtually identical to the F-12, except that the engine of the F-14 was rated at 1650rpm, rather than 1400rpm.

A 1939 Farmall A refurbished by Joe Schloskey, owner of Machinery Hill, a Phillips, Wisconsin, farm and industrial equipment dealer. Joe rebuilds one or two small tractors each year as fill-in work. He then adds a Woods mower deck and puts them on his sales lot. Thus equipped, these tractors are much in demand by those with above-average mowing requirements, especially anyone somewhat nostalgic for the finer old tractor.

Models A and C are featured in this 1952 Farmall advertisement.

rather than following the usual practice of beginning at serial number 501.

Despite vastly increasing competition, the F-14 sold well, with more than 27,000 units delivered in its two years of production. Competition in 1938 included the Henry Dreyfuss-styled John Deere Models A and B, direct competitors to the Farmalls. Minneapolis-Moline and Massey-Harris also introduced styled tractors. Allis-Chalmers came out with its Model B in 1938 and Model C in 1939.

Lettered Series

The real competition for all tractor makers came in June 1939 when a specter of the great tractor war of the twenties arose: Henry Ford was back in the tractor business. The late Elmer Baker, Jr., a staff writer for *Implement and Tractor* magazine, was quoted as saying, "Henry Ford had the time, money, and inclination to poke sticks at the McCormicks. He loved to, we've heard from the horse's mouth."

This time, the stick was the new Ford Model 9N tractor. This 2500lb tractor, selling for a mere $600, could plow more than 12 acres in a normal day, pulling two "fourteens"—better acreage than the expensive (more than $1,200) F-30 could do.

This unbelievable performance was made possible by the Ferguson implement system, the first volume-production application of the hydraulic three-point hitch. The system caused the weight of a variety of implements, plus their draft and suction loads, to bear down on the rear wheels, greatly improving traction.

The 9N was not a row-crop tractor in the true sense of the word, but its wide front did incorporate downward-extending kingpins that gave it fairly good crop clearance. Its cultivator was rear-mounted—and many a wise corn farmer would not take a chance to even try it.

According to extant reports, it worked quite well, however. The outcome is that Ford sold more than 10,000 9Ns in the six remaining months of 1939, despite the rush to production.

More than 220,000 Farmall A and Super A tractors were built between 1939 and 1954, attesting to their popularity. The Super A, introduced in 1947, was the same as the A, except hydraulic power was added for implement lifting. The Farmall A used essentially the same engine as the F-12 and F-14 Farmalls. It was available in both gasoline and kerosene versions. Rubber tires and a four-speed transmission were standard equipment. A higher crop-clearance Farmall AV version was available for cultivating such crops as asparagus. The A was considered a 16in one-bottom plow tractor. Most Super A tractors also had engines with a higher normal speed rating of 1650rpm, rather than the 1400rpm of the standard A.

The rush caused such severe production problems that the first 700, or so, 9Ns were shipped with cast-aluminum hoods, the steel stamping equipment not being ready in time. Almost 100,000 more of the little gray Ford-Fergusons were completed by the end of 1942, even with production curtailed by World War II. And just as the Farmall changed the configuration of the conventional tractor to that of the row-crop type, the Ford-Ferguson began to change it back to the wide-front type.

International Harvester was not caught napping by the competition this time. Seeing the trend toward more functional and eye-pleasing design, Harvester engaged the services of Raymond Loewy, a noted industrial designer who later gained worldwide renown with his rakish design of the Studebaker car line. Loewy was commissioned to overhaul the entire Harvester product line, from the company logo to product operator ergonomics.

By late 1938, the same year that John Deere introduced styled tractors, Harvester introduced the new TD-18 crawler tractor. The TD-18 was undeniably striking in its new, bright-red, smoothly contoured sheet metal hood and grille. Just months later, a new lineup of wheel tractors was announced, carrying the styling motif even farther with contoured fenders and styled wheels. The 1939 Loewy Farmalls still look stylish today.

Farmall A

The first and most radical of these new tractors was the Farmall A, which used the same engine as the F-12 and F-14 but governed at 1400rpm. Its most unusual feature was that the engine was offset to the left and the operator seat

Farmall B tractors were either dual or single wheel, narrow-front configurations, whereas the Farmall A was always a wide-front. Although the basic weight of the B was less than a ton, another ton of ballast could be added to provide traction and stability. The Farmall B was produced from 1939 to 1947.

Dan Langy maneuvers his 1941 Farmall B on his four-acre spread near Lena, Illinois. This 1941 Farmall B originally sold for a little under $650. The B was available in either kerosene or gasoline version. In Nebraska Test Number 331, the B developed a maximum belt horsepower of 16.8 and a maximum drawbar horsepower of 12.1. It also exerted a maximum pull of 2377lb, 64 percent of its weight. The Farmall B was essentially the same tractor as the A, but did not look like the A. The A had a long axle on the right side and a wide front. The Farmall B had two long axles and a narrow front. On the B, the engine was in the middle, rather than offset to the left as on the Farmall A. As shown here, however, the driver's seat is still offset to the right to provide an unobstructed view for cultivating.

and steering wheel were offset to the right. This gave the operator an unobstructed view of the ground beneath the tractor where the cultivator would be operating. Loewy called this concept "Culti-Vision." He reasoned that cultivating delicate crops was a major application of a tractor of this horsepower, and so shaped everything around this task.

Thus, the A was necessarily a wide-front machine to give the offset engine stability, but it retained the all-purpose functions for which Farmalls had become famous. It was equipped with both a belt pulley and a PTO, but the belt pulley was in the back, rather than at the side.

The new A was available with either gasoline or kerosene engines,

but as with all the Lettered Series tractors, gasoline predominated. The kerosene version used a compression ratio of 5:1, rather than the 6:1 of the gas engine. The thermo-syphon liquid cooling system was continued. This system operated on the gravity principle, rather than using a water pump; radiator shutters were used instead of a thermostat. Later versions of the A did use a pump-type system, however, and many have been converted over the years.

The A featured two wheel brake pedals on the right side of the platform that could be actuated individually or locked together. A Donaldson oil-bath air cleaner was standard equipment, as was a high-tension magneto with an impulse coupling. A Delco-Remy gen-

erator and electrical system were optional. The system included lights and a starter. Rubber tires were standard, as was a four-speed transmission with a road gear giving a top speed of 10mph.

The Farmall AV was the identical tractor, except it had longer front kingpin extensions and 36x8 rear tires. This arrangement provided an additional 6in of clearance for such crops as asparagus and sugar cane.

Farmall Super A

In 1947, a Super A version replaced the A. The Super A was identi-

This 1941 Farmall B is owned by Mary Lou and Dan Langy of Lena, Illinois. Except for the wheel arrangement, the B was the same tractor as the A. In fact, they were interspersed in the same serial numbering system.

cal to the A, except it had a built-in hydraulic system called "Touch Control," Harvester's first system for raising and lowering implements at the touch of a small lever. It consisted of three elements: an engine-driven gear pump, a double work cylinder, and a valve unit. Two rockshafts operated four rockshaft power arms to separately control left- and right-side implements.

Most Super A tractors had 1650rpm engines giving a substantial power boost. Production of the Super A continued through 1954.

Farmall B

The Farmall B was essentially the same tractor as the A—so much so, in fact, that the Bs were interspersed in the same serial numbering sequence. Model Bs do not look like Model As, though. The A has a long rear axle on the right and a short one on the left. The B has two long axles, one each on the left and right. Therefore, on the B, the engine is in the middle, rather than offset to the left as on the A. Nevertheless, the driver's seat is offset to the right and the steering column proceeds along the right side of the engine, as on the A.

All Model Bs were narrow-front, either single- or dual-wheel, and so followed in the tradition of the row-crop tractor. Rear wheels on both the A and B were reversible, to provide for row width changes of 28in. Both the A and B sold for about $600 in 1939, directly challenging the Ford-Ferguson 9N.

The basic B weighed about a ton, but adding a ballast could bring the weight up to almost two tons. Thus equipped, the B had little trouble with a 16in bottom pull-type plow. Other specialized implements included all of those for the A, except those requiring hydraulic power, as the B, unlike the Super A, was not made with internal hydraulics. Also, there were no Industrial or high-crop versions of the B.

Farmall C

The Farmall C more or less replaced the B in 1948. The same 113.1ci

This Farmall B is equipped with an aftermarket seat. Such seats, sold both as optional accessories and by other companies, greatly enhanced comfort and safety. Most farm equipment of this period used the simple, stamped steel pan seat. After ten hours of bouncing across plow furrows in such a seat, any farmer would welcome an improvement.

Instrumentation on the Farmall B was simple. The knob controlled the level of generator output. In the early forties, most tractors, including the Farmall B, used cutouts, rather than voltage regulators. Charging rate was upped when the lights were used.

engine was retained in either the gasoline or distillate configuration, as was the four-speed transmission. The big difference between the A and B Series and the C was that a steel rail frame was included in the C. The A and B did not have frames, but relied on the cast-iron

Unlike the Farmall A, the Farmall B had cultivator mounting pads at the front of the engine. The little B was unexcelled for row-crop cultivation. Rear wheel tread widths could be varied between 64in and 92in.

engine drivetrain for structure; the front ends were mounted to the front of the engine. The disadvantage of this arrangement was the lack of mounting places for front-mounted implements.

Along with the new frame, which was somewhat like that of the larger H and M models, came truly adjustable rear wheel spacing with sliding hubs. The A and B Series relied on reversible wheels.

The Model C was also fitted with hydraulic Touch Control.

Farmall Super C

The Super C replaced the C in 1951. The main feature of the Super C was an increase in engine displacement from 113.1ci to 122.7ci, through 0.125in increase in bore diameter. This gave the Super C a 15 percent increase in horsepower. The Super C was rated as a two 14in bottom plow tractor.

The Super C had other interesting new features. A new ball-ramp disc brake system allowed optional drive sprockets to be mounted outboard of the brake units to drive planters in direct proportion to travel. The seat was made more comfortable, with upholstering and an adjustable double-acting shock absorber and a conical coil spring. And, the hydraulic Touch Control system was standard, rather than optional.

The Super C was available in either dual tricycle or adjustable widefront configuration. The C and the Super C can be readily distinguished from other tractors by their high steering-wheel position and the sharp angle the steering shaft makes as it proceeds past the left side of the cowling.

A Farmall C and a nice International pickup are shown in this ad which stresses 5-Star Service. The "See you at the polls" note at the bottom refers to the 1952 election in which Eisenhower was elected president.

Next page
The Farmall Super C replaced the C in 1951. Displacement in the Super C increased from 113ci to 123ci, giving it a much-needed power boost. The Super C could handle two 14in plows. Also new for the Super C were ball-ramp disc brakes.

The Farmall Cub was a unique approach to a utility tractor. It was the smallest in the International Harvester line, capable of pulling one 12in bottom. Introduced in 1947, the Cub was produced with little change until 1964. Variations, called International Cub Lo-boys, were continued for some time thereafter.

Mary Lou Langy's 1958 Farmall Cub. The Cub was the only Farmall with an L-head engine. It had a 60ci engine and a three-speed transmission.

Kathy Schultz of Deerfield, Wisconsin, poses with her 1957 Farmall Cub. The Cub is equipped with the unique one-armed front-end loader. Robert N. Pripps

Farmall Cub

For the tractor industry, 1947 was a watershed year. Enough time had transpired since the end of World War II for postwar designs to appear. The major companies knew they were in for a battle for market share, because there were just too many tractor makers competing. Furthermore, despite the war, the Ford-Ferguson was gaining momentum and sales at an exponential rate. International Harvester's response was to make improvements to its entire line and to introduce a new, smaller, less-expensive tractor, the Farmall Cub.

The Cub was aimed at the market the John Deere L and LA had been filling, meeting the needs of the vegetable grower, nursery, landscaper, and the small-acreage farmer still using only a team of draft animals. Interestingly, John Deere dropped out of this market in 1947 by replacing its small L and LA models with the Model M, designed to attack Ford head on.

The Cub was of the same configuration as the Farmall A, as cultivation of delicate plants was to be a priority job. Separately, it is difficult to tell an A from a Cub. Together, the Cub looks like a scale model. The most distinguishing visual feature of the Cub is the shape of the gas tank, which is rounded, rather than tear drop-shaped, as on the other Farmalls.

The 1500lb Cub used a unique little 59.5ci four-cylinder side-valve (L-

Next page
Owner Jon Kayser and the author's son, Greg Pripps, stand by Kayser's 1956 Farmall Cub Lo-Boy to show how low it really is. The Lo-Boy was designed primarily for mowing. The low stance gave it stability on the hills and the ability to slip under shrubs. Robert N. Pripps

head) engine, rather than the valve-in-head type used by the other Farmalls. This 10hp engine was also used in combines, pumps, blowers, and other implements. In the 1950 version, operating speed of the engine was raised from 1600rpm to 1800rpm, giving the Cub about 10 percent more power.

Seven or eight implements were custom built for the Cub, including a one-armed front-end loader. The tractor was equipped with magneto ignition, but an electrical system with

A 1948 Farmall Cub. The Cub was introduced in 1947 for the nurseries, vegetable growers, and the landscaper market. The Cub, like the Farmall A, was off-set to the left with the driver and steering wheel on the right. This concept was called "Culti Vision" by the Madison Avenue types, in reference to the great view the operator would have of a belly-mounted cultivator. The Cub used a unique 59.5ci side-valve engine operating at 1600rpm. This one is owned by Jon Kayser, a Case-IH dealer in Dell Rapids, South Dakota. Robert N. Pripps

starter and lights was also available. Other optional equipment included a rear PTO and hydraulic Touch Control system. The Cub, and its variations, continued in Harvester's inventory through 1964.

Farmall H

The Model H Farmall, introduced in 1939, replaced the F-20. Its main competitor was the John Deere B, which had been introduced in a styled version for 1938.

The engine developed for the H was a more modern high-speed unit of 152ci displacement, operating at a rated speed of 1650rpm. As such, it was in the 25hp class, the same as the older F-20. This power gave the H the capability to handle a 14in two-bottom plow or to drive a 22in thresher with relative ease.

The H was introduced at the same time as the big-brother M, sharing frame and layout, so that mounted implements were interchangeable.

Most Model Hs were equipped with gasoline engines, but distillate

Next page
A 1956 Lo-Boy Cub. Chrome hood insignias were used on later models, same as on the big tractors. Later Cubs were not Farmalls, but carried the "International" designation. The Cub Lo-Boy model had a height of only 63in as compared to the regular Cub, which stood 76in high. Otherwise, they were the same, using the same C-60 engine. Later Cubs, such as this 1956 model, had an rpm increase, which slightly raised the horsepower. Robert N. Pripps

The long and short of it. . . . John Kayser's Model HV high-crop and his Cub Lo-Boy stand side by side. The HV stands almost a yard taller. Robert N. Pripps

The Farmall H was a completely redesigned sequel to the Farmall F-20. The striking Loewy styling was both aesthetic and functional. Although it had about the same horsepower as the F-20, the H had a completely new engine that used a water pump, instead of the older thermosyphon system.

A fine example of classic tractor restoration, this 1942 Farmall H, serial number 97552, is owned by Leslie K. Bergquist of Maynard, Minnesota. Leslie did the restoration himself and says the tractor has "family ties."

This Farmall H was originally the basis of a cotton picker. Since converted to a standard Model H, it is now owned by Bill Rollinger of Pecatonica, Illinois. The only difference Bill can notice is in the configuration of the rear axle housings. Because of its infrequent usage, it still has the original S-3 Firestone tires.

versions were also available. Most were equipped with rubber tires, except those affected by the rubber shortages of World War II; during the war, many Model Hs were sold on steel wheels or with rubber fronts and steel rears. Most Model Hs were of the tricycle configuration, but wide-front, high-crop versions were also available. The Model H and the Model M used water-pump cooling systems; the earliest of these did not have pressure radiator caps.

Farmall Super H

In 1952, the Model H was upgraded to the Super H. The major difference was an increase in engine displacement to 164ci from the previous 152.1ci—boosting power to more than 30hp. This gave the Super H a true two-bottom (16in) or three-bottom

(14in) capacity. Basic weight increased about 700lb, but the Super H could be ballasted to around 8000lb.

The Super H was available in tricycle, adjustable wide-front or fixed wide-front high-crop versions. Hydraulics were optional. The Super H was equipped with the new International Harvester disc brakes, which used ball-ramp, self-energizing devices, in which the motion of the tractor tended to increase clamping forces on the discs.

Farmall M

The mighty M was the "big brother" to the H; they had the same frame and layout so that mounted implements could be interchangeable. It was the top of the Farmall line from

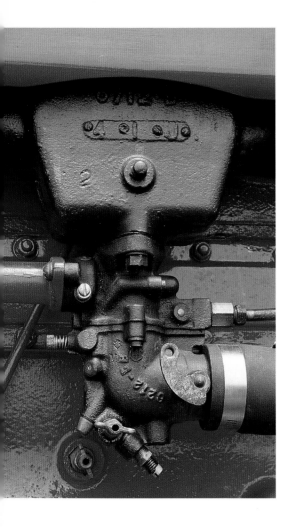

International Harvester made its own carburetors and governors. These are on a
Farmall H. Most other tractor companies
jobbed out components such as these. The
H did use a Delco-Remy starter, a Rockford
clutch, and a Donaldson air cleaner.

Farmall H serial number FBH377741
owned by Jon Kayser of Dell Rapids, South
Dakota. The Farmall H was made virtually
without change from 1939 to 1953. It was
introduced as the successor to the F-20. The
H used a 152ci engine operating at
1650rpm. It was rated for two 14in plows or
a 22in thresher. Although most were of the
dual tricycle configuration, wide-fronts (as
shown here) and high-crop versions were
also available. Jon's dad bought the tractor
new in 1952. Someone bought it from Jon's
dad and owned it for about six years before
Jon bought it back. It still has the original
tires on the back and its engine has never
been overhauled. Robert N. Pripps

International Harvester made its own magnetos, this one on a Farmall H. It is of the high-tension type, with an auto impulse coupling.

1939 to 1954, popular with large-acreage, row-crop farmers. Sales averaged more than 22,000 units per year.

The big 247.7ci engine, loafing along at only 1450rpm, produced enough power to easily handle three 16in bottoms. Fuel consumption was remarkably low; the M could be economically used for lighter chores, as well. Options included hydraulics, belt pulley, PTO, starter and lights, rubber tires, and a swinging drawbar.

The diesel MD was added to the line in 1941. The block part of the diesel engine was essentially the same as that of the gasoline engine. For diesel, aluminum pistons were used and the piston rings were thicker. A five-main bearing crankshaft was used, rather than the three-main bearing version of the gasoline engine. The head was, of course, completely different in that the compression ratio was more than dou-

The Farmall HV was a special high-clearance version of the famous Model H: note the high-arched front axle. The standard rear tires on the Farmall HV were actually smaller than on the regular Model H: 9.00x36 instead of 10.00x38. The difference was accommodated in the chain final drive, however, as the top speed of 15mph was the same for both versions. Jon Kayser's Farmall HV is serial number FBH-V 303312, making it a 1949 model. Robert N. Pripps

bled to 14.2:1. It also contained the diesel starting system that allowed the engine to be started on gasoline and, when warm enough, switched over to diesel.

The engine was started on gasoline with the diesel governor control lever (throttle) closed and with the compression relief lever pulled. Pulling this lever did four things: the combustion chamber was enlarged, providing a compression ratio of 6.4:1; intake air was diverted through the starting carburetor; the ignition circuit was completed; and the carburetor float was released, allowing the carburetor to fill with fuel. After a minute of gasoline

Previous page
Jon Kayser sits atop his 1949 Farmall HV at his Dell Rapids, South Dakota, Case-IH dealership. The overall height of the Farmall HV is 10in higher than that of the regular H. The high-arched front axle and the special chain final drive provide a 30in crop clearance. Kayser had been a Block Man for the International truck territory in 1966 when his father-in-law had encouraged him to take over the then-closed dealership. He got into antique tractor collecting in 1988, and now has about ten tractors. Robert N. Pripps

operation, the compression relief lever was pushed in and the diesel throttle was opened, and operation switched to diesel.

Although the MD cost half again as much as a gasoline M, most farmers found it well returned their investment. The MD used about one-third less fuel than the frugal M. Those of us old enough to remember the introduction of color television will also remember that diesel fuel was a little more than half the price of gasoline in those

The Farmall HV uses a special chain final drive to raise the rear axle above tall crops such as sugar cane, cotton, and corn. The rear tread of this 1949 Farmall HV is adjustable from 60in to 72in. The front is adjustable from 60in to 66in by reversing the wheels. This is somewhat limited as compared to the standard Farmall H with adjustable wide-front. Robert N. Pripps

Previous page
A 1953 Super H. Improvements over the Farmall H included a 164ci engine, a pressurized cooling system, and a deluxe hydraulic-snubber seat. Standard features included a swinging drawbar; an electrical system with generator, starter, and lights; a power takeoff and a belt pulley; and a hydraulic implement lift. Optional equipment offered included a hydraulic remote control, wheel weights, an hour meter, high-altitude pistons, magneto ignition, and fenders.

Dan Langy aboard a Farmall Super H owned by Frank Bunker of Milwaukee, Wisconsin. The Super H had a 29 percent power increase over the original H, making it a three-plow tractor.

days. The combination meant the price difference could be made up in about 1500 hours—about ten months for the average row-crop farmer in the forties.

The M could be ordered in high-crop, wide-front, or tricycle configuration.

Farmall Super M

In 1952, the Super M replaced the M. Engine displacement was upped to 263.9ci, giving the Super M a 22 percent power boost in the gasoline version and a 32 percent boost in the diesel version. It was also available with a liquefied petroleum gas (LPG) engine; during the fifties, this was a popular inexpensive fuel in many areas. It was also a cleaner fuel; no sludge or deposits were left in the engine, which meant about double engine life between overhauls.

The big news with the Super M was the MTA version, with the "TA" designation indicating "Torque Amplifier." The Torque Amplifier was a Harvester innovation in farm tractors, and the name became more-or-less generic as other brands picked up the idea. In operation, the Torque Amplifier provided a 1.482:1 ratio increase when actuated, resulting in an on-demand

Although considered a mid-sized tractor, the Farmall Super H could be ballasted to a total of 8000lb. The Super H was produced for fewer than two years; it replaced the Farmall H in 1953 and was replaced by the Farmall 300 in 1954.

Next page
"I've always enjoyed steel-wheeled farm tractors," says John Poch of New Holstein, Wisconsin. This 1940 Farmall M is in his collection of nineteen steel-wheeled tractors that he has acquired over the last eighteen years. His wife, Mary Lou, shares his enthusiasm.

Bill Rollinger's 1949 Farmall M, with Char-Lynn power steering. As with the Farmall H, the M could be obtained with either a distillate/kerosene engine or a high-compression gasoline engine.

power downshift to get through a tough spot without stopping to shift the main transmission down. It functioned much like "passing gear" in an automobile's automatic transmission.

The Torque Amplifier used a clutch-controlled planetary gearset that provided direct drive and an "underdrive" ratio for each of the transmis-

sion gears, effectively giving the Super MTA ten forward speeds and two in reverse. The MTA was the first Farmall with a live PTO.

Numbered Series

By 1954, the Korean War had ended. Eisenhower was president. Joe McCarthy was censored by the US

Senate. The economy was good, especially for the midwestern farmers who were finally making money in a peacetime economy.

Harry Ferguson had just won (after a fashion) his lawsuit against young Henry Ford for $340 million for loss of business and patent infringement. Ford had abrogated the Handshake Agreement his grandfather made with Ferguson in 1939, which had resulted in the Ford-Ferguson tractor. The outcome of the suit was that Ford paid Ferguson $9 million and agreed to stop using some of Ferguson's design ideas,

but the settlement did not include a prohibition against the use of the three-point hitch system. It was this system, which transformed the force required to pull an implement into weight on the rear wheels, that made the Ford-Ferguson the overwhelming sales leader for any size tractor. The fact that this system was not protected by the settlement meant it was up for grabs by all the other tractor makers.

The twelve major tractor makers had also become aware of a mood change in the row-crop farmer: these farmers wanted more power. The light-

The diesel option raised the price of the Farmall M from around $1,100 to just under $1,700. Most farmers who could afford the initial price found that the diesel paid off in fuel savings. The diesel provided 2.4 more horsepower hours per gallon of fuel than did the gasoline version. Also, diesel fuel cost only about two-thirds as much as gasoline in 1940.

duty use of cultivators on row-crop tractors for weed control was diminishing in favor of chemicals. Tractors were being used for higher-power applica-

The Farmall MD is such a capable and economical tractor that many are still at work on the farm. This 1946 example, owned by Aaron Woker, of Pearl City, Illinois, has been more-or-less put out to pasture, replaced by 806 and 1486 Internationals.

tions, such as multiple gang plows, followed by discs and drags, all hooked together. The first of the four-wheel-drive tractors since 1936, the Wagner,

had been introduced, which boded the type of tractor of the future.

More power was the name of the game. Tractor dealers were selling high-altitude pistons for engines used at normal altitudes. Aftermarket turbochargers were installed and governors were set higher. The demand for more power was not only heard for the largest tractors, but across the entire line.

For International Harvester, things were happening too fast. In

Next page
Aaron Woker's 1946 Farmall MD. The block part of the diesel engine is the same as on the gasoline version, but the diesel used five main bearings, rather than three. Pistons and rings are also beefier. Farmalls, like other International Harvester diesel tractors, have dual combustion chambers. A compression relief lever opens a partition between them, lowering the compression and exposing spark plugs for starting on gasoline. Once running and warm, the partition is closed and the engine switches over to diesel operation.

1953, John Deere introduced its Model 70, a top-end, row-crop tractor with more than 50hp. The Farmall Super M, brought out just the year before, offered only 44hp in the gasoline version. Besides, the Model 70, as well as the rest of the Deere line, could be equipped with "Power-Trol," Deere's

The Farmall Super M was noted for unexcelled lugging power. Engine torque peaked at about 360lb-ft at just under 1000rpm. The torque curve was essentially flat from there down to 750rpm (gasoline version). Combine that with the torque amplifier of the Super MTA, and there was not much that would bog it down. The standard rear tires of the Farmall Super M were 13-38s. For the fronts, 6.00x16s were used. The Super M (gasoline version) had a shipping weight of about 5600lb. With the optional wheel weights and calcium chloride liquid in the rear tires, the weight could be as high as 9000lb.

version of the weight-transferring three-point hitch. Harvester marketing knew that something had to be done for 1954 just to stay in the game.

Thus, the Numbered Series debuted in mid-1954, giving the impression that since the designations changed, this was a whole new lineup. Not much was done technically or cosmetically, but there was more power, at least in the larger Farmalls. Harvester managers could not, however, bring themselves to copy Harry Ferguson's three-point hitch. With dis-

Englishman John Friend is shown here plowing with his 1958 BMD, using a 1950s David Brown plow.

Next page
Manufactured in Doncaster, England, this Farmall BMD is pictured at the South Somerset Agricultural Preservation Club Show.

dain, they had treated it as a gimmick not needed by a real tractor, and now it seemed they were psychologically incapable of accepting it when it was handed to them as a gift. The fact that the three-point hitch was a real benefit to any size tractor, especially the smaller, lighter types, escaped them— and Harvester engineers came up with the "Fast Hitch."

The Fast Hitch was a two-point hitch that allowed for rapid coupling of hydraulically lifted mounted implements. It worked well enough, but it was, of course, incompatible with the three-point implements being standardized by other manufacturers and such industry groups as the American Society of Agricultural Engineers. It wasn't until 1958 that International Harvester offered three-point hitches as an optional alternative to the Fast Hitch.

Farmall 100

The Farmall 100 was essentially the same as the Super A, except the engine displacement was increased from 113ci to 123ci and the compression ratio was increased from 6.0:1 to 6.5:1. The rated speed was dropped from 1650rpm to 1400rpm. Although the Super A was not tested at Nebraska, it is estimated that these changes canceled each other out. Nevertheless, the 100 was rated for one 14in plow or two 12in plows.

Farmall 200

The Farmall 200 replaced the Super C. Both had a 123ci engine

227

Previous page
This 1958 British-built BMD has the optional adjustable wide front. Farmalls were also built in France and Germany.

operating at 1650rpm, but the compression ratio for the 200 was increased from 6.0:1 to 6.5:1, and therefore registered a little more horsepower in the Nebraska Tests. Other than changes to the grille and nameplates, the 200 was the same as the Super C.

Farmall 300

Real improvements in utility and productivity were incorporated into the 300. This tractor received the Fast Hitch implement lift, which made changing from one implement to an-

A 1958 Farmall Super BMD. This British-built version of the Super M is shown plowing in the wet September ground. At the wheel is John Friend of Pylle, Somerset. John uses the BMD regularly for plowing, baling, and rolling.

Previous page
The Super M had a 22 percent power increase over the Farmall M (gasoline version). The MD diesel version saw a 32 percent boost. The power increase was mainly due to a displacement increase to 264ci from 248ci. The Super M was also available in an LPG fuel version. Shown here is a 1952 Super M.

A Farmall 200, refurbished by Polacek Implement of Phillips, Wisconsin, sports a new Woods mower deck. Essentially the same as the Farmall C, the compression ratio of the 200 did increase from 6 to 6.5 to 1.

other faster and easier, and it had a live PTO and the Torque Amplifier. An increase in displacement and speed brought the 300's power up to more than 40hp. Otherwise, the 300 was essentially the same tractor as the Super H it replaced.

Farmall 400

As the replacement for the venerable M, the Farmall 400 was available

in either gasoline, LPG, or diesel model. A compression ratio increase on the non-diesel variants, plus breathing improvements, boosted power to more than 50hp for the first time—attaining parity with the John Deere 70. The Fast Hitch and Torque Amplifier were available, as was the live PTO.

Farmall Models After 1956

It was at about this point in the history of American agriculture—1963—that John Deere supplanted International Harvester as the largest

implement maker. Ford had persistently remained the supplier of the largest-selling single tractor model—more than 100,000 Ford 8Ns were sold in 1949—but as Ford diversified into multiple sizes after 1954, its total marketshare began to drop. The small, independent tractor makers all but disappeared—except for the makers of the four-wheel-drive monsters, such as Wagner and Steiger.

At Harvester, model numbers began to proliferate. The 100 and 200 became the 130 and 230, and the 300

In mid-1954, International Harvester introduced a whole new line of Farmalls. Shown here is a striking example of the result: the Model 300, basically replacing the H. Displacement on the Farmall 300 increased to 169ci from the 164ci of the Super H, through an increase in bore diameter of 1/16in. Rated engine speed was also increased to 2000rpm from 1650rpm, bringing the maximum belt horsepower up to 40, very close to that of the older Super M.

You don't have to be crazy to love old tractors, but some think it helps. Austin Hurst should know as he is a psychiatrist. His dad bought this Farmall 300 new in 1956, but sold it in 1969 when retiring from farming in northern Illinois. Austin bought it back in 1990. A friend of the family, John Bonjour, of Stockton, Illinois, overhauled it.

The Farmall 300 and 400 tractors were available in standard row-crop and high-clearance versions. Gasoline was the standard fuel, but the 400 was also available with a diesel or an LPG engine, and the 300 was also available with an LPG engine.

Next page
Most Farmalls of this era were delivered with dual narrow-front ends. The Farmall 300 was also available in a high-clearance and wide-front styles. With 40hp, the Farmall 300 was truly a three-plow tractor, but retained the maneuverability and utility of a mid-sized tractor.

A 1955 Farmall 300 with the optional wide-front front end. Owner William Kuhn bought this machine new. Now retired, he still uses the 300 on his small farm in Kinde, Michigan.

Air cleaner on an immaculately restored 1952 Super M.

and 400 became the 350 and 450. A big Model 600 was added in late 1956, but it was soon changed to 650. A white grille was added to all of these models. By 1958, a new sheet metal and grille suite were also added. The 130 and 230 became the 140 and 240, and the 350 and 450 became four models: 330, 340, 460, and 560. After that, the diversity of model numbers really took off.

By the late sixties, the numbers represented thoroughly modern and totally redesigned tractors. Big four-wheel-drive tractors were included in 1966; and in 1980, the Model 3788 was introduced. It was—and still is—one of the most advanced articulated four-wheel-drives made. It featured a "Control Center" cab aft of the articulation point and boasted four-wheel-drive traction with two-wheel-drive maneuverability.

The 1970s and 1980s were tough times for American implement makers.

Most, like Harvester, had not plowed enough profits back into plant upgrades and cost-reduction technology. Stockholder unrest caused many management changes as dividends fell. Bank interest rates went out the roof. Although the inflation rate, paralleling interest, made everything cost more tomorrow than today (which encouraged buying), money sources dried up and farmers were simply unable to borrow needed money for new equipment.

In the midst of all this, the United Auto Workers Union struck Harvester. The strike lasted only six months, but Harvester never recovered from it and the other financial woes of the times.

Finally, in 1988, Tenneco made Harvester management an offer for the Tractor and Implement Divisions that they could not refuse. Tenneco already had a foundering implement company, Harvester's arch-rival Case, but rea-

The Farmall 300 had all the modern conveniences: torque amplifier, live PTO, fast-hitch, and, best of all, a dipstick for checking the oil.

soned correctly that by combining the two, they could salvage the best of both worlds. Although it has made for some strange bedfellows, by this writing, some outstanding new tractor models have appeared. May the outstanding heritage of these two great companies fully combine to keep America and its farmers the food source for the world.

International Harvester initiated the numbered tractors to replace letter designations in mid-1954. Several improvements brought the tractors up to date. Fast-hitch was one improvement; the live PTO and Torque-Amplifier, available on some of the last of the lettered series, were now extended down the line. Power was increased; the Farmall 400 exceeded 50hp, a first for Farmall tractors.

Instrumentation and ergonomics were much improved on the numbered Farmalls that appeared in mid-1954. The lighted instrument panel contained oil pressure, ammeter, and coolant temperature gauges —and there was a cigarette lighter! On the numbered series Farmalls, introduced in 1954, the Torque Amplifier was available for both the 300 and 400 versions.

Previous page
A Farmall 350, the sequel to the 300 in late 1956. Displacement increased from 169ci to 175ci, and a "traction control" feature was added to the fast-hitch. The operator could now control the amount of implement-induced download on the rear wheels, making International Harvester's two-point hitch equivalent to the three-point hitch with draft control. The 350 could also be powered by a Continental diesel engine.

John Poch of New Holstein, Wisconsin, sits atop his 1958 Farmall 450. John is no stranger to equipment operation; he works as a forklift driver at Lake to Lake Dairy.

The Farmall 450 was built in 1957 and 1958 in diesel, gasoline, and LPG versions. It was considered a four-plow tractor.

Previous page
Nick Austin's McCormick Super BWD6 at the Great Dorset Steam Fair near Blandford, England. This tractor was purchased new by the Twizel Down horse racecourse at Fleet, Hampshire. It was sold to Nick in 1990 after thirty-five years of reliable service.

A British-built Farmall B450 diesel, photographed at the Great Dorset Steam Fair in Wincanton, England.

Nebraska Tractor Test

Early farmers were more often than not the victims of oversold, under-designed tractors. Dissemination of consumer information in those days was nothing like what we enjoy today. Unless someone in your neighborhood had a particular type of tractor, you were not likely to hear much about it. This was also true of other pieces of machinery and of automobiles, as well. Second, living in a rural area meant being isolated. Newspapers came by mail several days after the publishing date, radio was in its infancy, and publication of farming journals was just beginning. And finally, there were no standards by which mechanical things could be measured.

Because there were so many of them in those days, farmers had particular clout with the legislatures. They began to clamor for a national rating system for tractors, so that at least the power capability of a tractor could be understood. Competitive tractor trials in Winnipeg and other cities in the United States and Canada pointed out disparities between advertising claims and actual performance. These trials left much to be desired, as the tractors were often heavily modified by the factory and an army of mechanics and engineers kept them running long enough to compete. National legislation became bogged down in politics, however, and never came to pass.

A Nebraska farmer named Wilmot F. Crozier, who had also been a school teacher ("to support the farm," he said),

purchased a "Ford" tractor from the Minneapolis outfit not related to Henry Ford. The tractor was so unsatisfactory that he demanded that the company replace it. They did, but the replacement was worse. Crozier then bought a Bull tractor. This, too, was completely unsatisfactory. Next, he bought a 1918 Rumely "Three-plow." The Rumely met—even exceeded—Crozier's expectations; not only did it stand up to the strains of farming, but it could regularly pull a five-bottom plow. Shortly afterward, Crozier was elected to the Nebraska legislature.

In 1919, Representative Crozier and Senator Charles Warner introduced legislation that resulted in the "Nebraska Test Law." The law required

that any tractor sold in Nebraska had to be certified by the state. The state was to test the tractors to see that they lived up to their advertised claims. The tests were to be conducted by the University of Nebraska's Agricultural Engineering Department. L. W. Chase and Claude Shedd devised the tests and the test equipment, which have since become standards for the world.

The first test was made in the fall of 1919, of a Twin City 12-20, but could not be completed because of snowfall. The first completed test was made in the spring of 1920, and a certificate was issued for the Waterloo Boy Model N.

The results of tests of Farmalls between 1925 and 1957 follow.

Farmall Tests Summary

Model	Test Number	Fuel	Max. Horsepower Belt/PTO	Max. Horsepower Drawbar	Max. Pull	Fuel cons.	Weight	Wheels	Year
Regular	117	Kerosene	20.1	12.7	2727	9.39	4100	Steel	1925
F-30	198	Kerosene	32.8	24.6	4157	9.61	5990	Steel	1931
F-20	221	Kerosene	23.1	15.4	2334	10.4	4545	Steel	1934
F-20	264	Distillate	26.8	18.8	2799	9.82	4400	Steel	1936
F-20	276	Distillate	26.7	19.6	2927	10.5	4310	Steel	1936
F-12	212	Gas	16.2	10.1	1172	9.54	3280	Steel	1933
F-12	220	Kerosene	14.6	11.8	1814	10.0	3240	Steel	1933
F-14	297	Distillate	17.0	13.2	2369	10.9	4900	Rubber	1938
Cub	386	Gas	9.23	8.34	1596	10.9	1539	Rubber	1947
Cub	575	Gas	10.4	9.63	1605	9.38	2393	Rubber	1956
A	329	Gas	16.8	12.3	2387	12.0	3570	Rubber	1939
A	330	Distillate	16.5	15.2	2360	11.9	3500	Rubber	1939
B	331	Gas	16.8	12.1	2377	11.9	3740	Rubber	1939
B	332	Distillate	15.4	12.0	2463	11.8	3700	Rubber	1939
C	395	Gas	19.9	15.9	2902	11.2	4409	Rubber	1948
Super C	458	Gas	23.7	20.7	NA	10.8	5041	Rubber	1951

Farmall Tests Summary

Model	Test Number	Fuel	Max. Horsepower Belt/PTO	Max. Horsepower Drawbar	Max. Pull	Fuel cons.	Weight	Wheels	Year
H	333	Gas	24.3	19.8	3603	11.7	5550	Rubber	1939
H	334	Distillate	22.1	19.4	3169	11.8	5550	Rubber	1939
Super H	492	Gas	31.3	26.0	4178	11.7	6713	Rubber	1953
M	327	Distillate	34.2	25.5	4365	12.5	6770	Rubber	1939
M	328	Gas	36.1	24.5	4233	12.2	6770	Rubber	1939
MD	368	Distillate	35.0	NA	4541	14.6	7570	Rubber	1941
Super M	475	Gas	43.9	37.1	5676	12.0	8929	Rubber	1952
Super M	484	LPG	45.7	39.5	6115	8.76	9145	Rubber	1952
Super MD	477	Distillate	46.7	37.7	5772	13.9	9338	Rubber	1952

Model	Test Number	Fuel	Max. Horsepower Belt/PTO	Max. Horsepower Drawbar	Max. Pull	Fuel cons.	Weight	Wheels	Year
100	537	Gas	18.3	15.8	2503	10.6	4338	Rubber	1955
200	536	Gas	24.1	20.9	3166	10.8	5331	Rubber	1955
300	538	Gas	40.0	30.0	4852	11.8	8257	Rubber	1955
400	532	Gas	50.8	45.3	6508	12.1	9669	Rubber	1955
400	534	Distillate	46.7	41.6	6415	13.9	9700	Rubber	1955
400	571	LPG	52.4	46.7	6374	9.78	9900	Rubber	1956

Some Famous Farmall Competitors

Model	Test Number	Fuel	Max. Horsepower Belt/PTO	Max. Horsepower Drawbar	Max. Pull	Fuel cons.	Weight	Wheels	Year
Fordson	124	Kerosene	22.3	12.3	2142	8.95	3175	Steel	1926
Deere GP	153	Kerosene	25.0	17.2	2489	9.18	4265	Steel	1928
Deere A	335	Distillate	28.9	24.6	4110	11.3	6410	Rubber	1939
Ford 8N	443	Gas	25.5	20.8	2810	11.2	4043	Rubber	1950
AC WD45	563	Distillate	43.3	32.5	5908	14.0	9700	Rubber	1955

Notes on Nebraska Tractor Tests:

Belt/PTO Horsepower: This is Test C horsepower, the maximum attainable at the PTO or belt pulley. If the generator, hydraulic pump, etc., were not standard equipment, they were removed for these tests. Note that Nebraska test data published during this period are not corrected to standard atmospheric conditions.

Drawbar Horsepower: Taken from Test G data, it is based on maximum drawbar pull and speed. The difference between this and PTO horsepower is due to slippage and to the power required to move the tractor itself. The heavier the tractor, the less the slippage, but the more power required to move the tractor. Factory engineers looked for the ideal compromise.

Max. Pull: Test G. The pull, in pounds, used for calculating drawbar horsepower.

Fuel Cons.: The rate of fuel consumption in horsepower hours per gallon taken from Test C conditions. The higher the number, the better.

Weight: The weight of the tractor plus ballast in pounds. Ballast was often added for Test G and other heavy pulling tests and then was removed for other tests to improve performance.

Wheels: Steel or rubber.

Model, Serial Number, and Production Year Summary

This list provides a means of determining a tractor's model year by listing the beginning serial number for the production year.

	Beginning Serial Number	Year	
Regular &	QC501	1924	
Fairway	QC701	1925	
	QC1539	1926	
	T1569	1927	
	T15471	1928	
	T40370	1929	
	T75691	1930	
	T117784	1931	
	T131872	1932	
F-30	FB501	1931	
	FB1184	1932	
	FB4305	1933	
	FB5526	1934	
	FB7032	1935	
	FB10407	1936	
	FB18684	1937	
	FB27186	1938	
	FB29007	1939	
F-20	FA/TA501	1932	
	FA/TA3001	1933	
	TA135000	1934	To TA135661
	TA6382	1935	
	TA32716	1936	
	TA68749	1937	
	TA105597	1938	
	TA130865	1939	To TA134999
	TA135700	1939	
F-12	FS501	1932	
	FS526	1933	
	FS4881	1934	
	FS17411	1935	
	FS48660	1936	
	FS81837	1937	
	FS117518	1938	
F-14	FS124000	1938	
	FS139607	1939	

	Beginning Serial Number	Year
Cub	FCUB501	1947
	FCUB11348	1948
	FCUB57831	1949
	FCUB99536	1950
	FCUB121454	1951
	FCUB144455	1952
	FCUB162284	1953
	FCUB179412	1954
	FCUB186441	1955
	FCUB193658	1956
	FCUB198231	1957
A and B	501	1939
	6744	1940
	41500	1941
	80739	1942
	none	1943
	96390	1944
	113218	1945
	146700	1946
	1982964	1947
Super A	25001	1947
	250082	1948
	268196	1949
	281569	1950
	300126	1951
	324470	1952
	336880	1953
	353348	1954
C	FC501	1948
	FC22524	1949
	FC47010	1950
	FC71880	1951
Super C	FSC100001	1951
	FSC131157	1952
	FSC159130	1953
	FSC187788	1954

Prefix letters
A = FAA
AV = FAAV
B = FAB
BN = FABN
Super A = SA

	Beginning Serial Number	Year
H	501	1939
	10653	1940
	52387	1941
	93237	1942
	12250	1943
	15051	1944
	186123	1945
	214820	1946
	241143	1947
	268991	1948
	300876	1949
	327975	1950
	351923	1951
	375861	1952
	390500	1953

Prefix Letters
H = FBH
HV = FBHV

	Beginning Serial Number	Year
Super H	501	1953
	22202	1954

Prefix Letters
F-SH, SHV

	Beginning Serial Number	Year
M	501	1939
	7240	1940
	25371	1941
	50988	1942
	60011	1943
	67424	1944
	88085	1945
	105564	1946
	122823	1947
	151708	1948
	180514	1949
	213579	1950
	247518	1951
	290923	1952

	Beginning Serial Number	Year		Prefix Letters F-SM, M-TA				F-300	501	1954
Prefix Letters									1779	1955
M = FBK	MD = FDBK			F-100	501	1954			23224	1956
MV = FBKV	MDV = FDBKV				1720	1955		F-400	501	1954
					12895	1956			2588	1955
Super M	501	1952		F-200	501	1954			29065	1956
	12516	1953			1032	1955				
	51977	1954			10904	1956				

Farmall Tractor Specifications

Model	Year	Bore/Stroke (in)	Disp. (ci)	Comp. Ratio	Rated rpm	Forward Speeds	Basic Weight (lb)	Rear Tire Size (in)
Regular	1924-1932	3.75x5.00	220.9	4.5:1	1200	3	4100	40x6
F-30	1931-1939	4.25x5.00	283.7	4.5:1	1150	3	5990	42x12
F-20	1932-1939	3.75x5.00	220.9	4.5:1	1200	4	4545	40x6
F-12	1932-1938	3.00x4.00	113.1	4.5:1	1400	3	3280	54x6
F-14	1938-1939	3.00x4.00	113.1	4.5:1	1650	3	3820	
Cub	1947-1955	2.62x2.75	59.5	6.5:1	1600	3	1540	8x24
A	1939-1947	3.00x4.00	113.1	6.0:1	1400	4	2014	8x24
B	1939-1951				1400		2150	9x24
Super A	1947-1954				1650		2363	
C	1948-1951	3.00x4.00	113.1	6.0:1	1650	4	2845	9x36
Super C	1951-1954	3.13x4.00	122.7	6.0:1	1650	4	3209	10x36
H	1939-1952	3.38x4.25	152.1	5.9:1	1650	5	3694	10x36
Super H	1952-1954	3.50x4.25	164.0	6.0:1	1650	5	4389	11x38
M	1939-1952	3.88x5.25	247.7	5.7:1	1450	5	4858	11x38
MD	1941-1951	3.88x5.25	247.7	14.2	1450	5	5300	12x38
Super M	1952-1954	4.00x5.25	263.9	5.9:1	1450	5	5600	13x38
Super MD				16.5	1450		6034	
100	1954-1956	3.13x4.00	122.7	6.5:1	1400	4	3038	11x24
200	1954-1956	3.13x4.00	122.7	6.5:1	1650	4	3541	10x36
300	1954-1956	3.56x4.25	169.2	6.3:1	1750	5	4800	11x38
400	1954-1956	4.00x5.25	263.9	G 6.3 D16.5	1450	5	6519	11x38

Clubs and Newsletters

Books

The following books offered essential background on the International Harvester Company's origins and history, and about the tractors and equipment of the times. These make good reading and library additions for any Farmall buff. Most are available from Motorbooks International Publishers & Wholesalers, PO Box 2, 729 Prospect Avenue, Osceola, Wisconsin 54020 USA, or by calling 800-826-6600.

The Agricultural Tractor 1855–1950 by R. B. Gray. Society of Agricultural Engineers. An outstanding and complete photo history of the origin and development of the tractor.

The American Farm Tractor by Randy Leffingwell. Motorbooks International. A full-color hardback history of all the great American tractor makes.

The Century of the Reaper by Cyrus McCormick. Houghton Mifflin Company. A first-hand account of the Harvester and Tractor Wars by the grandson of the inventor.

A Corporate Tragedy by Barbara Marsh. Doubleday and Company. An intriguing account of the development of International Harvester Company and its ultimate sale of the farm equipment business to Tenneco in 1988. Much scholarly research and journalistic writing are evinced in this work; a "must read" for Farmall fans.

The Development of American Agriculture by Willard W. Cochrane. University of Minnesota Press. An analytical history.

Farm Tractors 1926–1956 edited by Randy Stephens. Intertec Publishing. A compilation of pages from *The Cooperative Tractor Catalog* and the *Red Tractor Book.*

Fordson, Farmall and Poppin' Johnny by Robert C. Williams. University of Illinois Press. A history of the farm tractor and its impact on America.

Ford Tractors by Robert N. Pripps and Andrew Morland. Motorbooks International. A full-color history of the Fordson, Ford-Ferguson, Ferguson, and Ford tractors, covering the influence of these historic tractors on tractor design.

Ford and Fordson Tractors by Michael Williams. Blandford Press. A history of Henry Ford and his tractors, especially concentrating on the Fordson.

Harvest Triumphant by Merrill Denison. William Collins Sons & Company Ltd. The story of human achievement in the development of agricultural tools, especially that in Canada, and the rise to prominence of Massey Harris Ferguson (now known as the Verity Corporation). Rich in the romance of farm life in the last century and covering the early days of the Industrial Revolution.

How to Restore Your Farm Tractor by Robert N. Pripps. Motorbooks International. Follows two tractors through professional restoration, one a 1939 Farmall A. Includes tips and techniques, commentary, and photos.

International Harvester Tractors by Henry Rasmussen. Motorbooks International. A photo essay on "Reliable Red."

Threshers by Robert N. Pripps and Andrew Morland. Motorbooks International. A full-color history of grain harvesting and threshing, featuring photos and descriptions of many of the big threshers in operation.

The Yearbook of Agriculture—1960. U.S. Department of Agriculture.

150 Years of International Harvester by C. H. Wendel. Crestline Publishing. A complete photo-documented product history of International Harvester.

Stemgas Publishing Company issues an annual directory of engine and threshing shows. Its address is: P.O. Box 328, Lancaster, Pennsylvania 17603; 717-392-0733. The cost of the directory has been $5.00. Stemgas also publishes *Gas Engine Magazine* and *Iron-men Album,* magazines for the enthusiast.

Clubs and Newsletters

Newsletters providing a wealth of information and lore about individual brands of antique farm tractors and equipment have been on the scene for some time. More are being published each year, so the following list is far from complete.

Antique Power
Patrick Ertel, editor
PO Box 838
Yellow Springs, OH 45387

Green Magazine (John Deere)
R. & C. Hain, editors
RR 1
Bee, NE 68314

M-M Corresponder (Minneapolis-Moline)
Roger Mohr, editor
Rt 1, Box 153
Vail, IA 51465

9N-2N-8N Newsletter (Ford)
G. W. Rinaldi, editor
154 Blackwood Lane
Stamford, CT 06903

Old Abe's News (Case)
David T. Erb, editor
Rt 2, Box 2427
Vinton, OH 45686

Old Allis News (Allis Chalmers)
Nan Jones, editor
10925 Love Road
Belleview, MI 49021

Oliver Collector's News
Dennis Gerszewski, editor
Rt 1
Manvel, ND 58256

Prairie Gold Rush (Minneapolis-Moline)
R. Baumgartner, editor
Rt 1
Walnut, IL 61376

Red Power (International Harvester)
Daryl Miller, editor
Box 277
Battle Creek, IA 51006

Wild Harvest (Massey-Harris, Ferguson)
Keith Oltrogge, editor
1010 S Powell, Box 529
Denver, IA 50622

GREAT AMERICAN
TRACTORS

FORD TRACTORS

Text by Robert N. Pripps
Photos by Andrew Morland

*To Janice, the wife of my youth and
my faithful companion these
thirty-six years*

Preface

The name Ford Tractor immediately conjures a vision of the little gray tractor that can be seen at golf courses, at airports and at small farms across the United States. Although the Ford name has been on a variety of tractors—from the simplest garden type to four-wheel-drive monsters—over the last seventy years, only those made between 1939 and 1952 were the true Ford Tractors; tractors made before and after those years must be identified in some other way besides the name Ford Tractor.

Three models were true Ford Tractors: the 9N, made from 1939 to 1942; the 2N, made from 1942 to 1947; and the 8N, made from 1947 to 1952. Although the 9N and 2N were basically the same, the 8N was a considerable refinement. Nevertheless, all three continue to be lumped together under the heading of Ford Tractor.

Ford Tractors seem to be everywhere, but fewer than one million were built for worldwide distribution. When introduced over fifty years ago, they revolutionized the tractor industry. This is the story of these little gray tractors, of their heritage and of the human genius that engendered them. It is also the story of their descendents, and of the Ford Tractor as it is today.

Acknowledgments

Without the specific help of certain people, this book would not have been completed. Therefore, I would like to gratefully acknowledge their contributions:

Keith Oltrogge, publisher of the bimonthly newsletter *Wild Harvest, Massey Collectors News,* for information about the Ferguson tractors.

Gerard Rinaldi, publisher of *The 9N-2N-8N Newsletter,* for using his computer to locate photographic subjects in my vicinity.

Palmer Fossum, Ford Tractor collector, restorer and parts dealer from Northfield, Minnesota, who is a storehouse of tractor lore and a genuinely pleasant fellow to be around.

Peder Bjerre, archivist with Variety Corporation (Massey-Ferguson's successor), who provided background and photos.

David Crippen, Joan Klimchalk, Cynthia Read-Miller and staff of The Ford Museum Archives at the Henry Ford Museum and Greenfield Village, who patiently dug out the black and white pictures appearing in this book.

Andrew Morland, photographer par excellence, who took the color photos (he made picture taking look easy, but I know it's not).

Michael Dregni, editor, and the others at Motorbooks International who put this work in print and bravely took the financial risk.

Like an overgrown gravestone, this 8N's nameplate signals the end of the senior Henry Ford's control of the Ford Motor Company, and the end of the famous Handshake Agreement that launched the N Series tractors. Very little time was spent on restyling the 8N to differentiate it from its predecessor, the 2N. About all that was done aesthetically was to eliminate the Ferguson System badge, add the Ford script and change the paint from all gray to a lighter gray for the sheet metal and red for the castings.

The Handshake Agreement

"You haven't got enough money to buy my patents," Harry Ferguson bluntly told Henry Ford. Ford was, by the by, possibly the richest man in the world at that time, 1938.

"Well, you need me as much as I need you," retorted Ford, "so what do you propose?"

"A gentleman's agreement," explained Ferguson. "You stake your reputation and resources on this idea, I stake a lifetime of design and invention—no written agreement could be worthy of what this represents. If you trust me, I'll trust you."

"It's a good idea," said Ford. And with that the two men stood and shook hands.

Thus was born an agricultural concept that would revolutionize farming. Not only is the squat, compact, insectlike tractor, with its integral implements, still very much in evidence more than fifty years later, but virtually every farm tractor built since the patents ran out or could be circumvented has embodied the Ford Tractor's principal element: the three-point hitch.

Until mid 1947, the correct name was Ford Tractor, Ferguson System or Ford-Ferguson. The similarity between Ford-Ferguson and Fordson, which was built by Ford in the United States between 1917 and 1928, caused considerable confusion.

Further complicating matters, in 1947 Ford abrogated the Handshake Agreement and began producing tractors without Ferguson. Ferguson then manufactured his own tractor, which

The Fordson Model N of 1932 owned by Brian Poole of England. This tractor has the water washer air cleaner.

was so similar that many recognized no difference. Suddenly there were Fordsons, Ford-Fergusons, Fergusons and Fords. Many old-timers still refer to them all as Fordsons.

Messrs. Ford and Ferguson had remarkably similar backgrounds, characters and temperaments. Both were Irish. Both were raised on farms—Ford in Michigan, Ferguson in Ireland. Both had a love for the land, a sympathy for

Harry Ferguson explains the workings of his System. On a kitchen table brought outside for his historic meeting with Henry Ford in 1938, Ferguson used a model to show how increased draft forces increased traction without the risk of back-flip accidents. Ford was so impressed that he entered into the now-famous Handshake Agreement with Ferguson on the spot. Together, they plunged into the development of the 9N Ford-Ferguson tractor.

farmers and their problems, a love for mechanical things and a disdain for the horse. Both had an almost mystical charismatic leadership ability that allowed them to enlist the extremely talented and loyal employees who made their businesses succeed.

Ironically, Harry Ferguson probably had more to do with the acceptance of the Ford Tractor than did anyone, including Henry Ford. It was the Ferguson System of implement integration that changed the tractor from a replacement for the horse to a truly useful and productive tool.

Harry Ferguson, left, appears with Henry Ford at the 9N introduction demonstration on June 29, 1939. This was a mere nine months after the Handshake Agreement that initiated the tractor—an incredibly short time by today's standards. Ford and Ferguson, both charismatic geniuses, complemented each other in temperament and worked together to get things done. Note the 8x32 tires; 10x28 tires did not become standard until 1942. The overall diameter is the same, but the later version has better flotation and traction. Except for the tires and the grille change in mid 1940, the appearance of the Ford Tractor changed little through 1952.

Emerson Borneman's working 8N, near Byron, Illinois, is typical of thousands of Fords that are soldiering on while their contemporaries and competitors have long since been relegated to the role of antiques. Seventy-three-year-old Borneman said, "If I couldn't have an 8N, I'd quit farming."

Heritage: The Fordson

In 1939, the entire history of the tractor spanned barely thirty years. Although traction engines had been around since the mid-nineteenth century, the origin of the word *tractor* is credited to two men named Charles of Charles City, Iowa: Charles Hart and Charles Parr.

In 1906, Hart and Parr made the first successful internal-combustion gasoline traction engine and called it a tractor. These early Hart-Parrs and other steam and internal-combustion traction engines were immense machines, weighing 10,000 to 80,000 pounds. Such monsters were useful only in large fields, and mostly for plowing or as prime mover engines for driving machinery via flat belts. The small landowner, common to most of the world's agriculture, was stuck with horses, mules or oxen.

But animal tillage was painfully slow. A team of horses could plow about two acres per day, and that took all the energy of a good plowman as

The Fordson's low weight, weight distribution and simple implement hitch resulted in a severe pitch-up, or back-flip, problem. The front wheels tended to lift when the plow contacted a solid object such as a buried rock. Despite ignition cutouts and clutch-disengaging accessories, about 150 fatal accidents had been recorded by the time this 1924 model hit the fields. The extended fender wing on this example was a block (of sorts) to back flips. This photo of Palmer Fossum's 1924 Fordson shows the way the engine casting was bolted directly to the transmission-axle housing for the first truly frameless design. This design is credited to Eugene Farkas, Ford's chief tractor engineer. Farkas may have been influenced by the Wallis Cub, with its one-piece belly pan structure supporting and protecting the main components.

well. Besides the sheer effort of man-handling the plow all day was the attendant job of harnessing and unharnessing the team, rubbing them down and generally tending to their needs. The biggest drawback to animal power, however, was that each year, a team of horses themselves consumed the produce of five acres. This encroachment on the cash-producing acreage was particularly hard on the small farmer.

Henry Ford and the Fordson

Henry Ford grew up on such a small farm outside Detroit in the late 1800s. As his interest in automobiles developed, he also expressed a desire, as he stated it, "to lift the burden of farming from flesh and blood and place it on steel and motors." In the early 1900s, he began to build experimental tractors from automobile components. Just four years after the founding of the Ford Motor Company in 1903, Ford made his first experimental tractor. He referred to it as his Automobile Plow.

In 1915, Ford built his first tractor from scratch. He considered it his second tractor and so called it the B. It had a 16 horsepower, two-cylinder, horizontally opposed engine, a spur gear transmission and three wheels—two front drivers and one rear steerer.

The Model B was never produced. It did, however, gain enough publicity to let the world know that Henry Ford was interested in developing a tractor. Although no public announcement was made, many farmers looked to Ford to do for the tractor what he had done for the automobile with his Model T car. Taking advantage of this expectation, a group of entrepreneurs in Minneapolis—which did include a man by the

name of Ford—organized The Ford Tractor Company. While these businesspeople did actually build and sell a few tractors, they really anticipated a settlement with Henry Ford for allowing him to use his own name.

Such was not to be the case, however, as the crafty Ford was not that easily taken. For organizational reasons, Ford formed a separate company to manufacture his new tractor, taking his young son Edsel as a partner. The name of the new company was Henry Ford and Son and the name of the new tractor was the Fordson, leaving, for the time being, the Ford Tractor name to the Minneapolis outfit.

The Fordson was launched in 1916. It was the first lightweight, mass-produced tractor in the world, and for the first time, the average farmer could buy and own a tractor. The heritage of the Ford Tractor was set with the Fordson, which was built by Ford in the United States between 1917 and 1928 and in the United Kingdom until 1946. By the end of its production life, there were about as many American-built Fordsons as there would be 9N, 2N and 8N Ford Tractors.

The most revolutionary feature of the Fordson was that it lacked a con-

A well-dressed and dapper Henry Ford shows off his Automobile Plow in 1907. The term tractor had not yet come into common use, having been coined by Hart-Parr only the year before. Note the classic right-hand-drive car in the background, probably a six-cylinder Ford Model K.

In about 1907, just four years after the founding of the Ford Motor Company, young Henry Ford sits atop his Automobile Plow, so named because it was made from automobile parts. It featured a two-cylinder transverse-mounted engine, chain and gear drive, and magneto ignition.

Next page
The fender wings of Palmer Fossum's 1924 Fordson. Note the tool and storage spaces provided. The Fordson name was a contraction of the company name Henry Ford and Son. In 1915, the Ford Motor Company was a stock company. When launching his new tractor venture with his son Edsel, Ford no longer needed the financial assistance of, nor the limitations imposed by, stockholders, so the new company was privately held. By 1920, Ford had managed to buy out the Ford Motor Company stockholders, so Henry Ford and Son was folded into the parent company, but the Fordson name was retained.

Fordson—the first mass-produced farm tractor. Clearly showing its heritage of the later N Series Ford Tractors, this 1920 version poses for a publicity photo. Also shown is the frameless construction, where the housings of the engine, transmission and differential are bolted together to provide the structure of the tractor. The Fordson was rated at 20 horsepower on the belt and 10 horsepower on the drawbar.

Henry Ford and son Edsel are seen at a Fordson demonstration in 1921. When the Fordson tractor was introduced in 1916, the Ford Motor Company was not wholly owned by the Ford family. Chafing under the restrictions of a board of directors, Ford launched his new Fordson tractor through a new and separate company, Henry Ford and Son.

ventional frame. Instead, the cast-iron engine, transmission and axle housings were all bolted together to form the structure of the tractor. Within a few years, this feature was copied by others, and with the exception of garden tractors and the large articulated four-wheel-drive units, most have been made this way ever since.

The Fordson had a 20 horsepower, four-cylinder engine, a three-speed spur gear transmission and a worm gear reduction set in the differential. Because high-ratio worm sets generally transmit rotation from the worm element to the gear element, no brakes were provided on early Fordsons. All you needed to do to stop was depress the clutch. The reason for this one-way rotation phenomenon is simply the efficiency, or rather the lack of efficiency, of worm gear sets. The sets used in the Fordson were about fifty percent efficient. This meant that of the 20 horsepower the Fordson's engine produced, only about ten survived passage through the worm set; the other ten came out as heat.

The initial version of the Fordson had the worm set right under the driver's seat, and after short periods of operation, the heat on the bottom of the driver became unbearable. Subsequent versions saw the worm placed under, rather than on top of, the differential, where it ran submerged in oil. The problem of the hot seat was eliminated.

By 1917, World War I had Europe in upheaval. The British Board of Agriculture, fearing mass food shortages, sought ways to dramatically increase the amount of land tillage, even though the army was placing mounting demands upon available horses. Two Fordsons were imported for testing in June of that year, and the tests proved the Fordson to be reasonably well suited to the British terrain and soil. Because of this and the unique mass production features of the Fordson, the Lloyd George government called for immediate British production.

Henry Ford, although a pacifist, generously made a gift of the patent rights for the tractor and agreed to establish a factory in Cork, Ireland, the town from which the Ford family had emigrated. As a stopgap, 6,000 American-made Fordsons were imported

The heritage of the subsequent Ford Tractor is clearly seen in this view of Doug Zillmer's 1922 Fordson. Fenders were options, but necessary for the operator's safety. The general size and shape are similar to those of the N Series Ford Tractors. Note the steering wheel location and angle. The operator's semistraddle position is also reminiscent. The Fordson engine produced 20 horsepower at the belt pulley and 10 horsepower at the drawbar, bringing about the sometimes-used cognomen of Fordson 20-10. The rear wheels of the Fordson are proportionally farther forward than those of the N Series Ford Tractors. This was done for two reasons. First, it allowed the operator to reach the control handles on the trailing implements, which would otherwise have been farther back to clear the wheels in turns. Second, it put a higher proportion of the tractor's 2,700 pounds on the drive wheels. Nevertheless, traction was one of the Fordson's weakest points. The Fordson had the dubious honor of registering the lowest traction efficiency of the 60 tractors tested by the University of Nebraska in 1920.

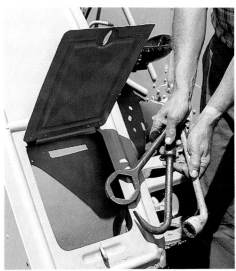

Palmer Fossum's 1924 Fordson has the original tool set supplied with the tractor. Total production of the Fordson reached 448,000 in 1924, and the 500,000th Fordson was built in mid 1925. The production price stabilized at about $400 (with the tool set).

until the Irish-made tractors began rolling off the production line. The few British tractor makers of the time reacted with considerable resentment. Importing and manufacturing the Fordson was the only logical choice for the government, however. No other way was available to reach the production volume required.

By 1928, when US production ended, 750,000 Fordsons had been produced. British production of the original Fordson concept, with refinements, continued until 1946.

The Fordson was, however, conceived merely as a replacement for a team of horses. Horse-type implements were attached to the tractor by a length of chain. The draft clevis was attached to the tractor's differential housing high enough for the implement to provide a downward pull to give added traction. This was common practice for tractors of that day, but it caused many back-flip accidents when the plow or other attachment hit an obstruction. Under these circumstances, the rear wheels could not slip, because of the downward pull of the implement, so the tractor reared up and flipped over backward. The high engine speed, the heavy engine flywheel and the inability of the wheels to slip caused the rearing action to be so rapid that drivers had no time to react. Often, drivers were pinned to the ground they sought to till.

Many farmers grew to hate the Fordson. Its name became synonymous with aggravation in agriculture. The reasons Fordsons became anathema were obvious and numerous. All machinery of that period lacked the considerable refinement found in the next generation, but these vehicles seemed to fail or attack their operators at the least convenient moment. In addition, many farmers had a relationship with their horses that stemmed from hours of toiling together. These agriculturalists hated to see the inevitable demise of horse farming and considered the Fordson a heartless substitute—which it was. Furthermore, many implements

This Dagenham-built 1938 Fordson Standard Model N, with oil bath air cleaner, works for owner Paul Matthews of Sturminster, England.

were made to be pulled by either horse or tractor, so the advantages of tractor power could not be realized. Finally, utilizing the full potential of the tractor engine's horsepower resulted in back flips, wheel slippage or damage to the implement.

Enter Harry Ferguson and the Ferguson System

Henry George "Harry" Ferguson was born in 1884, when Henry Ford was twenty-one years old. He was strong-willed, and had a penchant for confrontation with his father and schoolmasters. He left school at the age of fourteen to work on the family farm, where he came to hate the toil of agricultural work. In his late teens and early twenties, he worked for his

brother in the automobile business as a mechanic and race driver. He showed remarkable mechanical ability and possessed an innate engineering talent. He even designed, built and flew several monoplanes, just slightly behind the highly publicized activities of the Wright brothers from Dayton, Ohio.

Ferguson's most prominent attribute, however, was not his talent as an engineer, not his skill as a mechanic, not his bravery as a race car driver or airplane pilot; it was his high degree of perseverance. Ferguson's enduring claim to fame was his System: the integration of farm implements with the tractor. Through years of adversity, he stuck with his goal of perfecting and mass-producing his beloved System, which embodied principles

This example of the Dagenham-built Fordsons has the water washer air cleaner. Owner Keith Dorey of Wareham, Dorset, England, did the restoration.

found today on almost every farm tractor in the world.

"It is no more possible to design a plow which would be suitable for use with various sizes of tractors than it is to design a cart which can be drawn by a donkey or a Clydesdale, or a body that would be suitable for all makes of cars," Ferguson said, as he launched himself into the implement business. The first application of his System was a plow for the lightweight Ford/ Eros tractor, which was a conversion kit for the Ford Model T car. It was made by a St. Paul, Minnesota, firm

272

Harry Ferguson demonstrates his Ferguson-Brown tractor in 1938. The Ferguson-Brown was manufactured as a joint venture of Harry Ferguson and David Brown. It was the production version of Ferguson's Black Tractor, which was the first to incorporate the hydraulic three-point hitch and integrated implements. The Ferguson-Brown was somewhat smaller than a Fordson, and cost about twice as much, but its performance was enough better that it convinced Henry Ford to build the 9N Ford Tractor featuring the Ferguson System.

The three-point hitch is found on the business end of the Ford Tractor. This Ferguson System hitch and the low price provided by Ford's mass-production ingenuity ensured the 9N's success. Shown here is Homer Clark's 1940 9N, serial number 38975, in the trailer hitch configuration. Implements connect to the ends of the two draft bars extending aft from under the axles and to the spring clevis above the differential housing, making the three points.

273

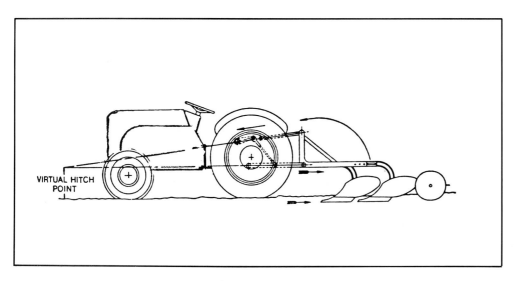

Several forces are at work with the Fer-guson-designed automatic Draft Control.

and consisted mainly of larger rear wheels mounted behind the normal axle on a frame extension, a much increased gear reduction and increased engine cooling. The Eros performed and sold quite well, and the Ferguson plow was a popular accessory.

The Ferguson plow weighed less than half as much as a conventional plow. Its ingenious feature was the way it hitched under the belly of the Eros tractor, forward of the rear axle. Thus the pulling force—the line of draft—tended to draw all four wheels onto the ground. Excellent traction was provided and any tendency for rearing was eliminated.

Ferguson's first application for his System was doomed from the start, however, not because farmers didn't like the plow, but because the market for the Eros tractor rapidly dried up. For it was 1916, the year Henry Ford and Son launched the Fordson.

But perseverance was Harry Fer-guson's long suit. Rather than fight the Fordson in the marketplace, Ferguson saw the vehicle as an opportunity to sell even more plows. At this time, the commitment had been made to build the Fordson factory in Ireland. Harry Ferguson learned that Charles Soren-son, Henry Ford's right-hand man for forty years, was coming to Britain to set it up. Plow drawings in hand, Fer-guson rushed to London to meet with him.

"Your Fordson's allright as far as it goes," he reportedly said to Soren-son—and while he gained little in rap-port with the man, he did at once get his attention. Ferguson's confidence, enthusiasm and aggressiveness carried the day. Charlie Sorenson lived to regret that first meeting, which ended with his commitment to support Fer-guson's development of a plow for the Fordson tractor.

After considerable difficulty with some directors of his own Harry Fer-guson Motors who simply wanted to adapt the huge inventory of Eros plows to the Fordson, Ferguson and his resi-dent genius Willie Sands came up with a completely new System concept. Called the Duplex Hitch, the plow was coupled to the Fordson by two parallel links, one above the other, attached to the Fordson above and below the rear axle differential housing. Thus, draft loads pulled down on the rear wheels, but also pushed down on the front wheels through the upper link, thereby eliminating the rearing tendency.

This mounting must be considered semirigid, as there were no hydraulics to control depth or to raise and lower the implement. The arrangement was said to be no better than acceptable because there was no provision for maintaining a constant plow depth as the tractor's front wheels went over undulating ground. Nevertheless, Fer-guson obtained a patent on the Duplex Hitch and later, a patent for a Floating

Skid device that tended to maintain the plow at an even depth.

Ferguson's next problem came from his inability to find suitable manufacturing arrangements in the United States. The plow was being produced, but not in high enough quantities to be profitable. Onto the scene came Eber and George Sherman of New York: Fordson dealers, entre-preneurs and confidants of Henry Ford. The Sherman brothers offered to team with Harry Ferguson to manufac-ture the plow with the Duplex Hitch in grand quantities.

Ferguson-Sherman Incorporated was established in 1925. Rumors that US production of the Fordson tractor would be halted by Ford began in 1926, and in 1927, the ax fell. The Fordson had ceased to be profitable and its fac-tory space was needed for the new Model A car.

Draft Control

While Harry Ferguson was busy with the Sherman brothers marketing the Duplex Hitch plow, his research team was working on improvements. The main thrust was in the area of hydraulics: a mechanism to raise and lower the plow and to control tillage depth. In particular, depth control was still a problem. The Floating Skid pat-ent worked well enough on the plow, but now the researchers were expand-ing the System to include other imple-ments such as discs, harrows and cultivators.

The research team began working on the principle that pulling force, or *draft,* was proportional to implement depth, assuming constant soil condi-tions. Draft forces were reflected to the implement attach points so that when draft increased, the implement should be raised hydraulically until the origi-nal draft was re-established.

Consider, for example, the task of opening new ground with a plow. The plow is set to run approximately 8 inches in the ground. As the tractor moves forward over the uneven ter-rain, the front wheels encounter a hump that raises the front end and allows the plow to dig proportionally

This is how to change wheel treads on the Ford-Ferguson tractor.

THE FORD - FERGUSON TRACTOR

WHEEL TREADS FROM 48″ TO 76″ — QUICKLY, EASILY

● Fast, easy changes of wheel treads in 4″ steps from 48″ to 76″ makes the Ford-Ferguson Tractor a truly practical row crop tractor with all the advantages of four wheel construction.

One important time saving feature in changing treads is that no adjustment of steering linkage is required when front tread is changed. Diagram shows why. The axle ends move rearward as

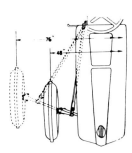

they are extended—distances between points where ends of radius rods and drag links are attached remain constant. Therefore wheel alignment always remains correct regardless of tread setting. This also makes possible offset front wheel for special work.

FRONT TREAD

● Center and end sections of the front axle are provided with a series of holes which permit the axle ends to be extended up to 72″ in 4″ steps.Change from 72″ to 76″ is made by reversing front wheels so disc is outward.

REAR TREAD

● The rear tread is widened by changing the position of the rims on the wheels in combination with changing or reversing the discs of the wheels, as illustrated below. Tread widths are possible from 48″ to 76″ in 4″ steps. Switch wheels, when necessary to permit tire tread to run in right direction.

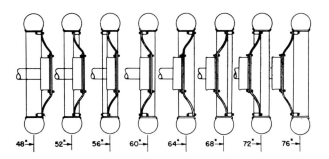

EIGHT WHEEL WIDTHS IN 4 INCH STEPS

From

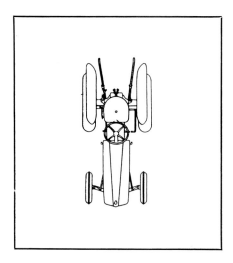

NARROW

48″ tread (52″ rear tread recommended for plowing and general work.)

To

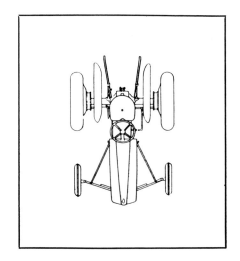

W I D E

Up to 76″ tread for row crop work.

THE FORD - FERGUSON TRACTOR

FRONT AXLE

• The front axle consists of a center section, pivoted directly to the engine, and two axle ends. All three parts are alloy steel, designed for high strength. Axle ends are adjustable on the center section, each being fastened by two bolts. Tubular radius rods extend from the axle ends

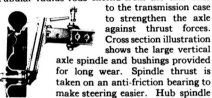

to the transmission case to strengthen the axle against thrust forces. Cross section illustration shows the large vertical axle spindle and bushings provided for long wear. Spindle thrust is taken on an anti-friction bearing to make steering easier. Hub spindle is pre-packed for lubrication. Special thrust face seal prevents dust from entering and greases from leaking out.

STEERING

• To reduce steering effort and make the front wheels respond quickly when steering wheel is turned, a bevel pinion and twin bevel sectors are used. Each sector is linked independently to one of the front wheels. To minimize friction, the steering column is mounted on two tapered roller bearings. The 18-in. steering wheel is made of hard rubber with a steel core.

CLUTCH

• This semi-centrifugal clutch has two outstanding advantages. It is capable of transmitting much higher torque than the engine develops, and yet a light pedal pressure is maintained through the use of centrifugal weights.

The clutch is a single plate type and is composed of two major units, the pressure plate and cover assembly and the clutch disc. The pressure plate is arched and triangular shaped so as

to give correct ventilation which is vitally necessary for good clutch operation.

The steel clutch disc has friction facing rings riveted on each side. There are six crimped steel

segments interposed between one lining and the disc which give the required amount of cushioning to insure smooth clutch engagement and long life of the friction facing.

A mechanical dampener incorporated in the hub of the driven member serves to insure quiet operation of the transmission and absorbs the shock of sudden clutch engagement.

• In cutaway illustration, *L* is one of the three release levers with weighted outer end *W*. Levers are mounted on pressure plate by needle roller bearings *B* and attached to cover plate by flattened pin and roller *R*. As engine speed increases, centrifugal force causes weighted outer ends of levers to attempt to assume a position in the vertical plane passing through *R*, which increases pressure against the clutch plate *P*. This adds to the pressure exerted by the six clutch springs *S*.

Clutch disc diameter.................9 inches
Friction area......................75.3 sq. in.

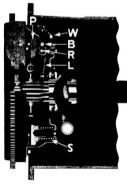

Both the clutch release bearing and pilot bearing are prelubricated type ball bearings and require no further lubrication.

• The clutch pedal works so easily that it can be operated by a small boy or girl. The long pedal provides increased leverage which reduces the pressure required. Clutch pedal and left brake pedal are side by side. The clutch pedal also applies the left brake when it is depressed past the point where clutch is completely disengaged.

No adjustment is required on the clutch other than to maintain a required amount of free travel in the clutch pedal.

Driveline specifics are given for the Ford-Ferguson tractor.

deeper. Instantly, as draft increases, the plow is lifted. As the front wheels drop off the hump, the hydraulics return the plow to its original position.

That is how it worked in theory. The task of the researchers was to come up with a simple, reliable and inexpensive way to accomplish this as rapidly as humps were encountered. They began their efforts using the Duplex two-point hitch arrangement. Draft forces were sensed in the bottom link. This worked well enough that in 1925, Ferguson obtained a patent entitled Apparatus for Coupling Agricultural Implements to Tractors and Automatically Regulating the Depth of Work, known simply as Draft Control.

Draft Control solved only part of the problem, however, as semirigid implement mounting aft of the rear axle also had lateral positioning problems. If, for example, the front wheels were steered to the left, the rear-mounted implement would swing to the right. In the case of a cultivator, this meant ripping out the very plants you sought to steer away from.

At this point, Ferguson's team realized that using two side-by-side lower links instead of just one would cause the virtual, or apparent, hitch point to be far forward of the actual attach points at the back of the tractor, so that the virtual lateral hitch point could be projected forward to the front axle. The two lower links now provided the draft, while the single upper link provided the download on the front wheels. All three links were equipped with ball joints on the tractor ends to allow for flexibility. The automatic Draft Control sensor was incorporated into the upper link.

In 1928, Ferguson began searching for a manufacturer to build a tractor incorporating his new three-point hitch. He did succeed in interesting the Morris Motor Company of England, but before the deal was signed, Morris canceled. The English firm had come to the same conclusion others were reaching, that world economic conditions were not good for new ventures. In 1929, Ferguson was again foiled by the stock market crash and the Great Depression.

The Black Tractor

Undaunted, Ferguson and his research team began designing their own tractor incorporating the three-point System. The hydraulics were to be built in, not just added on.

Interesting a manufacturer would be much easier, reasoned Ferguson, if he had a prototype to demonstrate. When the drawings were finished, he began contacting companies specializing in the parts required.

For the transmission and axle, the choice was the David Brown Company, a family-owned business that had begun in 1860 and grown into the largest gear producer in Great Britain. As it happened, that initial order began a chain of events that led to David Brown's becoming one of the world's foremost tractor companies, subsequently folded into Case/International Harvester. But in 1933, the David Brown Company was merely a parts supplier, one of several contributing to Ferguson's prototype.

Perhaps influenced by Henry Ford's "any color so long as it is black" philosophy, the prototype was painted black, and it was named the Black Tractor. Much testing and development was accomplished on this vehicle before satisfactory performance was realized. Eventually, David Brown committed to manufacturing the production tractor in a joint-venture company called Ferguson-Brown, Ltd. Sales were disappointing, however, because of the worldwide depression and because, although the love for them was largely lost, there were almost 800,000 Fordsons in the field. Switching to the Ferguson-Brown meant buying all new implements as well.

Nevertheless, Ferguson pressed on. In January 1938, one of his associates entered a Ferguson-Brown tractor in a comparative plowing demonstration at the Rowett Research Institute in Aberdeen, Scotland. Luckily, snow fell the night before the demonstration, and only the Ferguson-Brown (with its weight-transferring System) and a four-wheel-drive outfit were able to plow. Farmers went away amazed.

Still, sales were so low as to be unprofitable, and soon disagreement erupted between Brown and Ferguson. Brown wanted to build a bigger tractor; Ferguson wanted to increase production to the point where the price could be lower, building to inventory

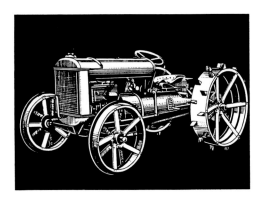

The 1933 Ferguson Black Tractor was the first prototype Ferguson tractor. It was named the Black Tractor simply because of its black paint scheme.

The 1936 Ferguson-Brown incorporated the Ferguson System with Draft Control.

until sales developed. When the two reached an impasse, Brown began making the changes he deemed necessary. In mid 1938, a frustrated Ferguson sailed for America to demonstrate his System to Henry Ford.

The Handshake Agreement

Henry Ford never intended for his company to be completely out of the tractor business when US production of the Fordson was halted in 1927. As hope returned to economic horizons, he began experimenting with new designs. He also kept in contact with the elder Sherman brother, Eber. The Shermans had continued in the tractor business by importing British-built Fordsons, and they were also involved with Harry Ferguson in building and marketing the Ferguson plow for the Fordson.

Not one to miss an opportunity, Harry Ferguson made sure that Eber

Sherman came to Great Britain early in 1938, to see a demonstration of the Ferguson-Brown tractor and implements. It was Ferguson's point of view in his disagreement with Brown that mass production was the key, and who knew more about mass production than Henry Ford. And how would Ferguson get to Ford? Eber Sherman, of course.

Sherman dutifully reported to Ford what he had seen. He suggested that Ford might be interested in the remarkable System. Of course Ford was interested, and Ferguson was invited to meet with him. Thus, in the fall of 1938, Ferguson and several aides brought a crated Ferguson-Brown tractor and implements by ship and truck to Ford's Fair Lane Estate.

It was a bright blue October day when the demonstration began. The tractor had been meticulously prepared. Only a small group was present: the Ferguson team, the Ford team, the Sherman brothers and the truck driver who brought the tractor from New York.

The demonstration was convincing. The diminutive Ferguson-Brown, about eight-tenths the size of a Fordson, clearly outperformed both a Fordson and an Allis-Chalmers with the same-size plows.

Ford took on a serious attitude and called for a table and two chairs to be brought out. Ferguson had a hand-sized model of the tractor, with which he was able to clearly explain his System to Ford as they sat at the table. The result of this conversation was a handshake, sealing a gentleman's agreement that Ford would make tractors and deliver them to Ferguson. Ferguson would have implements made by other sources to his designs and would be responsible for setting up dealerships and marketing. Further, it was agreed that either could terminate the agreement at will and without explanation.

From this Handshake Agreement, as it came to be known, came the immensely successful Ford Tractor. Also came much confusion about what the agreement covered and who was responsible for what. Nevertheless, as long as Henry Ford was in charge of the Ford Motor Company, the agreement worked.

This 1926 Fordson from the Fossum Collection has a homemade cab and is equipped with the Ferguson Duplex Hitch plow with its Floating Skid depth control device—the forerunner of the three-point hitch. US production of the Fordson ended in 1927 or early 1928, when the tractor's factory space was usurped by the new Model A car. Fordsons were also produced in Ireland and England, English production continuing until 1946.

The Tractors of the Century: N Series

Just three months after that bright blue October day of the Handshake Agreement, experimental models were ready for testing. Another six months saw completion of the 9N prototype, which incorporated all the important features. This prototype was taken to Fair Lane, where Messrs. Ford and Ferguson gave plowing demonstrations to a group of invited guests. Performance was spectacular, despite all the compromises Ferguson had to accept in order to achieve the mass production goals Ford required.

The Model 9N tractor

The 9N hit the dealer showrooms early enough in 1939 that over 10,000 were sold yet that year. The launch price of $585 included rubber tires; an electrical system with a starter, generator and battery; and a power takeoff. Headlights were optional.

The engine was a four-cylinder L-head type with 120 cubic inches of displacement, a 3.187 x 3.75 inch bore and stroke, and a 6:1 compression ratio, which produced 28 horsepower at 2000 rpm. Remarkable for its time, the tractor included as standard a large-capacity cartridge-type oil filter and an oil bath air cleaner. Also unusual for its time, but much appreciated, was an automotive-type reverse-flow muffler. Early Ford publications suggested the possibility of mounting a radio, because of the tractor's low noise level.

While most tractors of that day used magneto ignitions, the 9N had a direct-driven distributor with an integral coil. Magneto ignitions of the 1930s were cantankerous and troublesome and often induced kickback into the hand crank, resulting in many a broken arm. Needless to say, the mod-

ern ignition system and self-starter were welcomed.

An ingenious front wheel tread adjustment adapted the tractor to the width of crop rows. The front axle consisted of a center section that overlapped two outboard stub sections to which the wheels attached. Radius rods from the tractor body held the axle in place, a practice typical of Ford cars in those days. Steering linkages ran parallel with the radius rods down both sides of the tractor. The center and end sections of the axle were provided with a series of holes and two bolts for each side. The angle of the center section allowed the axle length to be varied by changing the amount of overlap, without the need to change, or even detach, either the radius rods or the steering linkages. This feature was not found in the 8N or subsequent Ford tractors; apparently, it was a concession to Ferguson patent claims.

Rear wheel tread could be changed by changing the position of the wheels on the rims and by reversing the wheel discs.

The key feature of the tractor was the Ferguson System. The three-point hitch allowed eighteen different implements to be either attached or

Note the 8x32 rear tires on this 1939 Model 9N Ford-Ferguson, serial number 364; size 10x28 tires became standard equipment in 1942, and 11.2x28 and 12x28 tires can also be used. Note also the horizontal grille spokes reminiscent of Ford car and truck grilles of the period. This grille type was made of cast aluminum and was used until 1941. The new grille, with vertical spokes, was made of steel, as aluminum was rapidly becoming a strategic war material.

This 1939 Ford-Ferguson 9N, serial number 364, owned by Palmer Fossum of Northfield, Minnesota, is a beautiful example of the earliest version of the classic Ford Tractor. Significant features include a cast-aluminum hood, grille and dashboard. Harold Brock of Waterloo, Iowa, a former Ford employee involved with developing the tractor, told Fossum that cast-aluminum hoods were used on the initial batch because stamping equipment for steel was not ready in time. The aluminum hoods and grilles proved to be quite fragile and have largely been replaced over the years.

Henry Ford introduces the new 9N to the press in June 1939. Besides plowing demonstrations given by himself and Harry Ferguson, Ford had the eight-year-old boy standing by the tractor show the ease with which the tractor and plow could be handled. To the amazement of the crowd, the boy's furrows were as straight and even as those of experienced plowmen like Ford and Ferguson. Note the identifying features of the early Ford Tractor: the smooth rear axle hub, cast-aluminum horizontal-spoke grille, four-spoke steering wheel and squarish manifold casting.

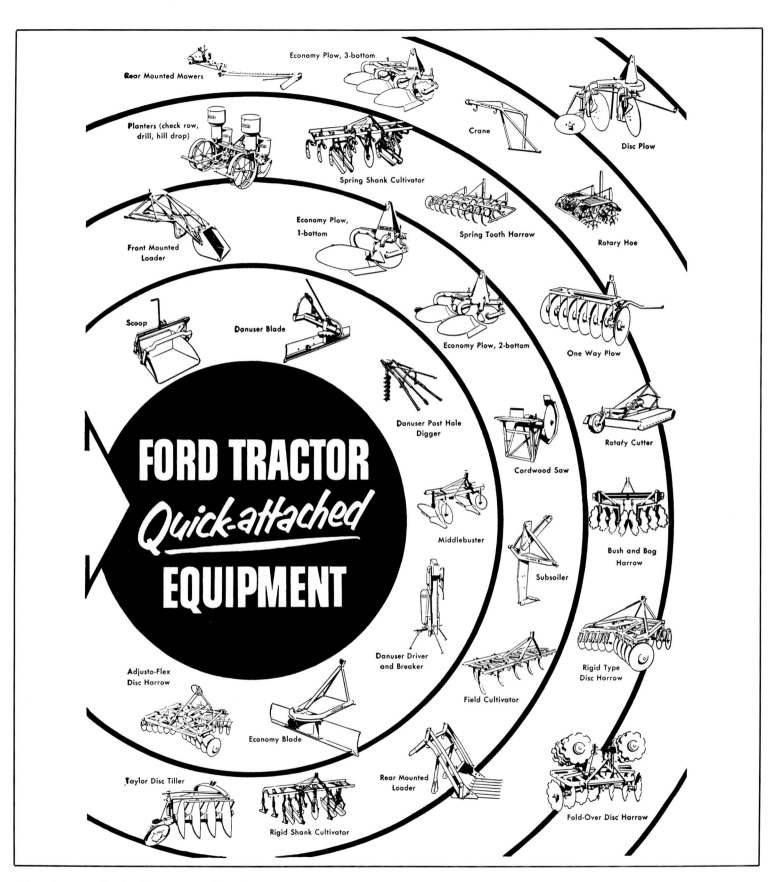

Advertisement displaying a range of Ford
Tractor equipment.

removed in about a minute. The hydraulic system enabled the tractor to carry an implement to the field and then to regulate its working depth with the patented Draft Control.

To say that the 9N was a success would be an understatement. The model's low price, about half that of equivalent tractors, alone accounted for some of its acceptability. Before World War II, some 17 million horses were still employed in agriculture. Farmers had ceased to question the cost-effectiveness of the tractor versus the horse, but the usurpation of production capacity by World War II kept down the number of 9Ns sold. Then, in 1942, after producing 99,002 Model 9Ns, Ford changed to the 2N version.

The Model 2N tractor

The pedigree of the 2N has more questions than answers. Opinions vary as to what differences there were between the 9N and the 2N, and why the model designation was changed. Until the subsequent 8N, model numbers were not commonly used in identifying the Ford Tractor. Only in parts catalogs were the differences noted.

Some authorities now speculate that the 2N designation simply indicated the incorporation of changes that improved life, reduced cost or simplified assembly. Others state that the 2N, correctly designated 2NAN, was a wartime kerosene-burning version, of which most examples have since been converted to gasoline. The most believable assessment appears to be that the 2 indicated 1942, and the 2N was introduced as a stripped-down wartime version with steel wheels and no electrical system. Then, as the wartime materials situation eased, the configuration more or less reverted to that of the 9N.

In today's parts catalogs, there are no parts indicated as being peculiar to either the 2N or the 9N. Identification can be made by serial number, or by the 9N's lack of the external hood-side panel attach fasteners found on 2Ns and 8Ns just ahead of the front axle, and by a four-spoke truck-type steer-

Harry Ferguson shows his plowing skill at the 9N press introduction in June 1939. The event was organized by the Ferguson-Sherman company at Ford's Fair Lane Estate. In typical Ferguson fashion, it was a well-planned gala event. Several new tractors were on hand with various Ferguson-Sherman implements. An area was fenced off so the 9N could demonstrate how well it operated in tight corners. The day's festivities for the 500 invited guests included a lunch served under large tents.

ing wheel found on most 9Ns. Otherwise, there are no visible differences between the 9N and 2N.

It was Ford's policy to incorporate changes and improvements throughout the year as necessary, but mostly at year-end. Accordingly, different configurations appear within the model designations, as well as within year-models. For example, the original 9Ns, introduced in 1939, have characteristics not found on later tractors:
• The instrument panel contains a starter button near the ammeter, the

Henry Ford, Harry Ferguson and the Sherman brothers, Eber and George, right to left, appear with the 9N prototype. The Sherman brothers joined Ferguson in manufacturing implements for the 9N and in setting up the dealer organization. Their relationships with Ford and Ferguson went back a long way. The Shermans had been Fordson dealers and the principal importers of Fordsons after US production was halted in 1927. They had also been in business with Ferguson building his two-point hitch plow for the Fordson. Notice the lack of name badges on the front of the tractor, although a place for the Ford emblem has been cast into the hood. Also notice the rear tire, between Ford and Ferguson; it seems to be a solid rubber type, with the tread attached by fasteners.

key switch near the oil pressure gauge and a red light to indicate when the ignition is on.
• The rear axle hubs are smooth.
• The front axle radius rods are I-beam type.
• The battery/fuel cap cover is not hinged, but is a snap-in-place type.
• Front axle grease fittings are on the forward side.
• The grille has semihorizontal spokes.
• The steering sector box, battery holder, grille, transmission covers, instrument panel and sometimes the hood (on the earliest models) are cast aluminum.

• The rear fenders have two crease bars instead of one.
• The left and right brake pedals are identical and interchangeable.
    The 1940 9N has several different features:
• A safety interlocked starter is introduced midyear.
• A hinged cover is used for the battery and fuel cap.
• A three-brush generator is installed.
    The 1941 9N incorporates these changes:
• The left brake pedal is now different from the right.
• Front axle grease fittings are moved to the rear for protection.

• A steel grille with vertical bars appears.
• A three-spoke steering wheel is introduced midyear.

In 1942, the designation was changed to 2N. Peculiarities of this year-model are as follows:
• The 10.00x28 rear tires become standard.
• The steering wheel is changed to a three-spoke with steel rod spokes.
• A pressurized radiator is introduced.
• A nonelectrical, steel wheel version with magneto ignition, hand crank starter and front choke is made available to save war-critical materials and keep production up.

In 1944, the last of the visible changes were made when the radius rods were changed to an oval tubular section and sealed-beam headlights were incorporated. Of course, some internal and construction method changes were made as time went on.

When this happened, for the most part, the old parts were dropped from the catalog. Hence, by now, most tractors have been updated to the latest configuration.

Models 9N and 2N summary

The original Ford Tractor (9N or 2N) weighed about 2,300 pounds, was painted a solid Forest Gray (darker than the 8N gray) and could work all day on 10 gallons of gas. It has two drawbacks: its brake pedal/clutch pedal placement and its three-speed transmission. Apparently, the engineers felt it more natural to put the left and right brake pedals on the left and right sides of the tractor. The clutch pedal is located on the left side with the left brake. Depressing the clutch fully also operates a linkage that actuates the left brake pedal. This is fine for stopping—you simply depress the clutch and right brake pedals. The

Palmer Fossum astride serial number 364, a 1939 Model 9N Ford-Ferguson. The four-spoke truck-type steering wheel was used through 1941. Besides carrying a full line of new and used parts for Ford tractors, Fossum is probably the number one Ford collector. He has over 50 Ford Tractors in his collection, including at least one of every year-model from 1924 to 1959. He also has a rare 1941 Ford pickup truck with a factory-installed Ford Tractor four-cylinder engine.

problem comes when a tight left turn is required from a stop. You must first release the clutch before using the left foot to actuate the left brake, and by then you are often already into the fence.

The limitations of only a three-speed transmission were largely overcome when the Sherman brothers

The 9N engine, shown here from the left side, was a four-cylinder L-head with a 3.187x3.75 inch bore and stroke, 119.7 cubic inches of displacement and a 6:1 compression ratio. It produced 28 brake horsepower at 2000 rpm bare, and 24 horsepower at the belt pulley with muffler, fan and generator installed. Note the original I-beam-type radius rod. The 1939 engines had no freeze plugs, so this must be either a 1940 or 1941, as a freeze plug is visible behind the oil filter.

introduced their Step-Up auxiliary transmission. Space was available between the clutch housing and the transmission, with a convenient split line at that point, which allowed the installation of a direct and high-range gear set—and, subsequently, a set of low-direct-high-range gears. With one of these auxiliary Shifters, the right ratio for the job could be found. Road

speed was increased from 12 mph at 2100 rpm to almost 18 mph. However, with the step-down (low-range) version, torque and bearing loads on the transmission, differential and rear axle can exceed design limits. In addition, torque at the rear wheels is great enough that back-flip accidents when pulling from the drawbar (not the three-point hitch) have to be guarded against.

Exit Henry Ford

By 1945, frail, eighty-two-year-old automotive pioneer Henry Ford resigned and his grandson, Henry Ford II took his place. By then, it had become obvious to many in Ford management that Ferguson held the clean end of the agreement stick. Much of the risk and investment were in the tractor end of the bargain. And, while tractors were provided to Ferguson at a fixed price, Ferguson did not offer a fixed price

through the dealer network. He could raise both the price of tractors to dealers and the price of implements. Ferguson also stood to profit most from the sale of parts and service.

In late 1946, Henry Ford II told Ferguson that the Handshake Agreement would end in mid 1947. Ford also announced a new, improved version of the tractor with a complete new line of Ford-produced implements. A whole new dealership organization was to be set up, independent of Ferguson.

The new tractor, the Model 8N, hit the dealer showrooms in July 1947. It was an immediate success, with almost 40,000 being produced by the end of the year.

Ferguson's reaction was twofold. First, with remarkable speed, he set up a manufacturing operation to make his own tractor, the Ferguson TO-20. In appearance, it was a dead ringer for the Ford 2N, even to the paint color,

288

but improvements made it comparable to the new 8N. Second, Ferguson launched a $340 million lawsuit against Ford for patent infringement and for damages caused by loss of business.

Six years later, in 1952, the suit was settled with an award to Ferguson of just less than $10 million. Over 200 lawyers had taken part, trying to sort out the complexities of the Handshake Agreement. The main militant against Ferguson's case was the success of his new tractor. It belied the damages-for-loss-of-business claim. Ford made some changes to the 8N to evade the patents, but the settlement was mainly for infringements. The next Ford trac-

tor, the 1953 Model NAA Jubilee, had major changes in the hydraulic system and other areas, as ordered by the court.

The Model 8N tractor

The new Ford 8N introduced in July 1947 was a classic engineering masterpiece. A 1948 model (hence the 8N designation), it was one of the most popular tractors ever produced. Improvements over the 9N and 2N models were numerous.

A slightly more powerful engine was used, with the compression ratio increased from 6:1 to 6.5:1. Otherwise, the engines were basically the same.

In 1939, a one-piece intake-exhaust manifold was used on the 9N engine, shown here from the right side. The generator was a simple shunt-wound type with a vibrator voltage regulator. In 1940, this was changed to a three-brush and cutout type.

Later, a side-mounted distributor and separate coil were provided, replacing the integral unit under the fan.

A four-speed transmission—a much-needed improvement—added greatly to the tractor's flexibility and productivity. First and second overall ratios were the same as before. These

289

Previous page

Homer Clark and this 1940 9N have been farming together for 50 years. Back in 1940, the National Farm Youth Foundation (NFYF) and Ford-Ferguson dealers awarded 29 new tractors as prizes in tractor operation and plowing contests. The contests were held in each of the 29 sales districts. Clark won this tractor, serial number 38975, in the Fond du Lac, Wisconsin, district. The Clark farm is in LaValle, Wisconsin, near Madison.

A line-up of transport trucks is loaded with 9N Ford Tractors. This photo was taken January 16, 1940, on the streets of Dearborn. The large number of tractors shown represents only about half of one day's production. The other half were probably shipped by railroad. Henry Ford determined the size of the tractor in order to fit the maximum number into a railroad car. The sign in the radiator grille of the lead truck, a 1939 Ford COE, reads, "Taxes paid by motor transports help keep down the taxes on your car."

In June 1940, a pair of 9Ns teams-up with a 1940 Ford truck to do some harvesting. The aluminum grilles were quite fragile; some were reportedly fractured by tall stubble.

were considered to be already ideal, first being selected on the basis of drive component strength and tire traction, and second being the best for pulling a two-bottom, 14 inch plow through normal soil. Third and fourth gears were on both sides of the old high gear. Third was the drag-harrowing gear; fourth was the road gear. Reverse was the ratio equivalent of third gear, rather than of first as on the 9N-2N transmission. This provided much faster back-ups, but also meant a lot of clutch slipping when maneuvering backwards in tight quarters. The Sherman-type step-up, step-down shifter found a useful home on the 8N despite the new four-speed gearbox.

In addition to automatic depth control (an original feature of the Ferguson System), the new 8N included

Position Control lever under the seat. The purpose of this control was to block out depth control and cause the implement to remain at a constant position relative to the tractor regardless of the draft load. This was a great convenience for such implements as the grader blade, cultivator, box scraper and so on. Draft Control was used for tillage implements where depth of work automatically varied according to draft forces.

After 1947, the top link rocker, which actuated the draft sensing mechanism, contained three moment arm positions rather than the previous one. This allowed macro adjustments in Draft Control sensitivity.

Although the brake mechanism for the 8N was improved over the 9N-2N system, the big news was that both

A 9N has the wheel and fender removed to show the three-point hitch mechanism. The control lever quadrant is beside the seat. Behind the seat is the leveling crank, which lengthens or shortens the right-hand draft link strut. Below the leveling crank is the Draft Control spring, against which draft forces work. If draft force increases to the point where the spring is compressed, the hydraulic control valve is actuated to raise the implement in the same manner as if the control quadrant lever were raised. When the obstacle is past and draft forces return to normal, the spring repositions the hydraulic control valve and the implement returns to its normal working depth. The tractor shown is a mid 1940 model, photographed on June 7, 1940. Note the safety interlock starter button, the hinged battery/fuel cap cover, the I-beam-type radius rods from the transmission case to the front axle and the smooth rear axle hubs. The Ferguson two-bottom plow is shown in the fully raised position.

pedals were now on the right side, positioned so that both could be depressed simultaneously for stopping or individually for maneuvering.

In terms of steering improvements, a new recirculating ball mechanism replaced the previously used sector gear setup. This resulted in reduced steering friction and backlash and provided for longer life. Steering wheel angle and height were also both increased on the 8N.

The new 8N was basically the same size and shape as the 9N and 2N, but it had light gray sheet metal and

An early 8N Ford Tractor is doing what it does best—plowing. Although over 400 implements would eventually be available, the Draft Control three-point hitch worked its best with the two-bottom plow. Many farmers of the forties plowed several hundred acres per year with 8Ns.

Early tractors, through 1941, incorporated significant changes throughout the model years. Features of the 1940 Model 9N were the hinged battery/fuel cap cover, an improved voltage regulator/generator and a safety starter button that was mechanically interlocked with the transmission lever in neutral.

Previous page
Homer Clark's 1940 9N was built late enough in the production year to include the midyear changes such as the safety interlock starter and the three-brush generator. Clark has also made some later-configuration changes to update his tractor. Because of the looming shadows of World War II, little was done in exporting the 9N. However, Canada, Cuba and Mexico each had one of the 38 Ferguson-Sherman distributors.

wheels with dark red cast iron. Accordingly, it soon picked up the nickname Red Belly. Also new were an air cleaner grille as well as red Ford scripts on either side of the hood and later also on the insides of the fenders. After serial number 290,271 in late 1950, 8Ns contained a multifunctional panel instrument that displayed engine revolutions per minute, ground speed at different gear selections and engine operating hours.

By the end of production in December 1952, 524,076 Model 8N units were produced. Over 400 implements were offered through the Dearborn Motors subsidiary. Besides those already mentioned, numerous other minor improvements increased life, ease of use or ease of repair. The price stayed amazingly low throughout production, eventually rising to about $1,200 in 1952.

Homer Clark's 1940 9N has a new grille of the later type, as the original aluminum grille was broken in a tornado.

Next page
This is a 1941 9N. The chrome trim around the ammeter, left, the oil pressure gauge, right, the shift knob, the choke button and the radiator cap would all disappear from the next year's model, the wartime 1942 2N.

75092-A

An early 1941 9N shows off its front-mounted snowplow and other features, including a new grille with vertical spokes, a larger generator, the nonsmooth rear axle hubs, liberal use of chrome and a Ford emblem trimmed in chrome on the front of the tractor. The snowplow was operated through cables from the lift arms of the three-point hitch, so the operator used the same control lever as for rear-mounted implements. A 1941 Ford car stands in the background. Behind the car are classic examples of the period's residential architecture.

The year 1942 was one of fairly major changes and saw a change in designation from 9N (signifying 1939) to 2N (1942). This 1942 2N Ford-Ferguson from the Fossum Collection has no electrical system, but has a magneto ignition and steel wheels. Tractors were considered essential war items, but production was only 16,487 2Ns in 1942, down from almost 43,000 in 1941 because of wartime shortages. Production of the tractor without rubber tires or copper in the starters and generators helped keep numbers up. Production reached 21,000 in 1943 and 43,000 in 1944, and most examples had tires and electrical systems by then, showing that material problems were largely overcome as the war progressed.

Advertising of the forties stressed that the Ford-Ferguson was one lightweight tractor that steel wheels had not forced off the market: "It's rugged enough to withstand the shocks of operation on steel wheels—and the Ferguson System provides all the extra traction needed to do the job," said farm magazine ad copy. This Fossum Collection 1942 Ford-Ferguson Model 2N on steel wheels has a unique two-way plow attached, allowing back and forth plowing without a dead furrow. In ordinary plowing, the farmer starts up the field in the middle and comes back down the side.

Thus, as plowing continues, the farmer moves from the middle toward the opposite side and from the first side toward the middle. When the field is completed, the last furrow coming downfield laps over the original furrow in the middle, leaving a hump, or sometimes a gap. With the two-way plow, the farmer merely switches from one share to the other and spins around to return along the previous furrow, saving the time needed to drive to the edge of the field for the return and avoiding the hump or gap in the middle.

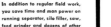
A 1943 ad for the Ford Tractor shows off the Ferguson System's abilities.

303

A BNO-25 Aircraft Tug, a variation of the 2N, does its thing with a B-24 Liberator. This picture was taken in March 1943, at the Willow Run airport, where Ford manufactured a record number of Liberators during World War II. The BNO-25 had a single brake pedal, no three-point hitch and heavy sheet metal. Another version, the BNO-40, had dual rear wheels. The rated drawbar pull was 2,500 pounds for the BNO-25 and 4,000 pounds for the BNO-40. With an empty weight of about 36,000 pounds, the Liberator was probably quite a load for the BNO-25.

Ford Tractors come off the assembly line at the Rouge Plant in 1944, some of the 43,443 built that year.

81664

A 1945 2N Ford-Ferguson demonstrates Ferguson's ingenious self-jacking system, which was operated by the three-point hitch hydraulics. The Jacking System was introduced to allow rapid adjustment of wheel spacing.

The handsome art deco styling is apparent in this photo of Leroy Folkerts' 1946 Ford-Ferguson. Styling was done by the Ford car styling department, and reflected the image of Ford cars and trucks.

Leroy Folkerts atop his 1946 2N Ford-Ferguson. Although this tractor is restored to showroom condition, it still does some work on the Folkerts' acreage. The 1946 model has all the improvements incorporated in the 9N and 2N; no improvements were made in the 1947 model. Over 97,000 2Ns were made in 1946 and 1947, so they are the most prevalent of the 9Ns and 2Ns.

Leroy Folkerts' 1946 Model 2N, serial number 225015, was one of some 59,000 Ford-Fergusons produced that year. The 9N-2N design was reaching maturity. Although the production rate was fairly steady, reaching a high of nearly 37,627 in the first six months of 1947, a major update was clearly required to keep the tractor competitive. Even with the subsequent 8N, Ford was never able to best International's Farmall for the number one sales spot. International had a line of tractors from small ones equivalent to the Ford to large diesel models. The idea for a tractor line of several sizes seems to have eluded Ford until 1954.

Previous page

This 1946 Ford-Ferguson belongs to Leroy Folkerts. Ford wiped out the competition for tractors under 30 horsepower with the 9N, 2N and subsequent 8N, but a lot of the competition's tractors were selling in the over 30 horsepower class, which kept Ford in the number two sales spot. However, the Ferguson System, with its penchant for improving traction, made a Ford with a plow perform as if it had 10 more horsepower.

This left side view of Leroy Folkerts' Ford-Ferguson 2N engine shows the shift lever for the Sherman Step-Up transmission, which greatly improves the flexibility of the Ford Tractor. The Sherman gives six forward speeds rather than three, and improves road speed from 11 mph to almost 18 mph. Putting the Sherman in neutral also allows operation of the engine without the power takeoff and hydraulics, and makes for easier cold weather starting by reducing the load on the starter (if the clutch is engaged). The 119.7 cubic inch engine was basically one half of the 239 cubic inch V-8 used in production cars and trucks. The original concept was to use production pistons, rods and so on, but in practice the tractor parts had to be beefed up a bit. The starter motor was interchangeable with that used on the small 60 horsepower V-8.

Leroy Folkerts owns this 1946 Ford-Ferguson. The Ford N Series tractor was made lower to the ground than contemporary competing tractors. While this was at least a perceived drawback for row crop farming, it was necessary for safety. When an implement, such as a plow, was raised, the overall center of gravity was considerably higher. A spin turn at the end of a row that was rapidly stopped by straightening the front wheels, and even applying the opposite brake, imparted a considerable roll couple. Add to this hillside conditions and the possibility of simultaneously dropping into a furrow, and the need for a low, squat stance is obvious.

Leroy Folkert's 1946 2N has the optional high air cleaner intake shown just ahead of the steering wheel. The standard intake was under the hood, where it was exposed to an extra amount of dirt thrown by the front wheels and fan. The optional intake was expected to receive cleaner air above the hood. There is a fine screen under the cap to keep out bigger particles, while the regular oil bath tank, below, takes out dust and dirt. Notice the new Ford accessory seat cushion. The standard metal seat leaves a lot to be desired in terms of comfort. The seat is adjustable by removing the attachment nut and moving the seat to a different hole in the seat spring.

316

On April 4, 1947, the 1,300,000th Ford-built tractor rolls off the Rouge line. The number includes 739,977 American-built Fordsons and some 300,000 British-built Fordsons. Production of 2Ns was nearing an end; in July 1947, that model would be replaced by the new 8N.

In July 1947, the first new 8N rolls off the assembly line at the Ford Rouge Plant. Although it looked much like the 2N it replaced, the 8N had a more powerful engine, an improved hydraulic system, better brakes, a new steering system, running boards and other refinements. A lighter

gray paint for the sheet metal contrasted nicely with bright red castings. Chrome appeared around the Ford logo on the front and the Ferguson System badge disappeared. Also new was the Ford script on the hood, and later on the rear fenders.

This 1947 Ford-Ferguson 2N Sugar Cane and Cotton Special from the Fossum Collection is a unique conversion that was popular in Louisiana and other southern states. It was designed to be a competitor for the Farmall F-12 and F-14 and the Case RC. The rear tires are 9x40s with special fender risers for clearance. The front tire is a 10x12.

The rear wheels of Fossum's Sugar Cane and Cotton Special have slots in the rims so that spacing can be changed. The wagon is a Ford Dearborn model.

321

FORD HYDRAULIC TOUCH CONTROL

includes constant draft feature

Lifting or lowering of implements is handled anywhere at any time without effort, just by touching the hydraulic control lever. An implement can be lowered to desired working depth and under uniform soil conditions, this depth will be automatically maintained.

Crossing a grassed waterway.

Lifts, lowers and controls implement in the ground at the touch of a finger.

Plus Ford Hydraulic Touch Control

Maintains uniform depth under varying soil conditions.

FORD HYDRAULIC TOUCH CONTROL

includes Implement Position Control

This great new Ford advancement means smoother operation, less wear on tractor and driver, easier, better work. In fields with reasonably smooth surfaces all you do is set the controls once—and uniform working depth of implements is automatically maintained, even when soil conditions vary.

See Your Dealer. Your nearby Ford Tractor dealer asks you to remember that he is headquarters for genuine Ford Tractor parts and for implement and tractor service second to none. He is a good man to know.

A 1947 ad presents the Ford Hydraulic Touch Control.

The classic 8N Ford Tractor with a Dearborn Implement box scraper. When Ford and Ferguson went their separate ways in 1947, Ford marketed its own line of implements under the trade name Dearborn Implement Company. The box scraper works much like the old horse-drawn slip scraper, except the tractor and three-point hitch do the hard work. Most versions of the box scraper can be turned around, so they can be filled while backing. Thus, they can be used to dig from a bank or in similar situations where you can't drive over the ground to be excavated.

Next page
A 1947 ad for Ford Tractors displays the three-point attachment.

Ford ®
TRACTOR

Saves time here to use in the field.

FORD TRIPLE-QUICK ATTACHING

You can attach or detach most implements in a minute or less. Arrows above show 3-point, triple-quick attachment. Even such a job as changing from mower to cultivator, or cultivator to mower, is easily done in 10 minutes.

Quick, Easy Attachment of Implements

ADD UP TO FASTER, EASIER FARMING

There will always be plenty of work to do on any farm . . . but there's no reason why as much of this work as possible shouldn't be made as fast and easy as possible.

This was the idea that Ford engineers had in mind when they went at the job of designing this great new Ford Tractor.

How well they succeeded is being proved every day now, as more and more farmers get an opportunity to see this new tractor, to put it through its paces, to turn it loose on their own farms.

That great combination—Ford Triple-Quick Attaching, and Ford Hydraulic Touch Control—is the last word in simplifying tractor operation, saving time both in barnyard and field, and in assuring you a better job with less work. You'll only need to try this combination once to realize how far ahead it is.

Owners of this new Ford Tractor are finding plenty more to talk about, of course. There's the new 4-speed transmission—four forward speeds and reverse, giving better selection of speeds to fit the work, and faster top speed. There's new, easier steering and improved braking. There's a total of 22 worthwhile advancements, each doing its share to make the new Ford Tractor a *better* tractor— and a better investment for you.

Your Ford Tractor dealer invites you to examine this new tractor and the many quality implements that have been designed especially to work with it. He'll be glad to demonstrate both tractor and implements to you.

We think you'll agree that your farm work *can* be made faster, easier and more productive—the new Ford Tractor way.

DEARBORN MOTORS CORPORATION, DETROIT 3, MICHIGAN

Dearborn
FARM EQUIPMENT

Dearborn Farm Equipment includes a wide variety of quality implements, specially designed by qualified implement engineers to operate with the Ford Tractor and field tested by practical farmers. Ask your Ford Tractor dealer to demonstrate them on your farm.
Marketed and serviced through a national organization of Dearborn Motors Distributors and Ford Tractor dealers.

NEW 4-SPEED TRANSMISSION gives you the advantage of a fourth forward speed, with stepped up top speed for road travel and faster operation in other speeds. New helical gears are in constant mesh, for easy, quiet shifting. Transmission cover plate is easily removable.

NEW BRAKE PEDALS, both mounted on right side. Either right or left brake can be operated with the right foot, or both operated together, leaving foot free for clutch. New Duo-servo type brakes give positive braking on either or both rear wheels.

NEW HYDRAULIC TOUCH CONTROL and linkage save both your time and your muscle. Implements are easily and quickly attached or detached. New attachment lugs plus provision for installation of swinging drawbar, permit more efficient use of a wide variety of equipment.

NEW SCREENED AIR INTAKE is conveniently located where dust is at a minimum. Has vented grille easily removable for cleaning. Special air cleaner extension (available as accessory) for use in extremely dusty conditions, is easily attached without drilling a hole in hood.

NEW AUTOMOTIVE TYPE STEERING GEAR provides steering ease comparable to your car. On turns, wheels hold true with minimum steering effort. Mechanism is readily adjusted for wear. This easier steering makes a big difference in a long day's work.

NEW SPRINGY, HINGE-BACK SEAT tilts up and back, giving you the relief of standup operation when desired. New 24" x 7" step plates, asbestos shielded on muffler side, provide foot comfort, make it easier, safer to get on and off.

A Quality Line of Basic Implements

Several of the implements now in the Dearborn line are listed at the right. Many more are being developed and will be ready soon. You will want Dearborn Implements because they are specially designed to operate with the Ford Tractor, and are of quality construction throughout. Expert implement engineers have designed them and practical farmers have thoroughly tested them.

Most Dearborn Implements may be attached or detached in a minute or so and take full advantage of Ford Hydraulic Touch Control for safe, easy transport to and from the field and almost effortless control of operation. Ask your Ford Tractor dealer for literature on implements now available, and watch for announcement of additions to the line.

Dearborn

FARM EQUIPMENT

- Moldboard Plow
- Disc Plow
- Rigid Shank Cultivator
- Rigid Shank Front End Cultivator
- Spring Shank Cultivator
- Spring Shank Front End Cultivator
- Single Disc Harrow
- Tandem Disc Harrow
- Rear Attached Mower
- Four Row Weeder
- Cordwood Saw
- Scoop
- Utility Blade
- Angle Dozer
- V Snow Plow
- Blade Snow Plow
- Front End Loader
- Sweep Rake
- Heavy Duty Loader
- 4 Wheel Wagon
- Post-Hole Digger

and many others

See Your Dealer.

Your Ford Tractor dealer is Ford Farming Headquarters in your locality, with all that this means in faster farming and less work and more income per acre. See him for a new tractor, for implements, for parts, for expert, on-the-spot service and for helpful suggestions. He is a good man to know.

MARKETED AND SERVICED THROUGH A NATIONAL ORGANIZATION OF DEARBORN MOTORS DISTRIBUTORS AND FORD TRACTOR DEALERS

Previous page
A 1947 ad showcases tractor features.

The half-track kit was a popular after-market accessory for both Fords and Fergusons. Besides this set made by Bombardier, the Canadian snowmobile and aircraft company, and installed on a 1948 Ford 8N owned by Fossum, the Arps track was also widely used. The additional traction and flotation are phenomenal. Operators report that the difference is like that between two- and four-wheel-drive. Although the tracks can be used for fieldwork, they are made for use on snow, mud or muddy concrete, such as for cleaning out a cattle yard with a front loader. The half-track can nicely handle the front snowplow implement and is also much in demand for use in maple sugaring.

326

A 1949 ad shows the line of implements.

This classic 1950 Ford 8N with a factory canopy was purchased new by Palmer Fossum's father on March 10, 1950. This was the tractor that infused Fossum with a love that has caused him to become a foremost collector of Ford Ns. The five-bow Ford accessory top has special brackets that fit on the fenders. The top is attached to the brackets with wing nuts; thus, it can readily be folded back, or removed when not in use. Besides being a desirable shield from the blazing sun, the canopy was also welcome when sudden rain showers came up.

Although the classic 8N appears to be longer and heavier than its predecessors, it is basically the same size and shape. The length, 115 inches, was supposedly set by Henry Ford himself, to fit the maximum number of tractors on a rail car. Ed Pochinski of Hatley, Wisconsin, has restored this mint 1951 8N over a period of years, obtaining parts and assistance from Strojney Implement Company, Ford-Ferguson specialists in Mosinee, Wisconsin.

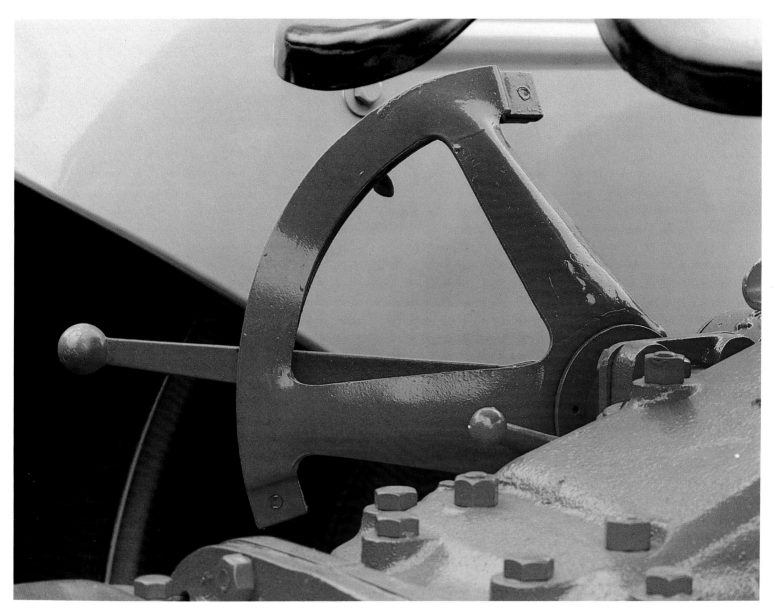

The Ford operators manual describes the 8N as follows: "The Ford two-bottom plow tractor is of the four-wheel type construction. A wide range of wheel spacings are provided. The short wheelbase and low over-all height give it greater flexibility and maneuverability. Implements are easily attached to the tractor by means of the 3-pin mounting."

One improvement incorporated into the 8N was the addition of Position Control to the previously available Draft Control. The Position Control lever is the small lever barely visible between the main control quadrant and the transmission housing. The hydraulics operate in the Position Control mode when the lever is in the vertical position, and under Draft Control when horizontal. Draft Control is commonly used with tillage tools, such as a plow. The implement will run at the set depth as long as the soil is uniform, but will rise or fall as draft forces increase or decrease. Position Control holds the implement at a constant position relative to the tractor, regardless of draft loads. Scoops, grader blades and grain drills are examples of tools that need Position Control.

A 1951 ad for the Ford Tractor emphasizes power and low cost.

TOP PRODUCTION!...
WITH LESS HELP!...AT LOW COST!

THE WHOLE FAMILY HELPS—Any member of the family can be a full-fledged tractor operator with a Ford Tractor. Triple quick-attaching of implements and Ford Tractor Hydraulic Touch Control make this possible.

GET MORE OF THE CROP—With no extra equipment the Dearborn-Wood Bros. Combine's header operates from 2 to 38" off the ground, to get lodged, low growing or rank crops. Big capacity. Bin, bagger models; PTO or Ford Farming Engine powered.

Ford Tractor POWER is Helping Thousands of Farmers Do Their Biggest Job

American farmers know what all-out production means. Long hours of work. Less and less help. Making use of every possible acre of soil and of every tool that will help to get the job done faster and better. Men coming out of retirement and getting back into the fields. Young people and women pitching in and doing the work of grown men.

This is the way the job was done before. It is the way it will have to be done now—in 1951.

To do more jobs and save more hours, Ford Tractors and Dearborn Implements, specially engineered to work with them, form an unbeatable combination. On farms short of help, the Ford Tractor which anybody, young or old, can use is a priceless "hired man." And on *any* farm, the handy, economical Ford Tractor can be a big factor in keeping production *up*, costs *down*.

We shall continue to do our best, through the nation-wide organization of Ford Tractor dealers, to help American agriculture do its biggest job.

LOW FIRST COST—LOW OPERATING COST
The low priced Ford Tractor has a remarkably low operating cost, too. The Proof-Meter (see arrow) not only proves this fact but permits you to cut costs still further.

Previous page
Most 8Ns are not county fair or parade items, but day-to-day working tools. This 1951 Model 8N, owned by Art Preston of Mauston, Wisconsin, is doing its duty with a mounted Dearborn hay rake. Art Preston is a retired Ford tractor dealer. It is not likely that this 8N will retire for a while yet.

The 8N tractors after serial number 290271 had an additional instrument in the panel: the Proof Meter. This was basically a time-recording tachometer with bands around the perimeter showing ground speed in the various gears and power take off revolutions per minute.

"Ford Farming" was the key phrase in the ad campaign introducing the 8N. It was printed on radiator grille covers and sold to owners for the purpose of keeping their radiators clean. This Ford accessory radiator grille cover is shown installed on Fossum's Sugar Cane and Cotton Special, a 2N conversion.

Ford and Ferguson Go Their Own Ways

Ferguson TE-20 and TO-20

Back in 1917, Henry Ford generously made a gift of the patent rights of the Fordson tractor to the British to help alleviate the World War I food supply problem. He also agreed to set up a factory for Fordson production in Cork, Ireland, under the operation of Ford's British subsidiary. In addition, Ford declared that he would take no profits from tractors made for the British government. The Ford subsidiary was practically an autonomous entity with a British board of directors, several of whom were in the government's Food Production Department.

In 1933, tractor production was moved to Dagenham, England, while the Cork facility was used to manufacture automobile components. According to Harry Ferguson, the Handshake Agreement of 1938 included the intention to stop Fordson production at Dagenham and begin British production of the new joint-venture tractor. Ferguson also understood that there would be a place for him on the British board of directors.

This was not to be the case, however, as the Ford directors in England would not go along with a model change

Strojney Implement's 1949 Ferguson TO-20 was Ferguson's answer to the 8N. When the Handshake Agreement between Ford and Ferguson was severed, Ferguson hastily set up manufacturing facilities for a US version of his English TE-20. The TO-20 was much the same, except for a US electrical system and some different casting materials. Although the Ferguson looked like a dead ringer for the Ford, very few parts interchange. Supposedly, Ferguson did this on purpose, to thwart the use of Ford parts in his tractors.

from the Fordson. Why not? Perhaps because of the wartime situation they faced, or perhaps because of the favorable royalty arrangement with the parent firm or perhaps because Fordsons still had a good market that they didn't have to share with products of the US factory. It was also quite likely that the directors were reluctant to work with the crusty Harry Ferguson, who, besides having the ear of Henry Ford, had a reputation for demanding his own way about everything.

Ferguson eventually accepted that the new tractor would not be made by the British Ford company and that there would not be a seat for him on the British board of directors. Accordingly, he began planning the manufacture, in England and under his own name, of a 2N-like tractor designated the TE-20.

One might wonder what Henry Ford thought of this undertaking. The truth is that he wasn't aware of it until it was a fait accompli. Henry Ferguson had sent him a letter outlining his pique with the British board of directors, but an aide to Ford had filed the letter without showing it to him. "We've got enough trouble making this Handshake Agreement work without this," the aide reasoned.

As soon as World War II ended, Ferguson negotiated a manufacturing agreement with Standard Motor Company. Production of the TE-20 began in late 1946 at the Banner Lane factory in Coventry, England.

The TE-20 was basically the same as the Ford-Ferguson 9N and 2N, but it had two important differences: an overhead-valve engine and a four-speed transmission. Additional minor changes and improvements included a pedal for the left brake on the right side

This 1948 Ferguson TE-20 with a Ferguson manure loader and spreader is from the Fossum Collection. Typical of the Ferguson genius, the spreader is equipped with a short stand under the tongue and a ring-type hitch. The tractor has an open hook attached to the drawbar. One could hook and unhook the spreader from the tractor without leaving the seat by lowering or raising the drawbar with the hydraulics. Thus, the tractor, with loader, could be used to load the spreader, and then to pull it to the field.

The 1949 TEA-20 owned by C. R. Middlebrooke of Otley, Yorkshire, England, is an agricultural show model; note the chrome steering wheel spokes and emblem. The shift lever and other parts are also chrome plated. The tractor was photographed at the Great Dorset Steam Fair.

The Ferguson TO-20's tilting hood allows easy access to many components otherwise obscured on the Ford. It does, however, preclude the use of most aftermarket loaders and bumpers unless specifically designed for the Ferguson. Some Fergies have had holes cut in their hoods for access to fuel and water caps when this tilting feature is blocked by a loader.

of the tractor as well as one on the left. A one-piece hood arrangement was also added with hinges at the front so that the whole assembly—grille and all—could be tilted, exposing everything from the radiator to the instrument panel.

In late 1946, Henry Ford II told Harry Ferguson that the Ford-Ferguson agreement would be abrogated in July 1947. This meant that Ferguson's

implement company, and his dealers, would be left out in the cold. The result was Ferguson's $340 million lawsuit and his decision to build a factory in Detroit to manufacture a US version of the TE-20, to be known as the TO-20.

It wasn't until October 1948 that Harry Ferguson drove TO-20 serial number 1 off the Detroit assembly line. The TO-20 was identical to the TE-20, except that it used a Delco ignition sys-

tem in place of the Lucas on the Continental Red Seal engine and it used cast iron rather than aluminum for the transmission housing. Aluminum was used in the TE-20 to better dissipate the combined hydraulic and transmission heat load; British oils of the time were less capable of higher operating temperatures than were US oils.

The TE-20 and TO-20 tractors quickly became a success. They were reliable and were priced competitively with the new Ford 8N. The TE-20s were imported throughout 1948 and 1949 until Detroit production of TO-20s could fill the demand.

One reason for the ready acceptance of the Ferguson was the fierce brand loyalty of owners in that period. If you were a Ford person, you wouldn't be caught with a General Motors

This 1951 Ferguson TEF-20, owned by R. B. Jones of Dorset, England, is powered by the quiet and smooth-running Freeman Sanders diesel engine. Freeman Sanders was an outstanding diesel engine designer. His improved combustion chamber design of 1935 resulted in cleaner exhaust and smoother running.

product on your place. Conversely, a farmer with Chevrolet cars and trucks wouldn't buy a Ford tractor even though he needed one. The appearance of the Fergies, as they came to be known, solved this dilemma for many farmers.

Because of their reputation for reliability, quite a number of Ferguson TE-20s found their way to Antarctica under the auspices of a British exploration program. Three of these vehicles, equipped with special tracked running gears, carried a Sir Edmund

Hillary expedition on a 1,200 mile trip to the South Pole.

The TO-20 was made in Detroit until the end of 1951. During 1951, the TO-30 was introduced and coproduced. This was basically the same tractor with a more powerful Continental engine and larger front tires.

Today, many Fergies are in routine use. The British-built TE-20s are becoming quite rare in the United States, although parts are generally available for all types through Massey-Ferguson dealers or tractor parts companies. Parts are not readily available for the TE version's Lucas electrical system, but by now, many tractors have had the Lucas system replaced by the Delco.

Ford NAA Jubilee

When the Ford-Ferguson lawsuit was settled in 1952, Ford engineers

had already been planning an improved tractor for introduction in 1953—Ford's fiftieth anniversary. Competition from the Ferguson TO-30, brought out in 1951, had been taking its toll on sales of Ford 8Ns. In addition, the lawsuit had made it obvious that a new hydraulic system would be required. And indeed, the court did decree that after 1952, Ford would have to use a completely different hydraulic control system.

Production of the new model, the NAA, began in January 1953. Prominent on the hood of the restyled tractor was a circular emblem that said Golden Jubilee Model 1903-1953, and the NAA quickly became known as the Jubilee. *Golden* referred to the fiftieth anniversary of the founding of the Ford Motor Company in 1903. *Jubilee* is a biblical term having to do with fifty-year periods (see Leviticus 25:11). (It is interesting to note that during the Jewish Year of Jubilee, there was to be no cultivation of the land.)

The Jubilee was somewhat larger and heavier than the 8N it replaced. Front and rear tread adjustments were accomplished in the same way and to the same extent, from 48 to 76 inches. The Jubilee had a 4 inch longer wheelbase, was about 4 inches higher and weighed about 100 pounds more.

Other than changes to the hydraulics, the most important improvement was the new Ford Red Tiger engine, an overhead-valve unit with 134 cubic inches of displacement and a 6.6:1 compression ratio that produced 31 horsepower at 2000 rpm.

The Ferguson lawsuit prevented the continued use of the old hydraulic pump with its supply-side control valve covered by Ferguson patents before the Handshake Agreement. In the old arrangement, the pump and control were under the seat in the transmission/differential housing. The pump was driven by the power takeoff mechanism only when the PTO and clutch were engaged.

The new pump was a vane type rather than the scotch-yoke type previously used. It was mounted on the right rear side of the engine, driven by a helical gear on the rear of the camshaft. Thus, hydraulic power was available whenever the engine was operating.

On top of the pump was a manual pump volume control called the Hytrol. This allowed smooth draft load sensing and smooth control of the three-point hitch with a variety of implements.

Also new on the Jubilee were a separate, independent hydraulic reservoir and outlets for providing hydraulic power to remote cylinders. A separate control valve was offered as an option.

A nonlive power takeoff was retained on the Jubilee as standard, but a continuous, or live, PTO was offered as an option. To provide the live PTO, a hydraulically actuated clutch was incorporated in the PTO drive. A separate pump was provided to actuate the clutch, driven by the Proof Meter cable.

AN IMPORTANT MESSAGE
TO OUR CUSTOMERS AND FRIENDS

We are happy to be able to tell you that the lawsuit brought more than four years ago against Ford Motor Company and Dearborn Motors Corporation by Harry Ferguson and Harry Ferguson, Inc. has been settled by agreement of the parties.

There are three points connected with this settlement which, as a present or possible future owner of a Ford Tractor, we want to make clear to you. Regardless of what you may hear to the contrary, these are the FACTS.

3 POINTS OF INTEREST
To Our Present and Future Customers

1 Ford Motor Company will continue production of the present Ford Tractor without interruption, and Dearborn Motors Corporation will continue to market them nationally as in the past. By the end of 1952, Ford Motor Company has agreed to make two simple changes, and only two changes, in the means of operation and control of a pump used in the hydraulic system in the Ford Tractor. After these simple changes have been made, there is nothing in the settlement of the suit to prevent Ford Motor Company from continuing the manufacture of the present Ford Tractor for as long as it may choose.

2 Ford Motor Company will continue to produce and Dearborn Motors Corporation will continue to supply, through its distributors and dealers, all repair parts for all past, present and future Ford Tractors.

3 Ford Tractors will continue to offer all the advantages of the present system of hydraulic control, the present method of attaching and operating implements, and all other features responsible for their wide popularity. Dearborn Motors will continue to offer its same complete line of implements.

A STATEMENT
By Mr. Henry Ford II

"In normal times Ford Motor Company would carry such a suit to a final conclusion in the courts. These are not normal times. Under the circumstances we were glad to get rid of the litigation to avoid the expense, harassment, and further interference with our tractor business involved in additional years in the courts.

"The settlement in no way interferes with Ford Motor Company's continuing to offer to the farmer the lowest priced tractor with hydraulic control and the present method of attaching and operating implements."

DEARBORN MOTORS CORPORATION, Birmingham, Mich.
National Marketing Organization for the Ford Tractor and Dearborn Farm Equipment

The Jubilee retained the recirculating ball steering gear and brakes of the 8N, as well as the 6 volt electrical system. The transmission was still four speeds, but the ratios were different. The reverse ratio was the equivalent of second gear, instead of third as on the 8N or first as on the 9N and 2N. Although 4.00x19 front tires were standard as on previous models,

A June 1952 ad from Ford announces the settlement of the Ford v. Ferguson *lawsuit.*

One man's faith in Justice makes this date memorable...

April 9, 1952

YEARS AGO a dream came true for Harry Ferguson. He obtained a patent on a device he had created—a hydraulic device that was to enable one man to do the work of many on the farms of America.

OTHER PATENTS were issued to this man, patents on devices that ended back-breaking farm tasks—that saved time and money. So good were these devices that eventually, by a handshake agreement, a large motor car company manufactured a tractor equipped with them. It was marketed as the Ford Tractor with Ferguson System, integrating tractor and implement into one efficient machine.

AS SOMETIMES HAPPENS, this arrangement terminated and Harry Ferguson, Inc. made and marketed its own tractor using the Ferguson System. The Ford Tractor continued to be made and sold, embodying some of the Ferguson patents and inventions.

THUS HARRY FERGUSON found himself in competition with his own creations. He believed deeply in justice and in the rightness of his claim against the Ford Motor Company. It was this man's faith in these things that found justification on this date . . .

April 9, 1952

ON THIS DATE the United States District Court for the Southern District of New York entered a final judgment, with the consent of all parties which ended four years of litigation between Harry Ferguson, Inc. and Ford Motor Company and others.

IN THIS ACTION, it was ordered and adjudged that:

1. The sum of $9,250,000 shall be paid to Harry Ferguson, Inc. as royalties on Patents Nos. 1,916,945; 2,118,180; 2,223,002 and 2,486,257.

2. Ford Motor Company shall not manufacture, after December 31, 1952, such tractors, and Dearborn Motors Corporation shall not sell any such tractors manufactured after December 31, 1952, as have
(a) a pump having a valve on its suction side, as for example in the present Ford 8N tractor, arranged to be automatically controlled in accordance with the draft of an implement, or
(b) a pump for a hydraulically operated draft control system for implement control and a power take-off shaft both driven by the lay shaft of the transmission, as for example in the present Ford 8N tractor, or
(c) a coupling mechanism on the upper portion of the center housing, of the form employed in Ford 8N tractors manufactured prior to November 22, 1949; and Ford Motor Company and Dearborn Motors Corporation must affix a notice on any long coupling pins, manufactured by them, to the effect that the pin is sold only for replacement on 8N tractors made by Ford prior to November 22, 1949. This notice will continue to be affixed until October 25, 1966.

3. Ford Motor Company and Dearborn Motors Corporation shall have a period of time, expiring not later than December 31, 1952, in which to make these changes.

4. All other claims and counterclaims are dismissed and withdrawn on the merits.

A COPY OF THE CONSENT JUDGMENT is available to anyone interested in reading it. This settlement between Harry Ferguson, Inc. and the Ford Motor Company resolves the issues. The inventions mentioned above with which this action was concerned will be found only in the Ferguson Tractor and in the Ferguson System in the future.

Harry Ferguson, Inc.

Detroit 32, Michigan

A June 1952 ad from Ferguson concerns the lawsuit's settlement.

In Jones' TEF-20, diesel power replaces the Continental engine of the original TE-20. Much historical data on the early Ferguson tractors is available from Keith Oltrogge, publisher of Wild Harvest, Massey Collectors News, a bimonthly newsletter for Wallis, Massey Harris and Massey-Ferguson collectors and enthusiasts, and from Peder Bjerre, archivist with Varity Corporation.

A Ferguson TE-20 on half-tracks works in Antarctica. Sir Edmund Hillary used Ferguson tractors on his historic expedition to the South Pole in 1958, and three Fergies made the round trip from the base camp to the pole. The altitude exceeded 9,000 feet, leaving the tractors with such limited power that the governors were reset to allow operation to 3600 rpm. Nevertheless, the Fergies performed flawlessly on the 1,200 mile trip. Hillary cabled back: "Despite quite unsuitable conditions of soft snow and high altitudes our Fergusons performed magnificently and it was their extreme reliability that made our trip to the Pole possible." The half-track running gear is still common for both Fords and Fergusons, especially in snow country. There are two main types: Bombardier and Arps.

6.00x16 tires were an option. These and other larger tires are almost universally found on Jubilees today.

Jubilees were made in 1953 and 1954. In 1955, they were replaced by the Model 600, which was essentially the same but without the Golden Jubilee emblem.

Beginning Jubilee serial numbers were NAA 1 in 1953 and NAA 77475 in 1954.

Later models

In early 1955, Ford announced five new tractors in two power classes, the 600 and the 800. Thus ended the era begun in 1917 wherein Ford was a single-tractor producer, and thus began the era wherein Ford would compete across the board. Liquified petroleum gas engines became an option later

that year for US tractors, and the Fordson Major Diesel was introduced in England.

The Workmaster and Powermaster lines—the 601 through 901 Series— were brought out in 1958, and later in the year came the 501. Each line had subseries numbers like 861, which indicated such things as the number of transmission speeds and whether or not the PTO was live.

American-built diesel engines also became available in 1958. First available was the 172 cubic inch four-cylinder engine. In 1961, a six-cylinder 242 cubic inch diesel engine was introduced in the five-plow Model 6000.

Today, Ford offers a complete line of tractors from riding mowers to huge articulated monsters. Throughout the intervening years, Ford tractor dealers have always carried an equivalent to the 9N–2N–8N. A Ford Model 1720 would be comparable to the 8N in horsepower and size, although it has a three-cylinder diesel engine, live hydraulics and a live PTO. It is also available with four-wheel-drive and with a hydraulic shuttle transmission, which allows selection of forward or reverse in any of the twelve speeds. If the $12,000 price tag is too much for your budget, however, your Ford tractor dealer is a good place to start looking for a true Ford Tractor—a 9N, 2N or 8N.

This new Jubilee hood emblem is available from Strojney Implement stock. The original emblems on the 1953 Ford Model NAA tractors had the words Golden Jubilee Model 1903-1953 written around the edge, signifying the fiftieth anniversary of the founding of the Ford Motor Company in 1903.

POWER *that Pur-r-r-s* when the going gets TOUGH!

Leroy "Bud" Peterson aboard his 1954 Ford NAA Jubilee in Northfield, Minnesota. The Jubilee reflects the competitive and legal pressures brought on by Harry Ferguson. Besides the lawsuit, competition from the TO-20 and then, in 1951, the TO-30 caused Ford to make almost a complete redesign for its new NAA model.

An ad shows the Ford Golden Jubilee tractor with Red Tiger overhead-valve engine.

An ad presents the new Ford tractor.

By 1956, Ford was no longer a one-tractor producer. Late 1954 saw the introduction of the 600, 700, 800 and 900 Series tractors. These were quickly followed in 1957 by the 501, 601, 701, 801, 901 and 1801 Series. The Fossum Collection's 1956 Ford Model 660 shown here is essentially the same as the Jubilee, with minor improvements. It was the top of the 600 Series line, having a five-speed transmission and a live PTO. Other models in the series were the 650 with the five-speed and no live PTO, and the 640 with a four-speed like the Jubilee's and no live PTO.

Robert Breitrick is at the controls of this 1956 Ford Model 800 owned by Scott Breitrick of Tigerton, Wisconsin. The Model 800 has 45 horsepower, enough to do most jobs on a family farm without too much overkill. It has live hydraulics, a live PTO and enough gears for most any job, yet it retains the low-slung compactness of the Ns. Diesel power was available in 1958.

Art Preston owns this 1959 Ford Model 981. With a 172 cubic inch, 47 horsepower engine, the 981 is an outgrowth of the 800 Series. It is designed to be convertible to a narrow front. It also has a two-speed (1000 rpm and 540 rpm) live PTO and a twelve-speed Selecto shift (shift-on-the-fly) transmission.

The 1958 Ford Model 501 Offset Workmaster from the Palmer Fossum Collection. The Workmaster was designed for single-row high-crop work, such as with sugar cane and grapes.

This 1958 Model 501 Offset Workmaster is part of the Fossum Collection. Designed for underbody-mounted tillage tools and an unobstructed view, the Offset is a departure from the Ford-Ferguson concept of rear-mounted implements, although the three-point hitch is retained. A substantial frame section is used, rather than relying on the engine structure to handle the loads.

The Workmaster used the 134 cubic inch Red Tiger engine of the Jubilee 600 Series, as well as the same four-speed transmission. This example also has a high-direct-low auxiliary transmission by Ford.

Two 12x38 rear tires help get the Workmaster up above the crops. The front and back wheels are adjustable in width to accommodate row spacing.

Next page

This 1963 Fordson Triple-D (Doe Dual Drive), owned by Steve Lester of Pilton, England, was built at Maldon, Essex, England. It was a farmer's idea to join two Fordson Majors together to make one articulated four-wheel-drive tractor. The Triple-Ds were expensive, but they sold quite well, anyway. Many have been converted back to separate tractors since the availability of large four-wheel-drive tractors has increased.

Ford Tractors Today

Since tractors are not registered in the United States, it is difficult to say how many of the 820,207 Ford Tractors built are still in use. One Ford tractor dealer's service manager revealed that until 1985, he had never scrapped one out. In the years since 1985, he had found several that he considered to be beyond economical repair.

All parts, including sheet metal and trim items, are available from Ford tractor dealers and from several parts suppliers (see list of suppliers at the end of this book). Farm stores carry tune-up kits, batteries and other routinely replaced parts such as mufflers and tires.

Many handy individuals are now refurbishing Ford Tractors for resale, some doing as many as one per month. In 1990, a refurbished 8N brought about $2,500. One that had been restored, or brought back to new condition, would sell for about $5,000. The 9N and 2N models, being somewhat less desirable as work tractors, usually brought about 20 percent less. Interest by collectors is rapidly increasing, however, as is the value of older tractors, if they are in essentially original condition. Neither the 8N nor the 9N and 2N are so readily available that the buyer can expect to do much comparative shopping, though.

Advantages and disadvantages of Ford Tractors

The demand for the Ford Tractor is high because it is the most widely known used tractor of its size (20 to 30 horsepower) with the hydraulic three-point hitch. New or recent-vintage tractors of this size are all diesel powered. While this has a fuel-consumption advantage, it definitely adds to the price of the tractor. A comparable new tractor will sell for over $10,000.

As for performance and cost of operation, aside from fuel consumption, the Ford Tractor will do the same job as newer tractors. Harry Ferguson criticized Ford's archaic side-valve L-head engine, but in fact, Nebraska Tractor Tests rated the 8N as being better on fuel consumption than either the Ferguson TO-30 or the 8N's successor, the Ford Jubilee, both with modern overhead-valve engines.

One drawback to the Ford Tractor as compared with later tractors is the lack of live hydraulics and power takeoff. On the Ford Tractor, the hydraulic pump is driven by means of the PTO mechanism, and the PTO is driven only when the clutch is engaged. This means that implements cannot be raised when the clutch is depressed. For many applications, this is inconvenient. For example, the operator must put the transmission in neutral and release the clutch in order to raise a grader blade before backing. The next model, the 1953 Ford Jubilee, has live hydraulics.

A second drawback, compared with later tractors of this size, is the

The Fossum Collection also contains this 1952 Ford 8N with a Funk six-cylinder conversion. Everything said for the V-8 conversion goes for the 95 horsepower six, except that the exhaust is single. Much more common than the V-8, the Funk conversion to the Ford flathead six was used with irrigation pumps, silo fillers, threshing machines, pull-type combines and the Sherman backhoe. Conversion kits went for about $850 when introduced in 1949.

The Fossum Collection includes this 1952 Ford 8N with a Funk V-8 conversion. The Funk conversion consists of gearbox adapters and adapters for front wheel attachment. The tractor is lengthened, so tie and radius rods are extended, and a hood extension is provided to reach the instrument panel. The hood and grille are raised, and an appropriate radiator is used. Fossum has two vertical straight pipes for the exhaust—the sound is magnificent!

Palmer Fossum drives his 1952 Funk V-8 conversion—the Ford bull, if there ever was one! This is a rare conversion; most used industrial, or truck, sixes. Kits were offered by Funk Brothers of Coffeeville, Kansas, which also produced, in the forties, a light aircraft known as the Funk B. The added power was welcome for such chores as belt-powering threshing machines or for heavy mowing, where a good part of the power went through the PTO.

lack of a rollover bar. While most welding houses could fabricate one, the inconvenience and cost probably mean that most owners will take their chances. Sims Manufacturing of Rutland, Massachusetts, is now offering rollover bar kits for Ford and other tractors originally sold without.

For some, a third drawback is the 6 volt electrical system. Conversion to 12 volts is not difficult; the same 6 volt starter can be used. The 6 volt system is adequate, however, and there is really little reason to change.

When Ford and Ferguson got their heads together back in 1939, their brain child was primarily a plowing tractor, designed to do one acre per hour. Today, Ford Tractors are rarely used

The engine of Fossum's Funk V-8 conversion is an 8BA, 100 horsepower 1952 Ford powerplant. The man who sold this tractor to Fossum said, "Remember that you have a 100 horsepower engine and a 30 horsepower transmission and rear end, and you won't get in trouble."

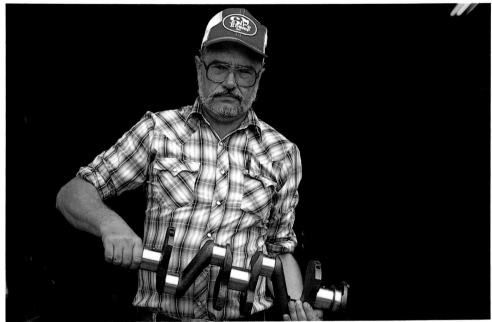

To demonstrate the extent of new parts available to the rebuilder, Bill Ficken, manager of Strojney Implement of Mosinee, Wisconsin, holds a brand-new crankshaft for the N Series engines.

Also available from Strojney Implement is this brand-new hydraulic cylinder and control. The availability of such new parts greatly reduces the risk to the rebuilder.

The new N Series cylinder head is another example of new parts availability for the N Series Fords. Ficken maintains that it is possible to create a new serial number tractor from parts. Major castings are the problem, although they are not so complex that new molds could not be built, if someone were really determined.

for plowing fields. Most are used for mowing or loading, equipped with front-end loaders and separate engine-driven hydraulic pumps. Of the 400 plus implements designed for the three-point hitch and power takeoff, the most common are the grader blade, posthole auger, landscape scarifier, rotary mower, lifting boom, saw rig (for cutting firewood), box scraper (for moving earth) and drawbar (attached either to the three-point links or to the differential housing, for pulling trailers or other light implements). Without 300 plus pounds of calcium chloride liquid installed in the tires, Ford Tractors used in drawbar pulling cannot exert as much pull as a heavier tractor.

How to buy a Ford Tractor

After the first glimpse at the general condition of the tractor, there are

Here's how to buy a tractor

Just ask yourself: "Will this tractor do the most jobs for me, *more* of the time, without wasting power? Is it easy to operate, and will it go from one kind of a job to another, quickly and easily?"

To *answer* yourself, you've got to *see* the tractor do *your* jobs on your farm. And above all, you shouldn't let "habit" guide your choice.

This time, call your *Ferguson* Dealer. Ask him to prove the ability of the Ferguson "30" in a Showdown Demonstration on your farm. Let him show you how many bottoms it will pull in *your* soil. See how quickly and easily you, or anyone, can change implements with Ferguson's *time-proved* 3-point hookup. Then disc, or do any of the other jobs you'll be doing throughout the year.

You (and your family) will discover that the exclusive Ferguson System gives you a lot more tractor for a lot less money . . . a lot more farming, with a lot less work.

Call your Ferguson Dealer today. Set up a Showdown Demonstration on your farm *soon*. Chances are, you've already missed too much . . . too long!

FREE BOOKLET tells you "How to Buy a Tractor". 24 pages of valuable information! Your Ferguson Dealer has your copy, or write: Harry Ferguson, Inc., Detroit 32, Michigan.   © 1953, H. F. INC.

Get your Showdown Demonstration of the Ferguson Manure Spreader and Loader. This exclusive Ferguson combination lets you load, hitch, haul and spread without leaving the tractor seat! Hydraulically operated, patented hook 'n' eye hitch lets you do this tough job alone, without drudgery.

No other tractor gives you *all* the Ferguson System advantages: Traction and penetration without power-stealing weight, finger tip and automatic draft control, front-end stability, and an exclusive built-in hydraulic overload release that saves tractor and implement if you hit a hidden rock or stump.

Seeing is Believing — Get Your Showdown Demonstration of the

FERGUSON "30"

several things to look for immediately: Is it a 9N or 2N, or an 8N, and can you live with the brake pedal arrangement of the 9N or 2N? Is there a Sherman transmission? A 9N or 2N is especially handicapped without one, and although the Shifter can be added, it will be costly.

Next check the condition of the sheet metal, grille and fenders. Problems here do not affect performance but are relatively costly to rectify and, if not corrected, affect your contentment with the tractor. A new grille sells for about $60. Each hood side panel is about the same.

Now examine the hydraulics. The controls of these components are connected through 6 inch holes in the cast-iron housings, which requires considerable skill and dexterity. Two initial tests will reveal whether expensive repairs are required: First, the three-point hitch should raise a substantial load easily—it should lift 700 pounds at the uniball points. Second, once raised, the load should not settle or leak down for at least ten minutes. Good hitches will hold up a two-bottom plow overnight.

For some reason, the exhaust manifold is a weak point. The manifold side of the manifold/exhaust pipe interface will often crack off. A new manifold will cost $50 to $60. Installation is not difficult, but heat may be required to loosen the bolts.

Check for free movement of the steering wheel, measured at the rim with the front wheels straight ahead. No more than 4 inches of free play should be accepted as tolerable. Check for slack in the tie rod ends, kingpin looseness and front axle/radius rod looseness. Check for front wheel shimmy when operating in road gear at high speed.

This aftermarket accessory swirl-type air cleaner, shown on a Fossum Collection 1952 Ford 8N, was designed to centrifugally separate the big chunks out and into the glass bottle, while the rest proceeded through the standard oil bath air filter.

You should be able to lock either back wheel with its respective pedal on virtually any surface. The brakes are easily adjusted, if the adjusting mechanism has not seized from years of corrosion. Check scraping, metal-to-metal sounds that would indicate depletion of the brake lining. A grabby brake indicates the same thing. Weak brakes are usually caused by axle seal leakage.

The clutch should operate without requiring undue force; it should engage smoothly and there should be no slippage when it is fully engaged. There should be an inch or so of free play on the pedal. On the 9N or 2N, be sure the clutch pedal actuates the left brake sufficiently to slide the left tire. Also make sure the clutch releases completely, so that there is no raking of gears when moving the shift lever from neutral while standing still.

The original rear wheels were built up around the rim of a hat, or box-section, with bolts attaching the rim to each wheel disc. If calcium chloride was used and if the tire ever leaked, the fluid found its way into this semi-enclosed area and corrosion commenced. Most of these wheels have already been replaced, but if the ones on the tractor you're looking at have not been, count on doing so at around $75 each. As corrosion eats through, the sharp edges produced will cut the tube and you will be plagued by slow (and not-so-slow) leaks. Collectors,

who want their tractors original, will pay a premium for good-condition box-section rims.

Check the radiator for leaks, dirty fluid and inadequate cooling (due to blocked passages). For 9Ns, this is not a pressurized system, so there is no pressure cap to inspect. A new radiator is about $150, and old ones are difficult to repair. A note of caution on cooling: Be sure the fan belt is tight and in good condition. If the belt slips, engine heat will boil the fuel in the tank directly above. The Ford has a good vent system, but if for some reason it should be restricted, the fuel tank could rupture, spilling fuel onto the engine.

The tractor should start readily, hot or cold, although the choke will most likely be required for every start. If the tractor is reluctant to fire up, the starter may need overhauling and may be taking too much of the available power, leaving too little for adequate spark. In addition, original starter drives tended to kick out too early. A modified unit is available and is easily installed.

Look for a resistor in the circuit across the ammeter. Some owners have removed this in an effort to get more power to the coil for starting. If this resistor is not in place, however, point life will be quite short.

Once the tractor has been started, check the operation of the generator by noting an indication of charge on the ammeter. Pre 1948 tractors have no

voltage regulator, as such, only a cutout system.

It is possible to jump-start the 6 volt Ford Tractor to a 12 volt source, although the practice should be considered a last resort. Remember, the Ford has a positive-ground system, opposite to today's convention, so the cables will be reversed on one end. For best results, do not run the engine on the 12 volt source vehicle during the jump. This allows the voltage to drop some from the rated. Attach the red cable to the positive terminal and the black cable to the negative terminal on the source battery. Attach the red cable to a good unpainted ground point on the tractor (not the battery terminal). Then, with the key on and the transmission in neutral, touch the black cable to the tractor starter terminal. Pull the choke while the engine cranks. Limit cranking to ten to fifteen seconds, with five minutes' cooling between attempts.

With the engine running, listen for smooth operation and lack of knocking or valve clatter. Oil pressure should be 30 to 40 psi. If smoke comes from either the tailpipe or the oil filler breather, a compression check is in order. Compression should be 90 psi minimum. A compression check will also reveal whether an engine miss is caused by a burned valve or by an ignition problem. Factory-rebuilt engines are available for about $1,300 plus your old engine. Parts for a do-it-yourself overhaul will run about $450.

Specifications

Fordson serial numbers and specifications

Beginning numbers

Year	Dearborn	Cork
1917	1	
1918	260	
1919	34427	63001
1920	100001	65104
	Rouge	
1921	153812	108230
1922	201026	109673
1923	268583	
1924	370351	
1925	453360	
1926	557608	
1927		
1928		
1929		747682
1930		757369
1931		772565
1932		776066
		Dagenham
1933		779154
1934		781967
1935		785548
1936		794703
1937		807581
1938		826779
1939		837826
1940		854238
1941		874914
1942		897624
1943		925274
1944		957574
1945		975419
1946		993489

Horsepower	20 @ 1100 rpm
Engine	251 cubic inch 4 cylinder L-head
Powertrain	3 forward gears
Weight	2700 lb

Model 9N specifications

Wheelbase	70 in.
Overall length	115 in.
Normal width	64 in.
Turning radius	8 ft.
Overall height	52 in.
Weight	2,340 lb
Front tire size	4x19
Rear tire size	8x32 early; 10x28 late
Front tread	48–76 in.
Rear tread	52–76 in.

Notes: Wheelbase is reduced as front tread is increased. Normal width is calculated at minimum tread width. Weight is with gasoline, water and oil, but with no weight liquid in the tires.

Model 2N specifications

Wheelbase	70 in.
Overall length	115 in.
Normal width	64 in.
Turning radius	8 ft.
Overall height	52 in.
Weight	2,340 lb
Front tire size	4x19
Rear tire size	10x28
Front tread	48–76 in.
Rear tread	52–76 in.

Notes: Wheelbase is reduced as front tread is increased. Normal width is calculated at minimum tread width. Weight is with gasoline, water and oil, but with no weight liquid in the tires. For rear tires, 11.2x28 and 12x28 tires can also be used.

Model 8N specifications

Wheelbase	70 in.
Overall length	115 in.
Normal width	64.75 in.
Turning radius	8 ft.
Overall height	54.5 in.
Weight	2,410 lb
Front tire size	4x19
Rear tire size	10x28
Front tread	48–76 in.
Rear tread	48–76 in.

Notes: Wheelbase is reduced as front tread is increased. Normal width is calcu-lated at minimum tread width. Weight is with gasoline, water and oil, but with no weight liquid in the tires. For rear tires, 11.2x28 and 12x28 tires can also be used.

Ford Tractors serial numbers

Model 9N

Year	Serial numbers
1939	1 to 10233
1940	10234 to 45975
1941	45976 to 88887
1942	88888 to 99002

Total production: 99,002

Model 2N

Year	Serial numbers
1942	99003 to 105374
1943	105375 to 126537
1944	126538 to 169981
1945	169982 to 198730
1946	198731 to 258503
1947	258504 to 296131

Total production: 197,129

Model 8N

Year	Serial numbers
1947	1 to 37907
1948	37908 to 141369
1949	141370 to 245636
1950	245637 to 343592
1951	343593 to 442034
1952	442035 to 524076

Total production: 524,076

Total 9N, 2N and 8N production: 820,207

Common N Series implements

Two-bottom plow
One-bottom plow
Disc
Spring tooth drag
Cultivator
Spike tooth drag
Sickle bar mower
Rotary mower
Saw rig
Hay rake
Grader blade
Front dozer, or snowplow
Box scraper
Posthole auger

Lifting boom
Scarifier
Rock rake
Flat-belt pulley

Ford Model NAA Golden Jubilee serial numbers and specifications
Beginning numbers

1953 .... NAA 1
1954 .... NAA 77475

Horsepower ...... 31 @ 2000 rpm
Engine .... 134 cubic inch
4 cylinder
overhead-valve
Powertrain .... 4 forward gears
Weight .... 2510 lb

TE-20 (imported) serial numbers
Beginning serial numbers

1948 20800
1949 77770

TO-20 (US built) serial numbers and specifications
Beginning serial numbers

1948 1
1949 1808
1950 14660
1951 39163

Horsepower ...... 22.53 @ 2000 rpm
Engine .... 120 cubic inch
4 cylinder
overhead-valve
Continental
Powertrain .... 4 forward gears
Weight .... 2,550 lb

TO-30 serial numbers and specifications
Beginning serial numbers

1951 60001
1952 .... T072680
1953 .... T0108645
1954 .... T0125958

Horsepower ...... 29.32 @ 2000 rpm
Engine .... 129 cubic inch
4 cylinder
overhead-valve
Continental
Powertrain .... 4 forward gears
Weight .... 2,840 lb

Sources

Central Tractor
3915 Delaware Ave.
Des Moines, IA 50316

Palmer Fossum
10201 E. 100th St.
Northfield, MN 55057

Goodman Tractor Supply
1200 East O St.
Lincoln, NE 68501

Strojney Implement Company
Mosinee, WI 54455

Tractor Supply Company
14242 C Circle Dr.
Omaha, NE 68144

Keith Oltrogge
Wild Harvest-Massey Collector News
171 East Main St.
Denver, IA 50622

Peder Bjerre
Varity Corporation
595 Bay St.
Toronto, Ontario M5G 2C3 Canada

Gerard Rinaldi
The 9N-2N-8N Newsletter
154 Blackwood Ln.
Stamford, CT 06903

Recommended Reading

Baldwin, Nick. *Farm Tractors*. London: Frederic Warne, 1977.

Fraser, Colin. *Tractor Pioneer*. Athens, Ohio: Ohio University Press, 1973.

Gray, R. B. *Development of the Agricultural Tractor in the United States*. St. Joseph, Michigan: American Society of Agricultural Engineers, 1956.

Larsen, Lester. *Farm Tractors 1950–1975*. St. Joseph, Michigan: American Society of Agricultural Engineers, 1975.

Williams, Michael. *Ford and Fordson Tractors*. Dorset: Blandford Press, 1985.

INDEX